More
Than a
Game

More Than a Game

Edited by John Wiebusch
Prologue by Jim Murray

A National Football League Book
Prentice-Hall, Inc., Englewood Cliffs, New Jersey

Library of Congress Catalog Card Number: 74-81177
ISBN: 0-13-600965-4

Prepared and produced by the Creative Services Division
of National Football League Properties, 10880 Wilshire
Boulevard, Los Angeles, California 90024.

First published in 1974 by Prentice-Hall, Inc., Englewood
Cliffs, New Jersey.

Printed by Kingsport Press, Kingsport, Tennessee.

Publisher: David Boss
Editorial Director: John Wiebusch
Executive Director: Jack Wrobbel
Managing Editor: Tom Bennett
Designer: Amy Yutani
Project Coordinator: Bill Von Torne
Production Manager: Patrick McKee
Editorial Assistants: Earlene Doran, Chuck Garrity,
 Harley Tinkham, Patricia Cross, Doug Kelly
Production: Felice Mataré

Contents

Prologue

by Jim Murray

Football is a fleet Sac-and-Fox Indian, a war party of one, fleeing across a playing field as if the Seventh Cavalry were after him. Football is Jim Thorpe.

Football is an overwrought coach in a tense locker room, biting off the ultimate pep talk: "Gentlemen, you are about to play a game against Harvard. Nothing you do in life will ever again be so important as what you do on that field today." Football is Tad Jones in the Yale Bowl.

Football is an overcoated romantic in a blustery press box, huddled over his typewriter, pecking out the deathless lead, "Outlined against a blue-gray October sky, the Four Horsemen rode again...." Football is Grantland Rice—and Sleepy Jim Crowley and Harry Stuhldreher and Elmer Layden and Don Miller.

Football is a shy redhead with a built-in change of pace and shift of direction a stalked leopard might envy. Football is "the Galloping Ghost." Football is Red Grange.

Football is a broken-nosed old coach, his bald head shining in the locker room lights as he recounts with brimming eyes the deathbed wish of a gifted athlete dying young. "One day, when the going is tough, ask the team to win one for the Old Gipper." Football is Knute Rockne. Football is George Gipp.

Football is love. And it's hate. It's fear. And it's courage. It's tragedy. And it's comedy. Grace and strength. Anger and joy. Football is emotion.

It's the American Game. It's "autumnal madness." It's Saturday afternoon and Thanskgiving morning. It's Sunday's heroes. It's Monday night.

Color it red, white, and blue. Set it to Sousa's music. Choreography by George M. Cohan. It's a grand old game.

It's the Yale Bowl and Yankee Stadium in hip flask and raccoon coat. It's Betty Co-ed and Corinne Griffith. It's Green Bay on a Christmas Eve and it's 20-below and snowing. It's the Orange Bowl on Super Sunday and it's 90 in the shade.

It's the Other Woman in a marriage. John's Other Wife is 100 yards long and 50 wide and has goal posts and he'd do anything for her.

It's Lombardi bellowing on the sidelines, a man of intellect in the body of a caveman. A soft heart in a cage of granite. He speaks of it as a game of love—in a locker room of bleeding, broken hulks. And no one laughs.

It's the Grand Old Man still scrawling "X's" and "O's" on tablecloths when he was 101 years old. It's an ageless game. It's Amos Alonzo Stagg, the patriarch of football.

It's the Ivy League. But it's also the Houston Oilers.

It's Walter Camp. But it's also Bear Bryant.

It's Frank Merriwell. But it's also Joe Namath.

It's forming in a circle to cheer the vanquished team. But it's also the locker room admonition "Winning isn't the only thing—it's everything."

It's an old country boy from a dry river town in Texas, ironically called "Sweetwater," firing a football that could ram through a keyhole and hit a receiver in the eye clear across the state, a pipestem-legged cowboy who threw a 28-inch hunk of leather around as though it were a grape.

It's a nasally New Yorker with a voice like geese honking, reminding the people of the number of Ralph Kercheval and Ken Strong, the glories of their past, the wonders of their future.

It's Super Sunday. And Black Monday. It's the New York Giants in sneakers on a frozen field dancing into the history books away from clumsy Chicagoans whose cleats slip on the glassy glacier that was the Polo Grounds that day in 1934.

It's the "Monsters of the Midway," the 1940 Chicago Bears, as unstoppable as a glacier, as frightening as an earthquake.

It's "Boola Boola" and "March, March On, Down That Field, Fighting for Eli!" It's Cole Porter, of all people, writing fight songs.

It's Bobby Layne, with five minutes to go, taking precisely four minutes and fifty seconds to score the winning touchdown and taking the whole team to the Copacabana afterward.

It's Tom Landry standing in the midst of 70,000 screaming spectators and looking exactly like a suburbanite trying to remember what his wife told him to bring home for dinner that night.

It's Brian Piccolo, dying bravely but fighting for yardage as usual, looking up into his wife's swimming eyes and murmuring, "Ain't this the shits, Baby?"

It's "Mr. Inside" and "Mr. Outside." The stuff of legends.

They didn't have to sell America on football. It was love at first sight. They took it to their bosom from prairie village to penthouse and skyscraper. From the White House to a log hut. From the sidewalks of New York to the palms of Waikiki. It's the story of the twentieth century quite as much as a recital of administrations, tariffs, dates of battles, treaties, concordants. "Detente" is the AFL merger.

Give us men who made our touchdowns, not men who made our laws.

It is a game Walter Camp invented, Teddy Roosevelt saved, Knute Rockne refined, Grantland Rice defined, and Pete Rozelle canonized.

It took over where vaudeville left off. It supplanted the Fourth of July picnic. The Thanksgiving Day classic was a football game. It was the Christians versus the Lions. Nero would have presided over a football game.

Hollywood faded before its glow. It became show business in its gaudiest application. Garbo? Bah! Give us Duane Thomas! Chaplin? Ha! Garo Yepremian was funnier. Hamlet? What's the matter with George Allen? Barrymore? The great lover? Ho! Tell that to Joe Namath. Paul Bunyan? I'll take Larry Csonka.

You talk of generals and battles? Robert E. Lee at Gettysburg? Grant at Richmond? Sherman? War is hell? No, no, give us Lombardi at the Orange Bowl. Shula at New Orleans. The battle of New Orleans was won by Tom Landry and Hank Stram, not Old Hickory.

Like spy stories? Read about the signing of Billy Cannon. The wooing of Too Tall Jones. You take Double-Oh-Seven. I'll take

Al Davis. The kidnapping of Csonka and Kiick and Warfield. The spiriting out of town of a number one draft choice through a motel window. Is that guy peeking into practice in a Roman collar really a Catholic priest? Or George Halas's spy? Do they pull the fingernails out of a guy traded from the Dallas Cowboys to the Washington Redskins? Or does he diagram the plays anyway? Is a playbook worth $2,500? Is the guy on the phone who wants to know if Gabe is hurt really an author? Does he write books? Or make book? Why does Jimmy the Greek know Namath is hurt when the writer on the beat doesn't?

Edgar Wallace would have loved football. Agatha Christie was missing a bet. Who needs sinister butlers when you can have furtive quarterbacks? What's more mysterious than a field goal on first and goal to go?

It's The Greatest Show On Earth. Barnum would have been an NFL owner. The biggest, closest-knit fraternity in the world is the NFL fan club. There is no brotherhood like the inmates of a saloon bus on their way to the home game. Rooting crosses color lines, religion is wiped out. Hell, the Rams *are* a religion!

See them now, huddled in tense concentration on the way to the Coliseum, the Stadium, the Bowl. Their minds are far from the strife of the streets, the mess in Washington. Their problems are larger. *Can* we contain Brockington? *How* is Snow's knee? Washington's hand? Is our linebacking corps solid? Will we be buying a round? Or kicking the dog? When it's over, will we be singing or cursing?

It's Big Business. And it's Small Town. It's for small boys. And it's for old men. The banker sits next to the shoeshine boy. "Take 'em in, John!" they both implore. "U" doesn't stand for State anymore. It stands for Johnny U. The greatest, boy!

Who would be caught alive on the streets the afternoon of a road game of the home team? A communist, that's who! A spy. A lousy, stinking un-American. With the Rams fighting for their life on television, who would be out prowling a supermarket? Officer, come get this man! He's acting suspicious. Who would be driving around the city on fourth-and-one and the Packers with the ball?

Women's lib? If you think so, baby. Whyn't ya go to yer mother's Sunday? The Dolphins are in San Francisco. I'll be eating in the living room. What's that, you say? It's either *you* or football? Ask me something hard. Don't start the dishwasher on your way out. Snows up the image. See ya around. Don't call up during the football season.

Hiya, Joe. Where's my wife? I dunno. Ain't seen her since kickoff back in September. Gabe went 14 for 18 that day.

Who can risk more for the home team? Marriage, job, health—they mean *nothing* compared to beating the Pack. What can bring on a greater depression than a one-point defeat? What produces the elation of a "We go to the Super Bowl!" Who prays harder than a fan whose team is on the 1 with a minute to play?

Who puts up with the discomfort of the season ticket holder who sits in the end zone from Sunstroke Sunday to Super Sunday? Is it raining? That's Vikings weather! Who cares if my shoes squish? Who cares if you spend the week "Ah-chooing!" into a Kleenex? Gotta *be* there, baby! Look, Alan Page *needs* me!

It's not a sport, it's a mania. It's not a recreation, it's an addiction. Psychologists, psychiatrists quietly go nuts. They can't find it anywhere in Freud. What is it? Father fixations? Infantile anal aggression? They try to explain it in terms of cheap, meretricious twaddle, the pipe-sucking prattle of professors. The guy with his nose in the program doesn't care. "Gid outta here!" he snorts. "I'm just trying to figure out who's playing strong safety and if he should be on the nose of the guard, ya dummy! I'm normal. I just wanna go to the Super Bowl, is all. What's kinky about that?"

It's the least individualistic sport there is. Baseball players go their own way between showers. You can go three for four and have a great day regardless of the team. You can hit your seven hundred and fourteenth home run and no one notices the club lost. Football players play for the team. You get a nosebleed for the *team*, not the Hall of Fame.

Players are public icons. Their pictures hang in the living rooms of houses full of people who never saw them except through binoculars. They do everything but light candles. America never had any royalty. But it does now. The Dolphins— or the Browns—are royalty. America's Olympus is the Super Bowl.

They said it was huckstered into mass-mania, but it's not true. It was an American obsession long before television trained a camera on it. It was Caswell Adams on the roof of the old Polo Grounds, telling of Tuffy Leemans and Tilly Manton and Mel Hein and Ken Strong, and a nation was hooked. It grew on its own. And, one day, its officials looked at it—and noticed the sleeves it was wearing were too short and it had grown out of its pants and its shoes were too tight. It was time to cut its baby curls. Television just said, me, too. Television is a follower, not a leader. It trains its cameras where everybody is already looking. In this case, the 50-yard line.

It is controversial. And Americans love controversy. The Great Debate was not what we should do about Vietnam. It was about what we should do about the field goal.

Watergate? Pshaw! The pressing problem in Washington is what to do about Sonny Jurgensen, not Ehrlichman. Who cares if Gerald Ford replaces Nixon? But if you want Kilmer to replace Jurgensen, you have a fight on your hands.

If Kissinger wants to do something, why doesn't he make peace between the NFL and the World Football League? Get Csonka back here. Stop frittering around with those silly little local wars. Never mind the Middle East. Shape up the Central Division.

Show me a politician dumb enough to schedule a State of the Union message in the middle of Monday night football. And I'll show you a guy who will get impeached, all right. World War III will be delayed a day owing to the Super Bowl.

The myths of the game die hard. They say it takes five years to make a pro quar-

10

terback. Okay, so how come Bob Waterfield made it in one month? And Joe Namath made it in a week? They say you have to be 6 feet 8 inches and 280 pounds. Okay, tell me about Floyd Little.

The dogma of the game rivals High Mass. It has its own ritual, its own rote. Was Latin ever any tougher than "red dog," "blitz," "down-and-out?" What's a "zig?" A "veer?" Who knows what a "post pattern" looks like? Where'd they get this sport—out of Lewis Carroll? Football is the other side of Alice's Looking Glass.

It's all as wonderfully nonsensical as the Wizard of Oz. Some day, they're going to take that tin suit off and it's going to be Bert Lahr instead of Merlin Olsen. It's Fantasyland. Fairy tale time. Disney is putting it on. All those characters will take their heads off and bow in the footlights and it will be Peter Pan and Bambi. Bob Griese and the Dolphins? Roger Staubach and the Cowboys? Naw!

Kids who used to go home from the Saturday matinees and act out the cowboys and Indians and *be* Ken Maynard or Buck Jones or Roy Rogers or John Wayne now go home and *be* Bob Griese or Franco Harris or O. J. "Okay, *you* be Manny Fernandez and I'll be O. J. Simpson!" "No! I don't wanna be Manny Fernandez. Why do I always have to be Manny Fernandez? This week, I'll be O. J. Simpson and you be Manny Fernandez! If I have to be anybody, I'd rather be Dick Butkus."

It's Walter Mitty's *ultimate* game. Pocketa-pocketa on the old Orange Bowl. In a million backyards from Perth to Perth Amboy, *somebody* is Bob Griese.

Our dreams are wrapped up in it. Who wants to be President if he can be Quarterback? Even the *real* President would rather be George Allen. George Allen doesn't want to be President. *He* wants to be George Allen, too.

Watch the fat old party at the next office picnic and touch football game. "Hey, look at me, I'm Otis Taylor! Okay, Lenny, lay it right in there! It's *six,* Lenny! I was *open,* baby! Watch for me! Watch for the move I put on that guy from accounting!" Breathes there a man with soul so dead who ne'er unto himself has said "Lookit me, I'm Mercury Morris!"

Where else can a man hold such power? Around the office, a schlemiel. On the 50-yard line, a kingmaker. Who fires the coach? Just ask yourself! Is it the owner? Don't be silly! It's *me,* baby! Little old me! Right there in the 50-yard line. "Call yourself a coach, Ewbank? By me, you're a dummy. My kid is a coach if you're a coach. Ya dummy!" Or, "All right, Mara, keep that coach and who you going to sell your hot dogs to? Not me! I ain't gonna be here to see that rockhead futz it up anymore. I should be working in the garage on Sundays, anyway. Who needs the aggravation of these guys who can't break a huddle. Get Allen and I'll come back to the games. Or Shula. Why don't you get Shula and get smart?"

Where else can you give advice to somebody making $200,000 a year more than you make? "Throw a flare, Namath, you dummy!" "They're in a stack, Gabe, even a baby could see that, you pin-brain!"

No one better get too big for his britches.

Easy now, O. J., 2,003 is good. Now, 18,000 more and you get to catch ol' Jim Brown. Now, *there* was a runner. Didn't need no blocking. What's so great about you, McCutcheon? Remember, Crazylegs played here. And I seen him. Look, Hadl, we seen Waterfield! You're no big deal. Van Brocklin, you ain't. You don't show me much, Plunkett. *I* saw Baugh! Shucks, we had Tuffy Leemans and Tilly Manton and Johnny Blood and Indian Jack and Riley Masterson and Cliff Battles. Beattie Feathers, for cryin' out loud! Ever see anybody catch Indian Jack from *behind?* Ever see anybody catch him from *in front?* Thorpe? Let me tell you about Thorpe. Sober, Thorpe was *invisible.* Drunk, and you still couldn't do nuthin' about him.

It's a talking game. You close bars with it. Or open stores. All during off-season, the argument rages: "He should of thrown a pass." "He should of punted." "Whyn't he try an end run?" "Yer all crazy! He should of tried a field goal! I know. My brother-in-law knows Tom Landry personally."

You only have to make the summit once. No matter what Joe Namath does, his epitaph will read "Joe Namath, who quarterbacked the Jets into one of the football upsets of the century, when he won Super Bowl III…"

You never really get old. Pop Warner is still alive. As long as a coach who learned from a coach who learned from Pop Warner is still alive. As long as kids' football is alive. On rainy nights, they tell you, Rockne walks under the Golden Dome. Even if he doesn't, if someone *thinks* he does—well, he *does.*

It's a sport for the poor. The rich men's sports declined, died. Crew sank. Polo was unhorsed. Tennis had to go to the arenas. Park Avenue couldn't keep it fed, nor the Main Line.

Football flourished in replenishment from tarpaper shacks of the cotton field, the cracked sidewalks of the ghetto, the company tenements of the steeltown. The sons of immigrants, the grandsons of slaves—the strong of back and fleet of foot—the once-despised minorities slapped the sons of riches out of the way and took over the sport. It ministered to group esteem of groups who had long lain deeming themselves unworthy, unequal. Who can feel inferior if he is Mr. Touchdown USA? Who can feel inferior if he can outrun, out-throw, out-think, or out-hit the cream of the country?

Is it a minor accomplishment? Then, why is it a multi-million dollar industry? Is it unworthy to be head of General Motors? Then, it is as worthy to be head of the NFL.

This, then, is Football in the seventh decade of the twentieth century. More than a game. Less than a religion. Somewhere between a faith and a frolic. A commitment. An involvement.

For some, it is a holy experience. For others, a mind of trouble. Winning is the only thing. But not everything. There's always next year. The dream will be fulfilled. The mortgage won't be paid. The taxes won't stop. But "We're number one!" "We won!" "We go to the Super Bowl!" is a healing all its own. A magic in its own right. A release, an escape. Your brother-in-law might make 10 times as much money,

might live in a fancy house on the hill compared to your shack in the valley. Never mind. *His* team lost. You call him up. "Hey, Stud, what'd you think of *our* Dolphins?" Let him eat his heart out. Let him have his Rolls, his summers in Europe. What if you have your Edsel, your summer in the steel mill. Did *his* team win? No, *yours* did. Hey, bartender, bring us another round here! To hell with your brother-in-law and his own bank. *I'm* buying. The Dolls won! "Hey, brother-in-law, wanna make a bet fer nex' year? Couldn' handle Zonk, cud yez? Har-har! Eat yer heart out! Ring fer the butler and cry. I'm havin' a beer with the Doll-fans! We're celebratin'!"

Food tastes better. Wives look prettier. The job looks easier. Even the boss smiles. We *won*, baby! What else matters? Here's to the best l'il ol' football team, the greatest coach, the greatest bunch of guys in the whole universe! *My* team! Drink up!

And that's the way it goes. That's what it's all about. From the frozen fastnesses of Green Bay to the sunglass seats of Miami, from the verdigrised pillars of Yankee Stadium to the upholstered magnificence of Dallas.

You belong to an elite group. Ace Gutowsky played here. And Dutch Clark. Beattie Feathers ran here. And George McAfee. Little Davey O'Brien. And studious Sid Luckman. "Hey, Joe, that Thorpe! He was somethin' w'ant he!?" "Sure was! I'll tell the cockeyed world. Had to send a horse to catch him!"

It is a game of "Bullet Bills" and "Slinging Sams" and "Juice" and "Jarrin' Johns"

and "Hustlin' Hughs" and "Joe the Jet" and "Bronkos" and "Horsemen."

Sunday is a day of worship. It's bobblehead dolls and bumper stickers and T-shirts and team colors and chrysanthemums and ribbons. It's rebel yells and Yankee twangs and tough Boston brogues and Texas drawls and Hollywood wise guys and side-of-the-mouths from the sidewalks of New York. It's Molly and me—and the Super Bowl makes three. We're happy in our Blue Heaven—Tunnel 8, Aisle 30 and a hot dog and a beer and "Take 'em in, John we're wit' ya!—win or tie!—Alla way!"

They have come from different backgrounds. From different ethnic groups and, in some cases, from different countries. Each has brought with him his own style and each has left his own mark. The might of Nagurski…the grace of Simpson…the poise of Unitas…the swagger of Namath…the passion of Lombardi…the compassion of Rooney. More than scores and more than games, when we think of professional football, we remember The People.

The People

by John Wiebusch

A Ranch to Build a Dream On

Y ou can stand by a fence there and listen to the silence, alfalfa rustling and bobolinks making love calls and low aching wood groans from a windmill off on a rise of land.

Cities change and people change but the landscape of this place is constant. Thomas Wolfe be damned, you *can* go home there. Or think you can.

Maybe that is because it has always been a place for pausing, not stopping. For eyes, not hands. The land here has always been the eternal artery to somewhere. The Frenchman, Bourgmont, passed through in 1724. He found only the nomads of the prairie, the Pottawatomi and the Kickapoo and the Kaw. Zebulon Pike passed through in 1806, on his eventual way to a peak in Colorado. The covered wagons passed through later, grinding out their trails, one to the northwest called the Oregon, the other to the southwest called the Santa Fe. Today it is trailers and campers and it is not much different now than it was then, except for the freeways.

The silence is away from the freeways, down a road that leaves a trail of dust behind you. Fields stretch out, brown now in the spring and full of furrows. And in a cluster of trees, a house, a barn, a granary. Grant Wood and Andrew Wyeth and Grandma Moses, they would love it here. Out here in Kansas.

R ay May discovered Kansas in 1971. He came to talk to a man about buying a horse and he ended up buying a half dozen horses. And a piece of land, 185 acres.

Ray May remembers standing out in the middle of that land on a day in March and thinking that this was the beginning of the dream. "Hot damn!" he said to no one and he walked through the exposed grain stubble of the year before.

Ray May bought his 185 acres, his ranch, with his share of the money from Super Bowl V. He was a linebacker for the Baltimore Colts and the Baltimore Colts were the champions of pro football.

"Funny," he says. "Here I was, the city boy all my life. Growing up in Los Angeles and going to school there, too (at USC). Playing pro football in Pittsburgh and Baltimore. Kansas, it was always just a place on the map in geography class. I never thought about it and I sure didn't think about going there. But here I was and it seemed like I'd come home. I couldn't believe it. It was just, well, love at first sight."

W akefield, Kansas, is nestled in a tiny fjord of the Milford Reservoir. The Milford Reservoir is a man-made diversion of the Republican River, which runs parallel to the border of Nebraska and Kansas before cutting a diagonal path through the farmlands of northeastern Kansas. There are places here with names like Strawberry, Buckeye, Greenleaf, May Day, Industry, Fact, and Enterprise and when they talk about going to town they mean places like Junction City and Clay Center and Manhattan.

It's not easy to get to Wakefield. You have to *want* to get there. First you fly to Kansas City in a jet. Then you go to Manhattan, which has a university (Kansas

Herb Weitman

State) and an airport, in a plane that has an engine that drives a single propeller. Finally, you rent a car in Manhattan and then you follow Highway 18 19 miles west to Junction City and then turn north on Highway 77 for 20 miles until you come to the bridge that crosses the Milford Reservoir to Wakefield.

Wakefield is the kind of place you drive through looking for the main street until you realize you're on it. The inevitable gas stations. The country store. The cafe.

In one of the gas stations you ask the man how you get to Ray May's ranch and he looks at you through squinted eyes as if to wonder why you'd want to know that.

"That direction," he says, pointing west.

"We already drove out there," you say, "and these directions here didn't help much."

"What you got there?" he says. You hand him a piece of paper with some poorly scrawled notes in one corner.

"Forget this," says the man. "All this is gonna do is confuse you. What you do is you drive out past those big silos on the left side of the road, you turn right first time you can and then you follow the dirt road around a curve through two intersections. Then turn left at the next crossroad and it'll be the first place on your right."

"Thanks," you say.

"Nothin'," says the man. He is leaning on the window. "Where you fellows from?"

"Los Angeles and St. Louis."

"A long way to come," says the man. "Hey, Herbie, these guys came from Los Angeles and St. Louis to see Ray May." Herbie whistles.

Ray May bought the ranch for his boys, for the youngsters from troubled places who had chosen him as their bachelor father. For the kids from Los Angeles and Baltimore and places in between who had some questions and needed some answers.

For Ray May it began in Los Angeles, too. At Denker Park.

"Understand, I had a good home life," he says. "I'm proud of my parents. But a big part of growing up, for me, was Denker Park and the kids there. We played our games together and we grew together."

He smiles and shakes his head. "Oh, it's not like we didn't get into trouble. We did. We'd help ourselves to cars and drive them until we ran out of gas. Once we stole a school bus and we got caught. It disappointed my parents something awful but they stood behind me. That's the thing so many of these kids don't have. They get into trouble and it's a dead end. It's like there's no turning back once you start

down the road. Now I believe if you do something bad you should pay the price. If you're man enough to steal then you should be man enough to take the punishment. But if you haven't got anybody to take you by the hand then, to help guide you, then brother, it could be all over."

Ray May began taking kids by the hand in the summers between his years at the University of Southern California. He was a defensive end there and his name was magic at Denker Park.

"The guys there," he says, "they needed some hope. They needed to be shown that there were ways of getting out. I'll tell you, I enjoyed it maybe as much as the boys did. I guess maybe I'm a giver and it went toward meeting my needs, too. It got to the point where I just couldn't stay away. That whole group of guys there in the mid-1960s, we already were like some kind of family. It was very gratifying, you know, making some kid who had been dumped on by his family feel just a little bit taller.

"When you get to feeling sorry for yourself, then you're in trouble. And it's easy to feel sorry for yourself when you grow up in a ghetto, when you don't get much of anything from anyone — love, a good meal, anything.

"One of the kids I've adopted we call Humbug. His name's Anthony Smith and he's from Los Angeles. This kid grew up in L.A.—he's 19 now—and you know that until a few years ago he'd never been to Hollywood, he'd never been up in the mountains, he'd never *seen* the beach. He was a kind of prisoner, and the only direction he was going was down. Well, Humbug not only graduated from high school but he came with me to Baltimore and now he's enrolled at City College of Baltimore. It's all up for him now."

Ray May's voice glows when he says it.

The land west of Wakefield is an undulating pancake, the road across it straight and narrow. On the right side are some cattle, black and white (are they Holsteins or Guernseys or something else?), scattered over a field with heads down. Ahead on the left are the big silos, and you brake and turn onto the narrow finger of a road that branches off to the right. The landscape is starkly spectacular, a kind of lonely beauty. Two hours before, in the low-flying plane, you saw it from above, a patchwork of earth shapes.

"Holy cow!" says your companion, the photographer, and you stop on the gravel siding to take some pictures. It is not the last stop. Ahead are sheep and cattle and a primitive country billboard. And silos and weathered barns and fences strung like stretched out cobwebs. It takes an hour to

travel the four or five miles to Ray May's Golden Nugget Boys' Ranch.

The modest collection of buildings are perched at the top of a gentle slope. A cabin-sized house with plastic sheeting on the outside of the windows. An interesting old stone barn. A ramshackle shed-garage. It seems a disappointment. It seems to be something less than the billing.

"This is the dream of my life," Ray May had told you on the telephone. Now you wonder if dreams are made of this.

To meet Ray May is to find out that they are.

He says, "Howdy," as if he has been saying it all his life and he pushes the black ten-gallon hat down on his head to keep it from the whiplash winds of the late morning. He is flanked by youngsters named Snooky and Cookie.

"First the ten-cent tour," he says. "Now maybe you look around here and you wonder just what it is I have in mind. I'll tell you. Over here will be the bunkhouses. We'll put in a barn and a corral, a stable, right up to the right side of where that shed is. Out back behind that will be a full-sized football field, a basketball court, a tennis court—you name it. A lot of work, a lot of money. It's going to take plenty of both. But sure as I'm standing here it's going to happen. Right, Snooky?"

"Right, Ray," says Snooky.

"It *is*," says Ray May and all of us are believers.

Up in the shed is a Chevy pickup, vintage early 1950s.

"Let's get this battery hooked up now," says Ray May. "Then you guys'll have something to run about in."

They work together, a communion of hands. It has been three months since the old truck has run and just attaching the battery is not enough. When it starts, Cookie and Snooky cheer and Ray May guns the motor and we are engulfed in black smoke. "In Los Angeles," he says, "they put you in jail for this."

Later, inside with Al Green sounds coming from the stereo, we talk about other things they put you in jail for. Like buying and selling drugs. Like stealing and robbing and burglarizing. Among other things.

"The big thing is respect," says Ray May. "If you have no respect—for your fellow man and for yourself—then you have problems. Most of the guys we have here started without it and it began right at home. That's where it is. You find a kid who has no respect for his home life and you put him out on the streets and you can't expect him to have respect for authorities, like police.

"It's a lousy situation and you can't change it overnight. You have to build con-

fidence in yourself to gain respect. And just being Mr. Nice Guy isn't enough. You've got to prove it by treating everybody the same, first-class. We have rules here—I make the rules and they're not easy. Right?"

Cookie and Snooky nod. "Man's a driver," says Snooky, and Ray May chuckles and continues.

"Like—and this is for real—if any of my guys are around here and I go anywhere, the guys go with me. Being together is a big thing in football and a big thing in life. These are guys—all of 'em —who were never part of a group interaction before. Either they were told they could or couldn't do something or they weren't told anything.

"And you've got to be there when they want you. They never had anybody who was there before, but now they do. You have to live with them and be with them and they have to know that you believe in them.

"Look, these are psyches that have been buffeted for a long time—ten, fifteen years. That's a lot of damage to mend quickly.

"One of the advantages I have over a lot of people is that I am believable because they know where I came from. You have to have experienced it or the kid's going to say, 'Man, you can't tell me what to do.' See, the unique thing about me is that I can relate because my life is some good and some bad, too. My parents, they're wonderful people. They raised three of their own kids and they adopted three other brothers. That's the example that I've got to follow and it's been a helluva inspiration. I'd like to give as much as my folks have given and that'll be my measure of success. Giving's my thing."

Ray May is the gift that keeps on giving. He began modestly, with three boys, boys now grown into young men and under his legal guardianship. But today the figure is nine, with the likelihood of more.

"We get this place going," he says, "and there's no reason why we couldn't handle, say, twenty-five kids or more out here. It will take money to do it but that's the only thing we don't have a lot of."

There is a reason Ray May does not have a lot of money. He spends it all on his boys. In the spring of this year he was putting four of them through college—at his expense. Joe (Peewee) Copes, 20, and Anthony (Humbug) Smith, 19, were at City College of Baltimore. John (Z Black) Smith, 20, was at Palmer Junior College in South Carolina and Michael (Superstar) Capers, 20, was at Cheyney State College in Pennsylvania. And the school expenses are almost incidental when compared with the travel expenses. Peewee, Z Black, Humbug, and

Superstar are all from Los Angeles and in school on the East Coast with new home roots in Kansas. Cookie, 17, and Snooky, 14, are from Baltimore and so is another youngster, Eric Williams, 13. Lester Rucker, 12, is from Los Angeles and Joe Griffin, 11, is from Universal, Colorado.

"The pleasures of life," says Ray May, "are seeing them here, working and playing together. Why most of these guys had never worked a day in their lives until they came here. Right, Snook? Right, Cook?"

Snooky and Cookie laugh and duck Ray May's sweeping right hand.

"C'mon," says Ray May. "I'll show you what I mean by work. This place may be the soul of the Boys' Ranch. I'll show you the heart—my friend Larry Patterson's place."

Larry Patterson is the man Ray May came to see about buying a horse 2½ years ago. The chemistry was instant. Larry Patterson told Ray May about the 185 acres that were only a couple miles from his own spread. They talked about working together on the dream and how it could happen.

Patterson is a horseman. He has reconverted and transplanted an old airport hangar in the middle of his property. It functions today as a combination barn, riding ring and stable.

"He is my brother," says Ray May. "Larry Patterson feels. He cares. We have a lot in common."

There is one thing Ray May and the boys of the Golden Nugget Boys' Ranch do not have in common with Larry Patterson. The color of their skin.

"Trouble," says one of the hands at Larry Patterson's place. "Your boys done taken that Chevy out and got it stuck in the mud."

"Where?" says Ray May and in an instant he is the angry father.

"Other side of the road," says the hand. "We'll take the tractor down and pull it out. It's in bad."

Ray May walks behind the tractor, stalking and steaming. Snooky is standing beside the truck that is immobile except for spinning wheels. Cookie is the driver.

"Look, man," Ray May says to Snooky. "You know what the rules are. You take this truck out, you ask first."

"Wasn't my idea," says Snooky.

Cookie is grinning nervously as Ray May turns to him.

"Okay," says the big man. "That's fifteen whups each."

"Fifteen?" pleads Cookie. "This wasn't worth that."

"Hell it wasn't."

The tractor pulls the truck loose and we follow it back up the driveway.

"I believe in strong discipline," says Ray May. "Call it old-fashioned, or what you like, but I believe that if you spare the rod you really do spoil the child. That all goes back to respect. You allow any rules to be broken once and pretty soon you've got rules being broken all over the place. After that you have a total breakdown and before you know it you're not in charge. That's true of all authority."

You ask if he equates himself to a strong football coach, to, say, a Vince Lombardi.

"Sure," he says, "we're alike in that we're both authority figures. A coach loses control of a team, he ends up with losers. Now I'm not talking about creating robots. I'm talking about living, breathing human beings applying themselves to a conduct code, helping each other, pulling for each other."

You ask if being a football player—a *star* figure—has made a difference in dealing with the boys.

"Not really. Hardly at all, in fact. Heck, when I came across some of these guys they had no idea who I was and what I did didn't mean a thing to them. Like Snooky. I picked him up hitchhiking in Baltimore one year. He'd just been in a fight and, I'll tell you, he didn't look good. We got to rapping and me, I figure that since he's a Baltimore kid he must know the Colts and so I say to him, 'You know who I am?' and he says, 'No,' and I say, 'Ray May.' He says, 'So?' The thing is, these guys all have a feeling of pride in what I do and in me as a football player, but that's not why they're here and I'm not about to push anything at them. This is not a hangout for jocks and jock lovers; it's a place for people and people lovers. If football happens here, fine. But we find a lot more things to do."

But surely Ray May must work at football—at staying in shape—in the offseason. A powerful figure of a man, he stands 6-3 and weighs 230.

"I run every day, yeah. 'Bout five miles. And that's a tonic that keeps me in condition. But I run alone. Everybody works and does his fair share, but no one's forced into doing things they don't want to do."

You wonder if the responsibility of being a surrogate father isn't a fulltime job. How does he find the time during a season that is six months long?

"It isn't easy," he says. "But given a sense of responsibility most of these fellows can function quite well independently. I mean all I can do is get them on the right track. After that they have to move on their own, applying those lessons they've learned."

And the future?

"Some day it will be a fulltime job . . . when I retire, whenever. By that point I'd like this place to be nationally recognized, a place where boys can come instead of going to reform school or jail. See, you get into these kids and you find out that their basic values are no different than you or me."

He is stroking the neck of a brown horse that is at the fence. The horse has a white star on its forehead. "Way to be, beauty," he says. "We'll get you a grooming today."

A voice from the hangar calls at Ray May. "Need your help," it says and we are running through the mud to the door. "That's my brother," says Ray May. "My brother Butch from Los Angeles."

Inside, an angry horse is resisting treatment for an infected front leg. Three men are unable to control the horse while the salve is administered. Ray May takes over on the left flank.

"Our man," says Cookie. "That's our man."

"He likes to be in charge," you say. "But is there a complaint department here?"

"Oh, sure," says Cookie. "You can come to him with anything and he'll listen nice as can be. Then he does just what he wants to do."

Snooky is there with Cookie and they laugh together. Until they met Ray May they did not know each other.

"He's all right," says Cookie.

"He's our man," says Snooky.

Cookie cocks his head. "You see all those awards he got? He show them to you?"

You say that he didn't point them out, that you only noticed and were impressed.

"Our man," says Cookie.

The honors include the Byron R. (Whizzer) White award (emblematic of excellence on and off the field), the Johnny Unitas award (for outstanding contributions to pro football and the community), the Big Brother of the Year award and a place on the U.S. Jaycees' Outstanding Young Men list.

"Remarkable," you said to him when you saw the awards but he shrugged them off by saying, "They're nice but their greatest value is that they make more people aware of what we're doing here. They spread the gospel. That's the main thing."

The ailing horse has been given its treatment and it limps away. Ray May wipes his hands together and shakes his head. "That's a nice filly," he says to his brother and another man. "I sure hope we can save it."

We move outside and we sit atop the three-rail wood fence that encloses the north corral. He is 28 years old, this "father" of nine, this man who cares.

"I look at these kids," he says, "and it does my heart good. Snooky and Cookie,

they'd be out on the street somewhere in Baltimore, up to no good probably. Instead, they're here and they're *living*.

"Another thing I remind these guys of is about the Man up there. Like Humbug, who's at City College in Baltimore and doing so well, he thought God was a monster when I first met him. And he'd just as soon have knocked your head off than as talk to you. And Z Black. He was so bad in high school in Los Angeles that teachers and counselors couldn't be encouraged. Not only did he graduate there but he's gone on to reach some kind of high at Palmer J.C. He graduates from the two-year program this year—and with honors yet. Z Black—we call him that because the color of his skin's ebony—has turned out to have quite a head on his shoulders. Of course I can say I knew it all the time."

"He did, too," says Butch May, Ray's younger brother. "He found Z Black at Denker and he said, 'What a waste of a human being.' "

"Z Black just needed a kick in the butt," says Ray May. "He just needed somebody to show him the way."

Ray May is squinting into the sun. The big hat is still perched on his head.

"I really believe there's good in everyone—and that's not just some naive assumption. It's based on years of working with people—people some folks said were 'bad' or 'incorrigible.' Baloney. All you've got to do is chip away at the concrete wall and sooner or later you get through. Like Snooky there. He's got fifteen whups coming but he's still my man. Right, Snooky?"

Snooky nods and says, "Right, Ray." He is working with a curry comb on the brown horse with the white star.

Twilight on the prairie. In the car, going back to Manhattan. Two voices.

"He'd be a great salesman. Or an evangelist."

"Yeah."

Silence.

"I don't think I've ever met anyone who believed so deeply in humanity . . . or the goodness of it."

"He *believes* it. And he makes you believe it. He makes this boys' ranch thing seem like, well—"

"I know. Like it wasn't a dream but a certainty."

"Some guy."

Rain, falling slowly, then a cascade. The clack of windshield wipers and the whoosh of tires on wet pavement. Thinking, they wouldn't be working with the horses tomorrow at Larry Patterson's place.

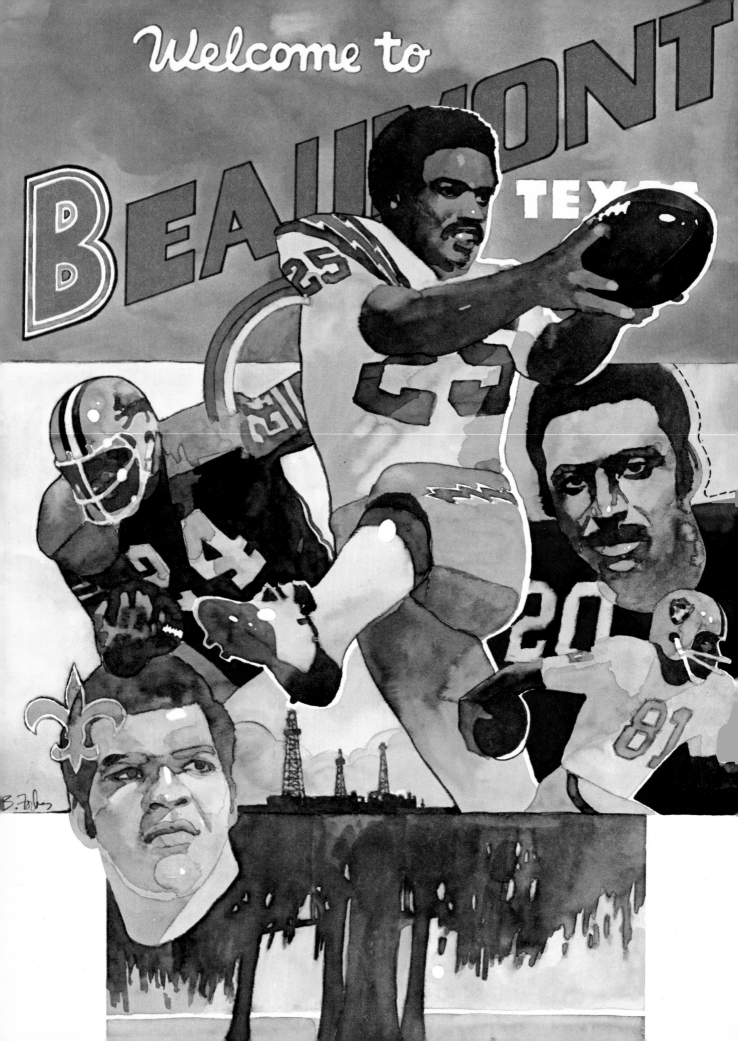

by Mickey Herskowitz

The Boys of Beaumont

"I don't care if Jim Brown himself stepped in there. They were nobody until they got tested by the Boys of Beaumont."

—JERRY LeVIAS, SAN DIEGO CHARGERS
AND HEBERT HIGH SCHOOL

It has a fine, sturdy, down home ring to it...the Boys of Beaumont. They were, and are, all of a pattern; all in the family, so to speak.

The phrase refers in general to the pool of talent that seemed to pour out of two black Texas high schools in the early 1960s. The schools have good, traditional southeast Texas names, Charlton-Pollard and Hebert (pronounced E-burt), and on the field they have worked up the kind of hate that lasts a lifetime.

"If a person died," says LeVias, "and the funeral fell on a Saturday when those teams were to play, well, they just postponed the funeral. Same thing with a wedding." The 1971 renewal drew 24,000 fans, more than some pro teams were drawing not too many autumns ago. It ended in a 6-6 tie. Poetic.

Domestic relations have been known to suffer unbearable tensions in the case of a mixed marriage. That is, one where the husband attended Pollard and the wife went to Hebert. "It is not unusual," says LeVias, "for husbands and wives to separate for the weekend."

This intensity of feeling has led, inevitably, to a point where football is regarded by the townspeople as slightly more important than one's left eye.

It is a fact that Beaumont leads the universe in the supply of professional football players (a distinction formerly held by Massillon, Ohio). At one point the list of established players was 13, including two white graduates from the city's integrated schools. This census does not include rookies who were on training camp rosters or neighbors who live down the road.

Merely by extending the coverage a few miles to incorporate what is known as the Golden Triangle you could enlarge the ranks to at least 20, among them the likes of Aaron Brown (Port Arthur) and Ernie Ladd and Garland Boyette (both from Orange).

To Willie Ray Smith, who came to Pollard back in the dark ages around 1957, such a deceit is hardly necessary. It is the proud boast of coach Smith that: "You can turn on a television set on a Sunday afternoon, and tune in any game in the country, and you'll hear the name of a boy from Beaumont."

Some of the names are Mel and Miller Farr, Jerry LeVias, Jess Phillips, Warren Wells, and two of coach Smith's own sons, Bubba and Tody. Blessed is the coach who provides his own manpower.

Actually, in only the thinnest sense is this a football story. It is a people story, about the hungry, the have-not, the child forsaken. It is football as social drama, as an escape hatch to fame and dignity.

It is about Willie Ray Smith's crusade. In 1957 he was persuaded to accept the head coaching job at Pollard largely out of curiosity. He could not understand how a team could contrive to lose every game for two years, during which it scored one touchdown. He considered this an affront to the spirit of man.

Bart Forbes

23

He found that before he could begin to attract the makings of a football team, he had to find a way to feed them. The kids were poor and many of them had empty stomachs and until then all football offered was more sweat and maybe a chance to break a leg. It was not exactly something they couldn't live without.

Pollard is a very old buff brick school across the street from the dockyards, in a very tough section. The students were bussed out of a ghetto on the other side of town to 'get there. By the time some of the families had paid the fare for four or five kids there wasn't much lunch money left. "Maybe a dime or fifteen cents," remembers coach Smith. "They had soda pop and a bag of chips. They had legs like sticks."

Smith headed downtown and talked the merchants out of a daily ration—a 100-pound sack of beans and a side of ham. "Mama would put a great big pot on the stove," said the coach, "and cook the beans and the ham overnight. In the morning I'd carry it all to school and we'd set up a table in the locker room."

At noon the kids would come, bringing their bowls from home, and they would take a serving of beans and ham hock and corn muffins and sit spraddle-legged and eat what was for many of them their only hot meal of the day.

That's how it began. Not all the kids were deprived. But all of them knew there was a better life out there…and what it would take to achieve it.

Across town, at Hebert High, coach Clifton Ozen was preaching the same doctrine. "We had it drilled into us," recalls Miller Farr, "that football could make us important. That it was the one best way to break out of the ghetto."

Behind Miller came his brother, Mel, and Jerry LeVias, a cousin, to give the theory truth. "It was our dream," says Miller. "Pro football was all we ever talked about. My brother and I would come in at night, after working out all day, and we'd have supper and we'd start to talk and we'd fall asleep at the kitchen table, our heads on our arms, talking football, just talking, talking."

The rivalry between Pollard and Hebert continued into the summer, with daily touch football scrimmages behind the swimming pool at Liberia Park. They played every day, all day, and out of these games Beaumont became to southern football what the Catskills, in the East, are to basketball.

The leaders were Miller Farr and Willie Ray, Jr., the oldest of the Smith brothers, the forgotten brother but perhaps the most talented of the pack. Ray drove a battered '55 Chevy station wagon all over town, col-

lecting football players from both schools. "Guys would be hanging out the windows," says Miller. "We always had enough for two teams and subs. We'd play for hours. By dusk we'd really be digging in. It was touch ball but it was tough. On the line of scrimmage they'd get real angry."

The action seldom stopped for injuries. Occasionally a player would retire to the sideline, and after minor repairs would return to the lineup.

One summer Willie Ray brought Gale Sayers down from Kansas. Later, George Webster was Bubba's guest from Michigan State.

"The word got around," says LeVias, "that if you wanted to get in shape you should go to Beaumont. You could get your thing together before you went to camp. But nobody awed us. I don't care if Jim Brown himself stepped in there. They were nobody until they got tested by the Boys of Beaumont."

They played more games than the Satchel Paige All-Stars, partly because there was so little else to do. If you were poor and black and lived in Beaumont in the early sixties, football was your entertainment.

But it wasn't all hardship and sacrifice. It was also pride and hope and the fellowship of pain.

Miller Farr remembers how it was to practice at night, on an unlighted field. "In the winter, when the days grew short, we'd keep right on working. By about five-thirty the cars would begin to pull up, fifteen or twenty of them, and they'd ring the field and turn on their headlights. Long after dark, we'd still be there, practicing in the glow of those headlights."

In March, 1971, Beaumont held a "Pro Day" honoring its gladiator sons. "Some of the people came up to me," says Miller, "to remind me that they said I'd always make it. They were some of the ones who used to drive out to practice and turn on their lights."

Of course, Beaumont ought to be known for more than the hardiness of its football stock. It was once that rare article, an authentic American boom town.

There, on a knob of land rising out of the swampy prairie on the outskirts of town, the liquid fuel age was born. It came to be called Spindletop, and the gusher that roared forth in January of 1901 launched the richest and maddest oil boom the earth had ever known.

It made men millionaires overnight and broke them before lunch. So quickly did Spindletop flood the market, so taxed were the city's sanitation facilities, that water was selling at one point for $6 a barrel and

oil for three cents a barrel. Land and oil leases were sold sight unseen. Saloons stayed open around the clock. Beaumont's red light district became the most notorious in the western hemisphere. Fortunes were won and lost on the turn of a card.

Much of the money left town, as money eventually does. Slowly it all faded, leveled off, and Beaumont returned to the hard work ethic of the quiet lumber town it once was. But the city always maintained a fondness for men who had vision, who were willing to spin the wheel, who could beat the odds.

And so in time the entire city discovered the black football players of Willie Ray Smith and Clifton Ozen, and celebrated them. Pride can drive as hard as riches.

Beaumont had always sent its share of good white football players to the major colleges. In the sixties it was still sending them: Billy Wright, Gus Hollomon, Johnny Fuller, Wayne McDermand.

But when Willie Ray Smith arrived at Pollard the young blacks were locked into the Texas soul brother circuit—Wylie, Prairie View A&M, Texas Southern. Some went to Grambling in Louisiana, where coach Eddie Robinson was knocking down doors.

"They had always had good black athletes here," says coach Smith. "But they'd play high school ball and drop out. Most of them didn't think about going to college. None of them had been to the Big Ten.

"I knew they had to have help. They had to have some options. High school football couldn't be the end of it. Too many of them were winding up as janitors, or they'd start hitting the wine."

He began to haunt every coaching clinic in the state, buttonholing the speakers, telling them about black football and the Boys of Beaumont. "Some of the coaches wouldn't even talk to me. But those who would listen, I knew I could sell them."

So Willie Ray, Jr., went off to play halfback for Kansas. Bubba and Jess Phillips joined Duffy Daugherty at Michigan State. From Hebert, Mel Farr went to UCLA and Jerry LeVias broke the Southwest Conference color line at SMU.

It was a little like running a marriage bureau.

"I just about forced Bubba to go to Michigan State," says coach Smith. "I felt like I owed Duffy something. At one time he had eight of my boys on his varsity.

"Funny thing, I tried to give Minnesota some of my players. Jess Phillips, for one. I wanted to spread them around and open up more opportunities. But an assistant coach at Minnesota said Jess couldn't play and Bubba was too lazy. They didn't want either one of them.

"One night before they were to play a game against Minnesota for Michigan State I called and reminded them that this was the school that said they couldn't play. I said, 'By all means, I want you to give them hell today.' And they did.

"The fellow at Oklahoma, Bud Wilkinson, he wanted Willie Ray. Oklahoma had just begun to integrate and he had signed his first black and he wanted Willie Ray to room with him. He needed a pair. And Willie Ray wouldn't go."

The one enduring disappointment of his career, a father's hurt more than a coach's, was the ill-starred career of his eldest son.

Young Willie Ray had been a quarterback and halfback with 9.5 speed. At Kansas he showed Gale Sayers how to cut. He tried out with the Chiefs, the Colts, the Packers, the Bears, and the Bills, finally giving it up after five knee operations.

His dad thinks he could still play, if a team were willing to gamble. "He was the best football player in the family, the best I've ever seen. And I know that it's eating him up. Here's the guy who paved the way for Bubba and Tody and he's never really had a chance."

Nowhere in his coaching successes, or his father's pride, can you detect traces of his own career that never was. Crippled in one leg by a boyhood hunting accident, he became a coach when the able-bodied went off to war. He was 26. He learned his football out of a book.

He is a firm, soft-voiced man whose discipline is impartial. "My father used to get bicycle tires and cut them in half," recalls young Willie Ray. "When we did wrong at practice, he would hit us with the tire."

The Smiths live in a handsome, all-brick home that Bubba bought for his mother, a gentle lady named Georgia, out of his first bonus check from Baltimore.

Bubba wasn't the first, and won't be the last, but he's the one you hear about, the giant who has a chance to be immortal. He has become a symbol to the Boys of Beaumont still to come. At 6-8, single, prosperous, he is highly visible. So are the others who broke through.

Jerry LeVias says there is a bond among them, a code that doesn't sanction less than one's best. "It's like this," says Jerry. "Miller Farr is my cousin. I was a year behind him in school. When I was still with Houston and he was with St. Louis, he tried to take my head off on one play. I paid him back by clipping him. After the game we just hugged each other."

It was LeVias, one notes, who is credited with having first described Beaumont as "The Pro Football Capital of the World." If you disagree, stay the hell away from Liberia Park.

by Charles Maher

Even His Best Friends Will Tell Him

Stan Caplan

Years ago, while officiating a Rams-49ers game in Los Angeles, Norm Schachter made a call against the home team. The fans, willing as always to examine one side of every question, let him have it.

Schachter's oldest son, Tom, then about 9, was in the stands. His father had a talk with him afterward.

"Tom, you've got to take it as an impersonal thing when the crowd gets on your dad like that. You have to realize these are home team fans and they get excited. Legitimately so. I know you probably hear a lot of talk in the stands and I hope you didn't take it personally."

"I took it personally," said Tom. "You blew the call."

Schachter, the NFL's senior official, is used to the zings and arrows. He's second-guessed on not one job but two. Once a high school principal, he's now an assistant superintendent in the Los Angeles school system, in charge of 52 San Fernando Valley schools with a combined enrollment of 60,000. A school administrator, like a football official, gets a lot of help from the sidelines.

Norm illustrated his predicament not long ago in an interview at his home. He said he'd be flying east to do a game and the guy in the next seat would be a football fan. He'd swear he'd seen Schachter somewhere before. A conversation would start and before long the guy would be asking for tickets, or for inside information on a game, or for an explanation of a disputed call the Sunday before.

"So I started saying I was a high school principal," Norm said. "But then all the militancy started in the schools and people would get on me about that. An educator can always get advice. So I took to saying I was an undertaker. It worked. Nobody would talk to me."

They talk to him plenty on the field. But they may not always be as angry as they look. Sometimes, they may just be playing to the crowd, as the mischievous George Halas was one afternoon in Chicago.

"I was working the Bears-Giants championship game in 1963," Norm said, "and Halas came out on the field at halftime. He ran up to me with his program and started waving it in my face. It looked as if he were really chewing me out but all he said was, 'Which way do we go in the second half, Norm?' I said, 'The other way, coach.' He got about ten yards away, then whirled and came storming back at me, waving that program in my face. When he got up to me he said, 'Thanks.' By now, the fans were really turned on. You should have heard them. I figured I'd be lucky to get out of there alive."

Then there was a game in New York. The Cowboys against the Giants. As Norm remembers, a division title was riding on it.

"Pete Gogolak came in to kick a field goal from the twelve. One of the Cowboys—I think it was Bob Lilly—broke through and blocked the ball. Gogolak, without breaking stride, caught the ball with his left foot as it came off the ground and kicked it again. Greatest bit of reaction I ever saw. Darned if the ball didn't sail between the goal posts."

"Was it good?"

"Well, sixty-two thousand people thought it was good," Norm said. "I guess everybody watching all over the country did. But I threw my flag. The Giants all charged me. 'What's the flag for?' they said.

" 'I don't know,' I said. 'But something's wrong.'

"And it was wrong. I'd reacted instinctively, as you do with experience. You can't kick a loose ball. If Gogolak had caught the ball with his hands, and had control of it, he could have kicked it again. But this was a loose ball. I called it a touchback and gave the Cowboys the ball on their twenty.

"Don Meredith (the Dallas quarterback) came running in and said, 'Nice call, Norm.' Of course, he had absolutely no idea what I'd called."

Another time Schachter was working a game in Cleveland. Frank Ryan, the Cleveland quarterback, had just gotten a doctorate in mathematics.

On second-and-nine, the Browns made seven yards. But the other team was offside.

Schachter: "Frank, you've got an option. You made seven, so it will be third-and-two. Or you can take the offside and it's second-and-four."

Ryan: "Second-and-four? Wait a minute, Norm. How do you get four?"

Schachter: "Well, Frank, you work it this way: You start with nine and take away five. That leaves four. Back home, we call that basic math."

Ryan called Schachter something else. But he was smiling when he did it.

Schachter had another ready comeback when challenged by Bob Skoronski on an unforgettable, unbearable afternoon in Green Bay. It was the 1967 NFL title game between the Cowboys and Packers. Game time temperature: 13 degrees below zero.

"I blew my whistle to start the game and that was the last whistle anybody really heard all day," Norm said. "All the whistles froze. I guess nobody knows that. We called the whole game verbally and with arm signals.

"Joe Connell, my umpire, tried to blow his whistle but he just got a little tweet. When he took the whistle out of his mouth, part of his lip came with it. I'd put a rubber nipple on mine so it wouldn't freeze to my lips.

"Television needed a time out in the fourth quarter so I called one. Well, it was really freezing now. Skoronski, the offensive captain for Green Bay, came running up."

Skoronski: "Norm, who the hell called that time out?"

Schachter: "I did."

Skoronski: "What for?"

Schachter: "For the players' pension fund."

Skoronski: "Great call. Great call."

Schachter remembered another title game, one that got people down on him for a call he didn't even make. "It was the sudden-death game between Green Bay and Baltimore in 1965," he said. "Don Chandler won it for Green Bay with a field goal. The call was disputed but I'm sure it was good.

"On a play like this, I don't make the call. I just relay the signal. I've got other things to watch. For instance, whether somebody runs into the kicker. But they thought I called it. I'm told that Chuck Thompson of Baltimore, who announced the game, ended his sports show for three months after that by saying, 'Good night, Norm Schachter, wherever you are.' "

Referees run into second-guessers everywhere. Before Super Bowl V in Miami, Schachter had breakfast at his hotel coffee shop.

Waitress: "May I have your order?"

Schachter: "I don't know whether to have ham and eggs or sausage and eggs."

Waitress: "That'll probably be the toughest call you have all day."

Schachter: "Well, let me have the ham and eggs."

Waitress: "You blew that one, too."

Years earlier, on the morning of a 49ers-Colts game in Baltimore, Norm was having breakfast in a hotel dining room. It was being remodeled and there was a partition right behind him. A waitress accidentally bumped it and it started to fall on him. Leo Nomellini of the 49ers, seated nearby, jumped up and grabbed the partition.

"Saved me from getting a hell of a bang on the head," Schachter said. "I said, 'Thanks, Leo. I appreciated that.'

"Leo was a good player. Worked hard. Seldom fouled. But that afternoon I caught him and called a penalty."

Schachter: "Leo, you're using your hands."

Nomellini: "I knew I should have let the damn thing fall on you."

Sometimes, the language is not that polite. A Minnesota player once blew his noodle and cursed at Schachter. Schachter called a 15-yard penalty. Norm Van Brocklin, then coaching the Vikings, asked Schachter at halftime what the penalty was for.

Schachter: "Number fifty-eight called me a son of a bitch, coach, and nobody calls me a son of a bitch except you."

Van Brocklin (smiling): "You son of a bitch."

That wasn't the worst thing that ever happened to Schachter in a Minnesota game. In 1969, the Vikings played the Colts on the second weekend of the season. For Schachter, it turned out to be the end of the season.

"I saw the right tackle for Minnesota miss his block and I knew the defensive end was going to get to the quarterback, Joe Kapp. I moved back, waiting for Kapp to get hit, and he got it, from the blind side. He fumbled. I went behind him to cover the play. The tackle who had missed the block was coming back to try to help out. I stumbled and he ran up my back. I heard a pop, like a gun."

The tendon on Schachter's right leg had snapped. "It was pulled right off the bone and severed," he said. "A Baltimore player picked up the fumble and went about seventy-nine yards, but Don Shinnick was holding so they brought the ball back. I'd been wiped out on a play that didn't even count.

"I did four and a half hours of therapy a day for the next year. I'd exercise in the morning ten or fifteen minutes, then ride the stationary bicycle five miles. On my lunch break at school, I'd swim about twenty minutes and in the afternoon I'd drag myself around the track about a mile. Then I'd use the whirlpool for a half hour and walk two miles at night. It was a four-shower day for me."

Schachter got into officiating in 1941, while coaching high school ball in Redlands, California. "I think it was a college scrimmage," he said. "They needed somebody to fill in. I liked it right away."

Norm went into the Marines in 1941, but he returned to officiating in 1942. He worked hundreds of football, basketball, and baseball games in the Los Angeles area. Then, in 1953, he got a call from Bert Bell, the NFL commissioner. Norm has not had many fall weekends off since.

"I fly about one-hundred twenty thousand miles a season," he said. "I guess I must have flown two million miles altogether. The league office tells us about ten days in advance where we're going and we leave home Saturday morning. The home team will leave a projector in the referee's name at our hotel and the league sends out a film of the game we worked the week before. We meet after dinner to look over the film, review our mechanics, and see if there's anything we might do better.

"Most of our officials don't really need the jobs. Most have been very successful in other fields. We have druggists, lawyers, deans of colleges, business people. Officiating is just something they enjoy doing.

"For me, it's more than a part-time job. I make up the tests they give officials and work on the rule book. It runs about eighty-seven pages now and we're redoing the whole thing. I spend about a half hour a day on the rules. You can turn to any page in the book and ask me about a paragraph and I can probably quote the rule. If you miss on a judgment call, that's one thing. Everybody's going to do that once in a while. But I'd hate to be wrong on a rule, to have forgotten something I should have known."

Schachter gave up coaching years ago but admits he still does a little of it—in his head. Before the offensive team lines up, he'll often call the play to himself, trying to anticipate what the quarterback will do.

"About nine times out of ten you can tell what they're going to do," he said. "I may change my position when I know something is coming up, but I'll change only slightly so the players won't pick up on it and key on me. I try not to go near huddles. When you've done enough games, you just about know what hole they're going to look for.

"In our job, you can't really watch the game. One of my prime responsibilities as referee is to watch the quarterback. The referee has overall command of the game and stands behind the offense. The umpire is behind the defense, close to the line. The field judge is downfield. The head lines-man runs the chains, keeps track of the downs. Across the field from him is the line judge. The back judge is on the same side, only downfield. None of us can really see the game. I mean the *whole* game. If you get caught up in it, you'll miss something in your own area of responsibility. I went over to the sideline one time and there was a young official standing there, really wrapped up in the game. 'Wow!' he said. 'Great play!' I knew he wasn't going to be around very long. He wasn't."

To keep his job, an NFL official must consistently be in position to make the correct call. To be in position, he must be in condition. Schachter works out every day, riding his stationary bicycle five miles.

But, everything considered, he probably gets his best workout on Sunday.

"I think we cover a good four or five miles during the afternoon," he said. "And that's not even counting after the game, when they chase us."

by Mickey Herskowitz

A Lion in Winter

The plaque on the wall behind Sid Gillman's desk offers a brief, but inspiring message: "Illegitimi non carborundum." Loosely translated from the Latin, it means "Don't let the bastards get you down."

In other years, in another place, "they"—and they know who "they" are—on occasion got to him. Sid admits it. There was a time when each season exposed new plots against his team, his league, his digestion. Rival owners romanced his players. Opposing coaches offended his instincts by turning their football fields into rice paddies. Referees were struck blind at the most crucial moments. The fans did not always understand that what he did was for their own good.

They can't touch him now. Not anymore. As he begins a new job, a second lifetime, really, the place of Sid Gillman is secure. The fact that his new job is with a team and an owner—the Houston Oilers of Bud Adams—with whom he had quarreled often, and with a good degree of zest, only serves as a neat footnote to the uncertain character of professional football.

For all the time to come, Gillman will be an epic figure in the history of what is now the American Football Conference (nee League). He built the San Diego Chargers, helped create the franchise, coached them through years of early glory, kept them alive when the wolf was threatening to have pups on the carpet. Beyond that, he established the standards that, on the field and in the front office, swept the rest of the league along and gave them a target at which to shoot.

Sid's work ethic determined the office hours for those who wished to compete. So it was that when Al Davis, a Gillman protege, was hired to rehabilitate the Oakland Raiders, he quickly shut off complaints about his own penchant for late night meetings. "Don't think you're working so hard," Davis would tell his grumbling staff. "The lights are burning in San Diego, too."

It is worth noting that the American Football League would have been 15 years old in 1974, if it had lived. Of course, it survives in the imaginations and memory boxes of those who went through puberty with it. Which means that it does live, nonetheless.

In his later years in San Diego, from which he departed in 1972, Gillman was at times referred to in print as "The Lion in Winter." There was affection in that phrase, and respect. It fit. Gillman has always been a lion of a man, a member of that breed of coaches—Lombardi, Paul Brown, Bear Bryant—who were the last absolute monarchs football may see.

Times and techniques and the men who play the game have all changed, requiring a frequent adjustment in coaching philosophy. But, by and large, the coaches who were winning big a few years ago evoked a common reaction from their players: fear. A former San Diego halfback once confided that, in the locker room before a game, in that moment when each man meditated in his own way, the prayer was never for victory or to be spared serious injury. The prayer was: "Please, God, don't let me be the first one to screw up."

The lash of Sid Gillman's discipline was

Gene Holtan

to be avoided at any cost. But it wasn't just the need to attain a certain level of performance that Sid drummed into his troops. They did not simply *play* for San Diego. They *represented* it. They carried the flag for an entire league. Once, he kicked the mammoth Ernie Ladd out of camp for sassing a waitress.

But we digress. The point is, this seemed a fair time, and the right source, to talk about the springtime of the American Football League. San Diego's old Lion in Winter was agreeable. He usually is these days, which surprises people who remember the Gillman of 1960-65 who was so intense and dedicated that he only had room in his brain for X's and O's. In those days Sid knew how to be charming, but he didn't always have the time.

Time was still in short supply, as he poured himself into the task of reconstructing the Houston Oilers. The Oilers were the 26th best team in pro football in 1972 and 1973. They won once in 14 games in both years. It is a rebuilding job that begins from the socks up. The clock has almost—almost—turned back to 1960.

So he sits at his Houston desk, a blue paisley bow tie undone and dangling from his neck, an unlighted pipe in his hand, and rearranges the papers and letters and contracts that tell him how far the game has traveled in 14 years.

In 1960 a "damned good" lineman earned $12,000. Today you can't even open a conversation for less than $30,000. In 1960 the Chargers didn't have enough clean uniforms to go around on picture day. Some of the unclothed threatened to quit on the spot, including a halfback named Paul Lowe, who was to become a great one. Gillman convinced him that a uniform didn't make the man. And Lowe played on.

In three accelerated years Sid Gillman would create a powerhouse in San Diego. Houston, with an NFL retread named George Blanda at quarterback, and Buffalo, with an exquisite character named Cookie Gilchrist, had their taste of honey. At Dallas, and later Kansas City, coach Hank Stram was turning out quality teams each season. And, finally, a Joe Willie Namath would come along to give the New York Jets, and the American Football League, the ultimate, howling acceptance.

From its creation, Gillman was the one, single, most respected professional the new league had. Although he had been fired as coach of the Rams, his team had won a division title in his first season at Los Angeles (1955) and his credentials were not to be dismissed. He was tough and demanding, a brilliant football organizer and inventive thinker.

He helped show the rest of the AFL how to design a staff, how to scout, how to draft, how to act with class.

To measure the contribution that Gillman made, you have to understand what a joke the American Football League was in the beginning in the public consciousness. Of the men who met in October, 1959 to announce its formation, the best known of the owners was Harry Wismer, the jolly ex-sportscaster who had claimed the New York franchise. Wismer's immortality had been assured the day, during a radio broadcast of an exciting football game, that he invented the 55-yard line.

The rest were men of wealth who seemed to have sought just another play toy. Their own distinctions were assorted. Barron Hilton had once had Zsa Zsa Gabor as a stepmother. Lamar Hunt was the son of a Texas oilman so rich that he, H.L. Hunt, had figured out that he wasted $300,000 worth of his time *each year* taking the wrappers off cigars.

Bud Adams was another Texas millionaire, as flamboyant as Lamar Hunt was conservative.

The Chargers had sprung to life, more or less, in Los Angeles, a fact that the city—and the team—would in many ways just as soon forget. It was a strange moment, even stranger 14 years later when you can look back, as through an album of baby photographs, and see where it has all led. Sid Gillman was out of a job in the winter of 1959. He was thinking about a new career in stocks and bonds. He liked the action and the thought of making a little money didn't make him unduly nervous. He had *heard* about a new pro football league, and skimmed over a story or two in the papers, but that was all.

Then Frank Leahy, once the very spirit of Notre Dame football, known among his admirers as "The Master," had been hired by Barron Hilton to run the Los Angeles Chargers. Leahy offered Gillman the coaching job. It seemed absurd, suicidal on the face of it. How could any man in his right mind return as coach of a team that didn't yet exist, in a league that was probably doomed, in a city where he had been fired?

No coach can resist an opportunity like that. So Gillman signed on. And within a month or two Leahy, who was having health problems, bowed out. The ark was Sid's. All he had to do was fill it.

"All we had," he recalls, "were rejects from the NFL and a few college kids we were able to sign. The other league had great fun at our expense in those days. But the slander they threw at us never bothered me. For the most part, I believed it. I knew what was over there. And I could see what

we had. There simply was no comparison.

"But one of the first steps we took paid off. I put in the biggest taxi squad anyone had ever seen, and a first rate scouting system. We had fifty players coming, fifty going and fifty more in mind. Our recruiting system was like a Montgomery Ward's catalog. We went everywhere."

In the early sixties, when tribal warfare broke out in Africa, Don Klosterman, then in charge of talent for the Chargers, took note of the situation: "We hear there are only three civilians left in Katanga Province—two missionaries and a Chargers scout."

Gillman's ideas were quickly copied. Taxi squads flourished everywhere, practically forming a third professional league. One year, in San Diego, Sid paid *full* salaries to seven taxied players. "The biggest mistake I had made with the Rams," he remembered, "was in not maintaining a taxi squad. We just ran out of bodies. Everybody was getting killed. We had people playing two ways. But back then, the theory was that it would make your veterans mad if you had players sort of waiting in the wings."

All the AFL teams suffered from problems deeper than the feelings of their employees. The teams had few stars and too few fans. Their search for talent frequently took on the character of a Marx Brothers movie. In Los Angeles, Gillman held a tryout camp that seemed to attract every truck driver and bartender in Hollywood.

The Chargers went on to win the West that original season, but the Los Angeles police would have been hard pressed to find any eye witnesses. They lost to the Oilers in the AFL's first championship game, and a few weeks later Hilton announced that the franchise would move south to San Diego. No one seemed surprised.

In the meantime, the war was escalating. To get players, who would become the stars, who would attract the fans, who would make the new league solvent, the Hunts and Hiltons and Adamses and Wilsons engaged the NFL owners in a kind of dollar Olympics. Suddenly college seniors were the new elite, the nouveau riche. Prices soared. Bonuses, salaries, and fringe benefits were the stuff of headlines and court actions.

It was a time of abductions, seductions, and inductions. It was a wild and tempestuous time for pro football, and the zanier it got the bigger it grew. It seemed that the crazies had taken over. Sid Gillman saw it happen, knew it had to happen, and was right in there swinging. But his instincts as a purist were aggrieved.

"You know," he says, thoughtfully, "you

can sit down with Klosterman and he can go on for hours about the funny things that happened in the early years. Klosterman could probably write a book about them. Me, I can't even write a paragraph. It wasn't funny to me. The funny things just went right by me. Most of what happened just drove me nuts."

Early in the war, in 1962, the Chargers signed a halfback from Virginia Union with the grand name of Hezekiah Ezekial Braxton the Third. Braxton became a legend before—and up to—the moment he signed as a pro, because of a conversation between his coach and a scout for the Dallas Cowboys.

"Is he a football player?" began the scout, routinely.

"Is he a football player?" echoed the coach. "Only one better and his name is Jimmy Brown."

"Can he run?"

"Can he *run*? He runs one step ahead of the wind."

"Is he tough?"

"Is he *tough*? He was responsible last season for seventeen stretcher cases, fourteen limpoffs, and eighteen positively-refused-to-return-to-the-games."

"Can he block?"

There probably was a pause. "Can he block?" repeated the old coach.

"Now, listen here, let me ask you a question. If he's blockin', that means somebody else is carryin' the ball, right?"

"Right."

"Mister," said the coach, "you just made your first mistake."

Sadly, Braxton's career in San Diego was brief, and he disappeared from the pro football scene.

Those were free and exaggerated years and pro football, for better or for worse, will never see their likes again.

One of the things that kept the AFL intact, thinks Sid, was the innocence and unselfishness of the owners, at a time when a little more knowledge and experience would have been fatal.

"We helped each other," he says. "We shared ideas, information. We worked together. Looking back, it was a beautiful thing. If one club had the rights to a player who might be more useful, say, might draw better, in another area, we shifted them around. That's how Boston let us have Ron Mix in San Diego."

As the AFL grew stronger, as each passing season brought the impression of more permanence, the old attitude of we're-all-in-this-together gave way to free enterprise. Gillman woke up one morning to learn that one of his prize linemen, Earl Faison, was being entertained by another AFL team.

Even now, years later, his voice rises at the thought of it. "Here he's our property," he says, "being tampered with by the owner of another team, openly, flagrantly. If that had happened in the National Football League, Pete Rozelle would have hanged them."

The Chargers were to be the dominant team of the AFL's first five years. Even today Sid thinks that his 1963 squad may have been the greatest the league has produced, and many less prejudiced observers agree with him. That team demolished Boston in the title game 51-10. It had Ladd and Faison, Lowe and Keith Lincoln, Mix and Walt Sweeney, a superb year by the reclaimed quarterback, Tobin Rote, and a great young receiver named Lance Alworth ("If Lance played the piano, he would probably sound like Artur Rubenstein.")

But the Chargers were headed for a period of attrition in the mid-sixties, and the dynasty talk was heard no more. "The rest of the league was gunning for us," says Sid. "We hit that stage where, for four or five years, we had little money to work with. It was all so costly. There were very few men who could stand the losses the owners absorbed in those years. At the draft, we'd have two blackboards, one with the names of players who would cost big money to sign, the other with those who didn't figure to come high. We always drafted from the second board."

Changes were taking place in San Diego, as they were throughout the league. Barron Hilton had sold out. "Barron is a marvelous guy," says Sid, "and my family loves him. But football, after all, was just a sideline for Barron."

The new ownership, headed by Eugene Klein, represented the kind of corporate wealth that was now moving ever more prominently into professional sports. A new stadium was in the planning stage. And finally, Sid Gillman would twice step out as coach of the team he created.

The second coming—and going—would be the more bitter. Sid quit late in the season of 1971. Before that, in 1969, Sid had retired on doctor's orders, felled by physical discomforts that included ulcers. "It was my design to give them," he said at the time, "not get them."

Sid did both in his career. John Hadl, the quarterback, as well as Paul Lowe, both developed ulcers, too.

Today the AFL years tend to run together for Sid Gillman. There were a plentitude of sweet moments and fast lines. He remembers the year the Pope called his Ecumenical Council, during the height of the war between the leagues. Sid quickly fired off a telegram to Pete Rozelle, commissioner of the aristocratic National Football League:

"POPE JOHN WAS A GREAT MAN BECAUSE HE RECOGNIZED THE OTHER LEAGUE."

And Rozelle wired back:

"YES. BUT IT TOOK A THOUSAND YEARS."

Ironically, Rozelle had been the publicity man for the Los Angeles Rams, when he was asked to check out a coaching prospect who had compiled an impressive record at the University of Cincinnati: Sid Gillman.

Few had more reason than Sid to celebrate when the merger of the leagues was consummated in 1970, and Baltimore, Cleveland, and Pittsburgh joined the American Football Conference to provide numerical equity. "We brought up three teams from the minors," observed Sid, getting in a last, friendly dig.

In the view of many, Gillman had given the new league its first touch of class. He had stressed the importance of developing their own stars. He had taught them how to organize.

At San Diego, he assembled a staff the likes of which hadn't been seen since the Allied invasion of Normandy. His coaches included Al Davis, Jack Faulkner, Joe Madro, and Chuck Noll. Klosterman, now the general manager of the Rams, was the talent hunter. In the front office was Al LoCasale, who came to Sid as a male stenographer and today, in Oakland, is regarded as one of football's more lucid minds.

Sid thinks back, and he knows the American Football League would not exist today if anyone had really understood how long it would take, how much money, how much in the way of sacrifice and, yes, ego.

"I can't separate it," he says. "The fight to get the franchise established, the '63 team that was just outstanding, and the whole story of San Diego, a beautiful town, but a conservative town, where I was told they hadn't passed a bond issue in a thousand years. And to me Jack Murphy was the key. His sports column. Without him the city wouldn't have a franchise today."

The Lion in Winter has indeed mellowed. "They" can't bother him now. The league is secure. So is his legend. "I'm a coach at heart," he says, "I've given up on league politics. But I have no complaints. I have spent the better part of my life among people who, in the things they do, are the most talented people in the world. You can't beat that kind of life."

Illustrations by Doug Johnson

Men in Motion

The game was once played strictly between the tackles. It was a struggle of huge men, masses in pads and helmets. Push and shove. Clutch and grab. Thrust and growl. It was primitive and lacking in beauty. It belonged to the rough-hewn men who played the old game of football and their ancestors, the brawlers and maulers of the steel mills and trainyards of working class America. It was intensely their game, a test of machismo much the same as two men wristwrestling across the bar or warring with bare knuckles in the alley out back.

But during the 1950s, the game began to change. The concept of offense was knocked out of kilter. No longer did teams find it necessary to drive 80 yards upfield on 20 or more running plays, spilling blood and shortening careers each step along the way. Teams introduced new formations designed to utilize the forward pass—once regarded as purely a footnote in the rulebook, reserved for desperate situations and pickup games on the sandlot.

With the birth of the passing game came a new breed of athlete—the wide receiver. Not big enough to run through the middle of the line, not strong enough to carry the ball 30 times a game, yet introducing new skills and creating new problems for the defense.

Today, they have changed the look of the game. It is no longer a hopeless tangle of bodies at the line of scrimmage. It is no longer strictly a game appealing to the brutes and bullies among us.

On these pages, artist Doug Johnson has captured the exquisite essence of the wide receiver. The smoothness of Paul Warfield …the elusive perception of San Francisco's Gene Washington…the blue streak trailed by Minnesota's swift John Gilliam. They are all masters of their art, yet each brings something new to his interpretation.

There are very fast men such as Olympic gold medalist Bob Hayes of Dallas, who comes off the line in a violent explosion of energy, fleeing toward a finish line only he can see. There are other receivers with little speed but extraordinary moves who leave faster cornerbacks embarrassed and beaten in the open field. Among the best at this are Miami's Howard Twilley, Oakland's Fred Biletnikoff, and former New York Jet Don Maynard, the all-time leading receiver in pro football history.

"I started in this league as a running back, then switched to wide receiver," says Washington's brilliant Charley Taylor, "and there is a big difference. When you're running the ball at the line, you know your assignment but you aren't really thinking—you're more reacting. But when you're a wide receiver running a pattern, you're thinking all the time—when you should make your move, how deep, where the defensive back is, and how to lose him. It's like a game within a game.

"It can be embarrassing when you make a mistake and drop a pass because you're right out there in the open for the whole world to see. But there's no feeling in the world like catching that ball behind the defense, then just running for all your worth into the end zone and hearing that crowd go wild. It's a high like nothing else I've known."

Paul Warfield

Gene Washington

John Gilliam

by John Wiebusch

Winning Isn't the Only Thing

In Toots Shor's place that night, he was king. Art Rooney, waving that cigar, laughing that big Irish laugh, signaling to Johnny behind the circle bar to do it one more time.

They were gathered around him, the worshipers and admirers and friends. A priest. A fight promoter. A fight manager. A fighter. A baseball manager. A horse trainer. A jockey. A millionaire industrialist. All the cronies.

It was good times and it was ritual. They knew him, all of them. They had been there before. They had heard all the stories.

They sat amidst the cigar smoke and they were with him. "Boys," said Art Rooney, "I'd like to win this one. It's been a long time."

They smiled and shouted and raised their glasses. "To number one," someone said and Art Rooney was smiling. "We are going to give them holy hell," he said. "We are going to bring home the bacon to Pittsburgh."

It had been 30 years. It had started in 1933. The Pittsburgh Steelers had gone at it all those times and they had come away with empty hands in every season. They had placed second four times—but never closer than three games behind —and they had tied for first once. In 1947, Pittsburgh and Philadelphia both finished with 8-4 records and they played it off in Pittsburgh. It was no contest. The Eagles won 21-0.

In 1963, there was another chance. The futility could be ended. The frustration could be over. If the Steelers defeated the Giants in Yankee Stadium the championship of the National Football League's Eastern Conference would be theirs. The Giants had three more wins than the Steelers but the Steelers had three ties and sometimes ties were as good as a victory. In the season of the slide rule, the Steelers could finish 13 percentage points ahead of the Giants with a victory.

Early in the year, in Pittsburgh, the two teams had met and the Steelers had won 31-0. But these were the Giants of Tittle and Gifford and Huff and in the north winds of Yankee Stadium they were favored to win.

"Every time the Giants score a point," said Toots Shor, "I'm going to take a little nip against the cold. I expect to be loaded by the middle of the third quarter."

Everybody laughed again, even Art Rooney. They all knew he was kidding. Toots Shor loved Art Rooney. Everybody did.

It is a line in the Steelers' pressbook, there on page 74. It is like a lot of lines in the Steelers' pressbook. It says losing. It says empty hands. It says: New York 33, Pittsburgh 17.

Time does not heal all things. Sometimes time leaves open wounds. In 1972, nine years since the Year That Almost Was for Art Rooney, the Pittsburgh Steelers, the team he owns, have not had a winning season. They have finished last four times and they have averaged less than four victories a year.

They have not broken any hearts.

39

Three Rivers Stadium sits on the low-lands of the Allegheny River. The Monongahela flows nearby and when it joins with the Allegheny it crashes together and moves west. Together, the Allegheny and the Monongahela become the Ohio River.

Art Rooney is pointing out to the still brown water that separates the stadium from the steel and glass of downtown Pittsburgh. He is standing in the parking lot that goes down to the Allegheny.

"That water looks pretty peaceful now," he says. "But that's because it's August and not April. You know, once, a long time ago, I darned near drowned here, right near this spot.

"I tell you it was something. In those days—this was back before they had flood controls—if you spit in these rivers, the flood came up. It wasn't unusual to paddle our way to school in a boat.

"Well, right here on this spot, right where this new stadium is built, there used to be a park called Expo Park. The Pirates played there before Forbes Field opened in 1909. My dad's saloon was right over there, across the street.

"This one year there was an awful flood and three of us were paddling our way to school in a canoe—a kid named Squawker Mullen, my brother, Dan, and me. We were taking that canoe right through the outfield in old Expo Park. Squawker was moving around in the canoe and I told him to sit down. Sure as shooting he was going to upset it—and sure as shooting he did. Squawker and Dan didn't have boots and a coat on, so they made it easily. But me, I had on boots and an overcoat. I'll tell you, it was my last gasp when I reached out and grabbed hold of that grandstand."

The memories are alive and he shakes his head. He looks toward the stadium that is only three years old and he shakes his head again. "That's some sports park," he says. "That's some place for a team to play. And maybe win a championship." He is winking and grinning.

With baggy pants and tousled hair, he seems an intruder in the graphic modern offices of the Steelers. The offices were put together by a designer and they look it. There are open spaces and bold paintings and stitcheries; there are glass-topped desks and fruitwood-paneled walls. They do not fit Art Rooney. The offices used to be in the old Roosevelt Hotel, just off a lobby of potted palms. In the old offices there were stuffed chairs with worn edges and pictures hung at random and an old air conditioner that worked occasionally and made a lot of noise when it did. Those offices fit Art Rooney.

"Pretty nice, huh?" he says to a visitor and he leads the way through a reception area as big as the whole lobby of the Roosevelt.

"It's beautiful," says the visitor. "But do you like all the order?"

"The image of the Steelers is changing," he says. "We're winning more now, we're playing in this stadium, we're selling a lot of tickets."

In another time, the Steelers were pro football's rag dolls and the attendance showed it. In the fifties, when pro football was growing, the crowds at Steelers' games were small; in the sixties, when pro football was mushrooming, the crowds were . . . well, embarrassing.

"I don't feel good about it," he says. "I didn't like losing games and I didn't like losing money. But I'll tell you something. And this is from the bottom of my heart: Whatever I lost in money I was lucky to be able to lose it. I'd pay to lose it . . . to keep in this game. I love it that much.

"And you know they've been mighty good to me here in Pittsburgh but then they've given me some raspberries, and that's all right. If I were sitting out there, I'd boo Art Rooney, too. But these are my people and this is my town and it does my heart good just to be here."

Over the years, he has had offers to sell and chances to move. Atlanta, Boston, Baltimore, New Orleans, Houston, Cincinnati. They all came around. Art Rooney said no to all of them.

"I couldn't leave Pittsburgh," he says. "I wouldn't leave Pittsburgh. My home's here."

The house in which he lives with his wife, Kathleen, the house where he raised his five sons, is a five-minute walk from Three Rivers Stadium. The house is three-story Victorian, a fascinating relic in a neighborhood that is mostly parking lots and rooming houses now. The Rooneys have lived in the house for nearly four decades.

"Before we moved to this house," he says, "I only lived in one other house in my whole life and that was just out the door and across the street from here. Not for all the money you could show me could you get me to move away. Kathleen knows that."

Art Rooney is a millionaire. He owns the Pittsburgh Steelers. He has a 365-acre farm in Maryland, the major part of whose population is made of 120 thoroughbreds. He has bought and sold major blocks of commodities and has interests in the stock market. His five sons control three major racetracks—Liberty Bell Park, Yonkers Raceway, and the Palm Beach Kennel Club.

Art Rooney wears baggy pants and lives in a neighborhood past its prime. He gives away quarters to the kids who come around and he sits on his porch and says that all he wants to do is make people happy.

It makes you feel good just to be around him.

The place that has been Art Rooney's life is the 22nd Ward now but once it was the First Ward. They called it The Ward and sure'n if you weren't wearin' green on the seventeenth of March you'd better have stayed away.

Art Rooney was the oldest child in the saloon keeper's family. There were six boys and two girls and their hair was red and their cheeks were freckled.

They were athletes, all of them, but Art and Dan were the special ones. They played baseball and the major league teams came around with contracts. They boxed and the promoters were excited. They played football and they were good enough to get offers from Knute Rockne at Notre Dame.

They played semipro baseball against the black teams, the Homestead Grays and the Kansas City Monarchs. They toured the carnivals, challenging the carny boxer ("I'll take on any man in the house. Now, who wants to be the first to try?"). They started a semipro football team called Hope-Harvey. They even played the Canton Bulldogs and Jim Thorpe once, and Art Rooney missed a field goal and Jim Thorpe ran it back for a touchdown and Canton won 6-0.

Oh, they had a grand time. Art and Dan playing all the games, going away now and then to try minor league baseball, going to school at Duquesne or Georgetown or Washington & Jefferson.

And going to racetracks.

Art Rooney was 23 years old when he went to a racetrack for the first time. It was a track in Ohio named Maple Heights. That was the place where the kid from The Ward fell in love with the horses.

In 1936, Art Rooney spent one afternoon at a New York track called Empire City and another at Saratoga. It was over a weekend and he won a lot of money. Maybe $250,000. Maybe $350,000. A lot of money.

"You bet with bookmakers then," says Art Rooney. "Racing's not the same today. All the romance is gone. They took away the characters when they brought in the parimutuel machines. Ah, the bookies, they were wonderful people. They were just folks."

He is asked about the weekend in 1936 and he says, "Don't believe everything you read in the papers." And then he is laughing and talking about it.

"We drove up from Pennsylvania and we got to Empire City just before the first race. I bet $20 with a bookmaker in the grandstand and won $700 or so. I felt sorry for the guy because it really clubbed him right off, so I went back to him to give him a chance to get even and I let the whole thing go. Well, I had three or four winners and I ended up breaking the guy.

"That was a Saturday and on Monday Saratoga was opening and so we drove up there and, anyway, I came close to sweeping the card. It was the best day I've ever had and Bill Corum, the sportswriter, was right there and he saw it and he wrote a column about it. Well, then the stories about me just kept getting bigger and bigger and one of the papers put a guy on me, to go around with me at the track. One day this reporter had me winning big and I says to him, 'Hey, what is this? I had a bad day yesterday. I lost. And you had me winning.' And this guy—oh, he was a funny little fellow—he says, 'Look, I like this assignment and it's only going to last as long as you win. Once you start losing, this assignment ends.' But heck, it made for good reading, all this talk about me being so lucky."

A few years ago a national turf newspaper had a series of articles on notable horseplayers.

One of the articles was about Art Rooney. It said, "Arthur J. Rooney of Pittsburgh is one of the greatest horseplayers of all time."

Walking down North Lincoln Avenue, the avenue on which Art and Kathleen live, you listen to him talk.

"There is the image of me as the benevolent loser. That even though my football teams have never won anything it doesn't bother me. Well, that's foolishness. I keep a lot to myself when we lose but you'd better believe that I hurt inside every time. When we lose, I don't want to talk about it and I don't want to read about it. I don't want to see any replays.

"Buddy Parker, who coached here for some years, said once that one day the Pittsburgh Steelers are going to get lucky and when they do it'll last for ten years. I'm waiting for that day.

"I thought sure that it would be 1963. But in that game against the Giants we got nothing but bad breaks. We missed a couple of passes that could have been touchdowns. On another play a fellow from our team was in the clear in the end zone and he dropped the ball. There was nobody near him. And then Gifford made a fantastic one-handed catch—like you would a

baseball—to give them a touchdown and they went on to beat us for the championship. That game is a sore spot. And that's the closest we've come. The closest.

"You know, in 1941 I went up to our summer camp in Hershey to watch a workout. The team had their new uniforms on. They looked terrible and when a sportswriter asked me what I thought I told him so. I said, 'The only thing different is the uniform. It's the same old Steelers.' The papers have never let me forget that. We lose and the headlines still say, 'Same Old Steelers.' It hurts."

He was awarded the franchise rights for Pittsburgh in 1933. It cost him $2,500 and the word is that he won the money at the track the day before. Art Rooney says he's not sure if that's true or untrue. He says it without smiling.

The modern era of football began in 1933. Bert Bell was awarded a franchise for Philadelphia that year and the National Football League, a scattergun collection of clubs for most of its first dozen years, stabilized and played its game in two divisions for the first time.

And the team that was owned by Art Rooney, the team he called the Pittsburgh Pirates—the same as his favorite baseball team—finished in last place.

"But it was fun," he says. "It was a lark. There was Tim Mara and George Halas and George Preston Marshall and Bert Bell and Curly Lambeau…a lot of fine folks.

"We knew that professional football would be a good thing in Pennsylvania but you see, up to then there had been laws they called 'blue laws.' This was going to be changed by the legislature. So they gave us a franchise and our schedule was made up, but a couple days before the first game they called me up and told me that some preacher said that the game shouldn't be allowed on account of the blue laws. The city council had to ratify the repeal and it wouldn't meet until Tuesday.

"But I wanted this new team of mine to open on schedule and so I went to see the superintendent of police, a man named McQuaid. I told him my problem and he thought it was silly. He said, 'Give me a couple of tickets and I'll go to the game. That'll be the last place they'll look for me if they want to stop it.'

"So McQuaid hid out at the game and we had three thousand, maybe thirty-five hundred, people there. It was a beginning. We didn't grow quickly, either. I mean our football team or our attendance.

"We plugged along, selling a few tickets here and there, trying to break even. We didn't make a lot but we didn't lose a lot, either. Our payroll for those early years didn't amount to much."

The early years are 39 years in the past. In the new stadium, the team has drawn more than 90 percent of capacity. The Pittsburgh Steelers are solvent and self-supporting and that much has changed. The complimentary ticket list has not. Some of the names on it came with the franchise.

They pared the list before they moved to Three Rivers in 1970. Art Rooney was gone when they did it. But he found out. His people got back to him. The priests and the policemen got back on the list.

His is a euphoria born of giving. He is a soft touch for a hard-luck story. And if you are a priest and you have a hard-luck story, well, mercy, you had better open an account.

The stories are legend…

Once he was in New York for some NFL meetings. There was a cab strike at the time and it was not easy to get away from the airport. Rooney managed to get one, however, and as he was leaving he saw a harried priest trying to summon a cab. Rooney ordered his driver to stop and pick the priest up.

They talked as they drove to Manhattan and Rooney learned that the priest was a missionary who had come to New York to solicit funds. Rooney asked who he was going to see and the priest named several wealthy men. He mentioned a friend of Rooney's and Rooney said, "Put him at the top of the list." He reached into his pocket then and he pulled out a roll of bills and pushed them into the priest's hand. "When you talk to him, tell him that Art Rooney started you off with ten grand."…

Once he was driving back from the track. He had had a good day. Along the way he saw a young priest on a corner, waiting for a bus. He stopped the car and offered a ride.

"You look worried, Father," said Art Rooney.

"I am," said the priest. "A fire burned out the roof of our church and I don't know where we're going to get the seventy-five hundred dollars to replace it."

"Here," said the driver. And he stopped at the next light and counted $7,500 out of a pocketful of money.…

Once a church in Pittsburgh was taking a special collection for an orphanage. The giving seemed generous but still the total was only $1,300.

Art Rooney, just returned from a few days at Saratoga, heard about it. He visited the priest and said he'd like to do his part for the orphans. The priest said, "Fine," and Art Rooney handed him ten thousand-dollar bills.

"I hope you came by this honestly," said the surprised priest.

Rooney nodded. "I won it on the horses," he said....

A few years ago they gave a testimonial dinner for Art Rooney. They were going to present him with a magnificent gift. A car or a boat or something like that. Art Rooney would have none of it. He agreed to the idea of a testimonial but only if all the money was given to the Crippled Children's Fund.

He doesn't want to talk about the giving. He says, "You didn't come all the way out here just to make me sound like some Good Samaritan, did you? Why, we should be talking about the people who have been here."

The people. The Steelers have often been accused of being a team without character. They have never been accused of being a team without characters.

Johnny Blood McNally. Whizzer White. Walt Kiesling. Joe Bach. Bill Dudley. Jock Sutherland. Ernie Stautner. Jim Finks. Lynn Chandnois. Bobby Layne. Buddy Parker. Gene (Big Daddy) Lipscomb. John Henry Johnson. To name a few.

Art Rooney delights in telling stories, in rambling through the past. But the fervor is unflappable when the subject is Johnny Blood. He played for the Steelers in 1934 and then he went away for a year and then he came back to play and coach from 1937-39. Ask Art Rooney about Johnny Blood and he grins and says, "Oh, my," and he begins to talk.

"You know he may have been the only coach in history who had the players looking out after him instead of the other way around. Once we played a game before the season in Los Angeles and John missed the train coming back.

"The team was going on to Charleston, West Virginia, for a game with the Eagles and we got there and we were there for the whole week and still there was no Johnny Blood. What happened was that he stopped off in Chicago on his way back—he was known to have a good time along the way—and it was Sunday and he saw that the Packers were playing the Bears and so he went out to the park. The Packers were his old team and he had a lot of friends there. Someone asked him why he wasn't with the Steelers and he said, 'Oh, we're not playing this week.' Well, no sooner had he said that than the fellow with the loudspeaker announced a first-quarter score: 'Philadelphia seven, Pittsburgh zero.'

"But I'll tell you, he was loved by the players. Of course they loved the loose rules. I don't think there ever was such a thing as a check-in time and at that time that was really something. Johnny Blood was something.

"One time we were playing New York and every time we'd get into scoring position John would put himself in the game and something would happen and we wouldn't make it. This happened a couple times and finally our captain went to the referee and asked him if he could reject a player and the referee told him yes. So Blood came into the game the next time we got close and they wouldn't take him. He ran off the field—now understand he's the coach—and he's hollering and shouting that he'd get even with the captain. So we scored and when they came off the field he said, 'Well, that's what I was going in for. I was going to tell you to call that play.'

"And doggone, you have to know about the game we had one time at Forbes Field when he got his leg cut wide open, right down the leg. And it was just laying wide open and he would go in the huddle and put his foot down and the blood would shoot all over. The rest of our ball players all got sick. They asked him to leave but he wouldn't and every time he'd take a step his shoe would fill up with blood."

Art Rooney's face is aglow. "He still comes back here at least once a year and we talk and we talk. We have a nice relationship."

The bond is special but it is not unique. Art Rooney will fire a coach (he fired Blood in the midst of a disastrous 1939 season) and release or trade a player. But it is never without pain. And although the business relationship may end, the personal one seldom does.

Whizzer White, who is known around the Supreme Court as Byron R. White, played one season for the Steelers. He visits Art Rooney regularly and once he said, "Art is the finest man I've ever known."

Art Rooney cares for people. He thinks about feelings. Walt Kiesling was the Steelers' coach three different times. Joe Bach coached the team twice—with a 25-year interim in between. "Firing a guy is brutal," says Art Rooney. "I feel for the families."

He accepts the role of the heavy reluctantly and infrequently. But he often has been the peacemaker, the intercessor between the volatile coach and the fiery player. Art Rooney has had a lot of both of them.

"Kiesling was as stubborn as a man could be," he says. "But Jimmy Finks was the same way. Now I think that Jimmy was a great quarterback—one of the best—and he was the life of our club in the early fifties. But he and Kies were always scrapping. I loved them both. Oh, that Jimmy he was a smart one.

"And Kies, my old friend, was around here for years. He was part of the franchise.

He was tough, oh my. I remember once before a game the players were going to strike. See, Kies gave one-hundred percent of himself and he didn't realize that there's few humans that can give one-hundred percent in sports or anything. So he was a slave driver. But I told these players that although he was hard as nails and difficult to get to know that when you did get through to him he was your friend for life. They played that game and finished the trip and it turned out that about five or six of the guys from that team ended up being his closest friends.

"But Kies had his funny little foibles and you weren't about to change him if he felt some way about somebody. Like Lynn Chandnois: He was a great running back in the fifties—I think Bill Dudley was the best we ever had but Chandnois was right behind him—but Kies thought he didn't give one-hundred percent and he was always against him. Once in a game with the Giants, Lynn ran the opening kickoff back ninety-seven yards to a touchdown. A little later he ran ninety yards for a touchdown and then after that he ran sixty yards for another touchdown. We won the game sixty-three to seven—it was just incredible—and after the game Kies dressed and came into the office. I'll never forget his words. He said, 'Can you imagine that lucky bum?' We had to laugh."

Kiesling's personal prejudices were one thing. You could laugh at those. A decision he made in 1955 is another thing. Art Rooney wails over that.

"We had Johnny Unitas in training camp—drafted him ninth out of the University of Louisville. That same year there was a kidnap scare and my twin boys were up at camp with the club at St. Bonaventure and they kept writing me back about how the best quarterback in camp was this guy Johnny Unitas. One of the letters said, 'But the only one he throws to is us and we're not on the team.' So Kies released him. He said, 'He can't remember the plays. He's dumb.' When you talk about regrets, there's one big one there. But I'll tell you, we seem to be experts here in Pittsburgh in trading away quarterbacks. You want a quarterback, you come to us. We drafted Sid Luckman and traded him away. We had Earl Morrall. We had Unitas. We had Len Dawson. We had Jackie Kemp. We had Bill Nelsen. I guess we didn't have much foresight."

He shakes his head over the might-have-beens. But his eyes are moist when he talks about Jock Sutherland and Big Daddy Lipscomb.

"Jock was one of the great coaches this sport has ever known. He was a genius at the University of Pittsburgh and when he

came here in 1946 we had won only two games combined in the two years before. He brought us to five-hundred in his first year and then we tied the Eagles for first the next year, '47, before we lost in that playoff game. Jock died the next spring. They found his car in a ditch and him slumped over the wheel. He had a malignant tumor on the brain. They operated…but it was too late."

And Big Daddy. "He was a great football player and we only got to see him for two years, '61 and '62. He was the kind of guy who would try anything, though. He did everything to excess. I don't believe he was on dope while he was with the team—the players would have known and they didn't. I have to believe he tried it and he took too much. Just two days before he died he called me and asked me to send him some money. I sent him $500 and when they found him most of that money was in his pocket."

Art Rooney is the president of the Pittsburgh Steelers but he has relinquished most of the active duties to two of his sons. Dan Rooney and Art Rooney, Jr. run the day-to-day operations of the club.

He still comes around the offices but mostly it is to admire. "I never was one much for details," he says. "The boys are way out in front on everything. The way it is with me is like when it's time for meetings and the draft and such, I'd just as soon not be out shooting the breeze with the sportswriters."

He was inducted into Pro Football's Hall of Fame in 1964. "I am lucky," he said to the gathering at Canton and then he said that, oh well, even though his team hadn't beaten the Giants the previous year, why he was too old to start fretting. He said the Steelers' day would still come.

And today, out there on the porch, he says it again. "I am lucky," he says. "I am lucky in life."

He has lived in the same city for 71 years. He has been married to the same woman for 43 years. He has owned the same football team for 39 years. He has lived in the same house for 35 years.

"Afternoon, Mr. Rooney." It is a boy of 12, maybe 13. He is wearing a Steelers sweatshirt.

"Richard," says Art Rooney, "you've got just three more weeks of this playtime before you start getting back to the school books again."

"Yes, sir," says Richard, and Art Rooney pats him on the shoulder. He is reaching into his pocket.

Ernie Davis

Jim Brown

by Jim Barniak

Thunder Out of Syracuse

At first glance, Archbold Stadium looks as if it was constructed to stage Greek drama or maybe protect Syracuse University from Indian attacks. Built in 1889, it has survived as the country's oldest football "bowl" and now, though seemingly choked off from the rest of the campus by high-rise expansion, it is still home for the Syracuse football team.

Down on the field, they are still going with real, live grass, a symbolic reminder that football is still your basic, old fashioned, rock-'em, sock-'em game. At Syracuse, they have not yet heard of all the new-fangled artificial surfaces. In fact, they have yet to get over the shock of the forward pass.

This is run country. To the left, right, up the middle, on third-and-18. You get the ball, you run with it. On that note, Archbold Stadium shall go down in history as America's foremost showplace of the run. Yes, this ancient combination rickety amphitheater and Fort McHenry North. It is the ground gainer's Mecca. Not the big Coliseum in Los Angeles or the stadium at Notre Dame or anything they've got in Texas. When you talk about the run, old Archbold is where it's at.

Almost as old as the stadium, certainly as sturdy and ten times as lively, is Floyd (Ben) Schwartzwalder who coached football at Syracuse for the past 24 seasons. He's going to retire at the end of the 1974 season and there is talk already that his successor will put in some passing plays. Well, they better be good because ol' Ben's running plays make up an entire era of football.

It started when a 16-year-old freshman named Jim Brown hit campus in 1953 and it let up only recently in 1967, when a brawling, half-track of a fullback named Larry Csonka left school to pursue a Super Bowl with the Miami Dolphins.

In between, they gave the ball to guys like Ernie Davis, Jim Nance, and Floyd Little. Together with Brown and Csonka, the five gained a career total of 11,720 yards at Syracuse. Almost seven miles. For the coach and followers of Syracuse football, they were the seven most beautiful miles in America—whether the powerful, generally short bursts of Csonka and Nance, the uncanny broken-field long gainers of Little and Davis, or the awsome thrusts of Brown.

And these were the big names, all of whom, with the exception of Davis, who died of leukemia shortly after graduation, went on to further glory and yardage records in professional football. There were others of the era who left their best running days behind them: Jimmy Ridlon, who turned to defense in the pros; Art Baker, who opted for the Canadian League; or German immigrant Gerhard Schwedes, a number one draft pick of the Boston Patriots in 1960 who simply didn't make it.

Throughout the era, there was something magical about the running plays at Syracuse. Out of healthy backs, coach Schwartzwalder would grab, say, an end, a guy like John Mackey, and give him the ball. Mackey has been called the greatest tight end in the history of pro football. He might have been a back had it not been for a history of calcium trouble in his legs.

But he got the ball occasionally and was the running hero in his final games in 1962,

Richard Huebner

leading an upset over Navy and Roger Staubach, returning a punt for a touchdown (a first for a Schwartzwalder-coached team at Syracuse) against George Washington and closing with a dramatic rush in a 12-7 win over UCLA.

Isn't it rather amazing that one school would produce such a flow of talent, all schooled to perfection in the art of carrying a football under arm?

Was some underground network of skulduggery at work here? Wide open recruiting? Did Jim Brown really major in basketweaving? Who told Floyd Little when it was fourth down? You can't run over and around people Saturday after Saturday and expect to be a hallmark in the humanities, you know.

On that count, Syracuse stands doubly proud. Jim Brown carried the mace at the head of the graduation parade, an honor symbolic of all-around campus excellence. Ernie Davis was granted the same honor. Mackey, Little, and Ridlon were honor students. Of all the great backs, Csonka was the only one who didn't earn a diploma. The burdens of supporting a wife and a child and the lure of a rich pro contract served to diminish his lust for academics.

Csonka says: "If you've got any talent, sooner or later it comes to the forefront. At Syracuse, you sure got the ball. If you could run with it, you got the chance to prove it and develop into something."

Since the senior heroics of Brown in 1956, there was a built-in intangible contributing to the success. Brown left as a legend. New backs coming in were confronted with a standard of excellence. If it wasn't Brown's records you were shooting for, or Davis's, then it was Little's and now Csonka's. And there were moments when the legend became powerful enough to become a tangible. This is recruiting.

Brown was influential in bringing Davis to Syracuse and Davis, in death, was to sway Little. And, as though it were the proper thing to do, jersey number 44 was passed along as part of the deal. However, getting it all started with Brown was, as coach Schwartzwalder suggests, perhaps a stroke of luck.

At Manhasset High on New York's Long Island, Brown was a 13-letter winner, only 15 years old as a senior and literally dominating his peers in football, basketball, baseball, track, and lacrosse. Oddly enough, the latter sport may have been the one that steered him toward Syracuse.

A local lacrosse enthusiast named Ken Molloy, a Syracuse alumnus and Manhasset attorney, became an ardent sideline follower of Brown and developed into a family friend. Naturally, he directed Brown toward his alma mater. But not before rounding up all the alumni on the island to help.

"Oh, there was a fine little to-do over ol' Jim," says Schwartzwalder, biting into a fresh cigar that he chain-chews. "There were those in the admissions department suspicious whether the boy could make it here academically. And, I couldn't get a scholarship for him because I had used up my enormous allotment. Twelve, you know. So, we turned the boy down.

"Well, you should have seen the commotion. All the alumni out on Long Island there are plenty upset. One fellow, a judge name of, eh, I should never forget this guy's name. Oh, yeah, A. Holly Patterson, he made it known that unless we admit Brown there's going to be a significant decline in alumni donations from that particular area. Well, they went back and forth about grades and scholarships and here they're talking about ol' Jim who, besides all the athletics, is the extemporaneous speaking champion of the island. You didn't know that, did you?

"Well, it all got settled. Ended up that the alumni set up a scholarship for him the first year. Then, after that, he got one from my enormous allotment. And after that, of course, all we hear was what a football factory we were turning into.

"I think a lot of people were more surprised when Jim got his diploma than by some of the things he did on the field."

Slightly withdrawn, somewhat moody, not exactly surrounded by the most talented teammates, Brown was not an instant smash as would later happen with Davis and Little. He talked of quitting school as a freshman and almost did as a sophomore when the coach angrily dispatched him to the second team.

"He was the strongest boy I'd seen," recalls Schwartzwalder. "He could climb them ropes we had, twenty feet in the air without ever changing the expression on his face. Anyhow, we had some boys who had trouble with the block and a quarterback who had trouble getting the ball to ol' Jim. I think maybe he got a little disgusted.

"Well, some days I'd find him dozing off on the practice dummies. Phew! All that talent just lying there doing nothing. Then one day he was late for practice. I put him right with the second group.

"I'll tell you, my phones liked to have lit up like this here cigar if somebody put a match to it. 'Hey, how come you fired Jim Brown?'

"We had a long talk after that, Jim and I. The first time really that we ever talked things out. After that, our relationship improved. I said, 'Jim, I'm asking two things of you. Get to practice on time and stay friendly with all of the offensive linemen.'"

Brown did that through some of the most spectacular 2,091 yards college football had ever seen. He gained 986 of them in his senior year in only 158 carries and led the team to the Cotton Bowl against TCU. Brown scored 21 of his team's 27 points in that game, but had an extra point blocked that would have given Syracuse a tie.

"Keep in mind," says Ben, "that Jim was doing a little pioneering back then. The hotel where we stayed in Dallas for that Cotton Bowl wouldn't let blacks in the elevators. We ended up getting Jim a room on the first floor. And remember that when he was a senior, he was just turning twenty. But he handled things just beautifully, on the field and off."

Probably as significant as any game that final season for Brown was a trip down to Elmira to visit with Ernie Davis, then at Elmira Free Academy and one of the most sought after backs in the country. Notre Dame was in the early lead until...

"The Mark Twain Hotel," says Schwartzwalder. "They were holding some awards thing for Ernie. Jim and I were invited. Up at the head table it's fixed, naturally, so ol' Jim is sitting next to Ernie. I could see them talking and I sort of moseyed by once. I could hear Jim say, 'Come to Syracuse.' I never heard nothing prettier."

In his book, *Off My Chest*, Brown talks about his first association with Davis:

"I told him about my early experiences at Syracuse. I told him I had had a bad time because some people assumed the presence of a Negro on the squad meant trouble. I told Ernie I had had a hard time proving myself, but that's why I think they will treat you well. Their attitude toward me was wrong. They are conscious now of the fact that they must treat everybody fairly."

Unlike Brown, who struggled as a sophomore and played on rag-tag teams until his final games, Davis was the star of the best team in the nation as a sophomore. He was warm and gregarious, even-tempered and though he lacked Brown's stallion power as a runner, he was quicker, a better thrower, blocker, and defender. And soon Ernie cut in on the legend.

Absorbing it all was a 19-year-old high school kid from New Haven, Connecticut, named Floyd Little. Ernie Davis was his idol. But, even though he was the finest runner in New Haven, Yale's included, there was no wide open path leading him to Davis's footsteps. Little was a confused kid. At 19, he became too old to play high school football in his last year at Hillhouse High.

Larry Csonka

Jim Nance

Floyd Little

He did get a visit from Schwartzwalder and Davis and as Ben recalls, ''There was Ernie with his arm around Floyd and giving me the A-OK sign, like we got him, you know.''

Not quite. Notre Dame was recruiting as feverishly and some alumni were able to send Floyd to the Bordentown Military Institute in New Jersey. Little was an awesome runner for two years there, scoring 20 touchdowns one season. Meanwhile, at Syracuse, Davis was spectacularly weaving toward the Heisman trophy.

But Notre Dame hung tough and appeared to be winning the recruiting race for Little. Then, in the spring of 1963, Floyd Little got a phone call from a friend telling him that Ernie Davis had died. The jolt dug deep. He wanted Syracuse now. Floyd Little wanted jersey number 44.

Until death, the script always seemed to come out right for Ernie Davis. Playing on a national champion as a sophomore. The Heisman trophy. Meetings with President John F. Kennedy. Running into the hot NFL-AFL bidding war.

He was the top pick of the Buffalo Bills and the Washington Redskins. When the Redskins chose to trade their number one pick to the Cleveland Browns (for Bobby Mitchell and Leroy Jackson) it all but ended the bidding. Ernie was going to join his idol and friend, Jim Brown.

''Won't this be something?'' said Cleveland Browns owner Art Modell at the signing. ''Jim Brown and Davis in the same backfield.''

On May 17, 1963, before he could play for Cleveland, Ernie Davis was dead.

''After twenty-three years, he felt fulfilled, picked out of a crowd,'' said Brown. ''He died the way he wanted to... inconveniencing nobody. I know of no greater humility. Ernie Davis was not afraid to die but was embarrassed from grieving his friends.''

Floyd Little remembers the impact Davis had on his family the day Ernie visited New Haven.

''I was considering only three schools seriously at the time—Notre Dame, Syracuse, and West Point,'' he says. ''After I visited each one, I'd come back and my mother and brothers and sisters and me would sit around and vote on the different issues. Likewise, when one of the people from a school would visit us.

''My sister Rose, she was sold on Ernie. She would periodically remind us that any school that could produce a person like Ernie Davis had to be a pretty good place. The day he died, well, that did it.''

After a couple of lost years in high school and two years at Bordentown, Floyd Little was a mature young man of 21 when he came to Syracuse. He became a team leader almost immediately.

"He even kicked me out of a team meeting once," remembers Schwartzwalder. "They told me he chewed the team out pretty good. We had a few lovers, if you know what I mean. Floyd used to tell them, 'You guys do pretty good picking up girls. I'd like to see you start doing as well picking up your blocks.'"

Little wasted very little time getting on with tradition. In his first varsity game as a sophomore, he turned Archbold Stadium upside down with a five-touchdown performance against Kansas. It was too much even for his sometimes ornery, cigar-chewing, ex-paratrooper of a coach.

Schwartzwalder won't admit to it, but there are hints that Little was his favorite. Floyd was, as mentioned before, an effective team leader. He developed study habits at Bordentown that would later turn him into an all-around college citizen, a solid example for teammates and other students to follow. After graduation, Little came back to assist the Syracuse football staff in spring drills. And during the racial turmoil that beset the staff and the campus prior to the start of the 1970 season, it was Little who refuted many of the blacks' grievances and came to the defense of his coach.

"The thing, away from the exploits on the field, that I remember most about Floyd," says Ben, "is that he had a strict moral code. People offered him money, ten bucks here, ten there, and he wouldn't take it. When the pro leagues merged when he was a senior, costing him a big bonus, I remember him saying, 'Ah, the leagues are paying too much anyway.'"

Little's career at Syracuse was enhanced first by the presence of Jim Nance and, later, by Csonka. Ben's running game now had a Mr. Inside and a Mr. Outside and the opposing defenses had big problems.

Nance, one of 10 children, son of a coal mine dynamiter, came out of Western Pennsylvania with a reputation as a good football player, a very good wrestler and an excellent eater.

Says Ben: "I looked at him and just knew he could run through the stadium. I said, 'Son, how tough's it going to be to get you to Syracuse?' He looked at me and said, 'Not tough at all. This is where I want to go.' Hmm. Now he's got me thinking he maybe ain't hungry enough. Lordee, that was as far from the truth as you could get."

Nance set some records, but mostly at the training table. He became a fierce, immovable wrestler, later to develop into an NCAA champion, but on the football field he had to battle his weight as much as the

defense. But he did slim down in his senior year to gain 951 yards, keeping the defense honest while Little, the super soph, ran around them for 828 yards.

Again Schwartzwalder stood out as the super recruiter. But what did he do?

"The so-called blue chippers," he says, chomping a hunk of cigar away, "I don't rightly know how to recruit them. My philosophy is take the kid who wants to come here. You take these kids, assuming they can play for you, of course, over the hot shots.

"Then, once you have them, say my ball carriers for example, you simply tell each one, 'Look, son, if you're any good, you'll get a chance to prove it here. I'll promise you one thing, I'm going to see that you get the ball.'"

Ben, in all honesty, did have to alter his philosophy, this in pursuit of Larry Csonka, a big hunk of farm boy out of Stow, Ohio. He had been receiving regular scouting reports on Csonka from assistant coach Bill Bell, but nothing that would implant visions of the next Jim Brown.

But Ben and his wife Reggie are native West Virginians and one of the few pleasures for the Schwartzwalders, outside of bridge and game films, are occasional trips back home to visit kinfolk. And, what the heck, Stow wasn't all that far from West Virginia.

"This story is the kind they used to make in the movies," says Ben. "As we're walking up the driveway to the Csonka place, there's a cat and a rabbit fussing on the front lawn. Out the front door comes Larry, he grabs the cat with one hand, the rabbit with the other and, I'm telling you, this kid's got quickness I can't believe.

"I gotta have him now, but we hear that he's locked up for Clemson. Don't you know it, but Larry's daddy is a fellow West Virginian. Well, I like to tell you, I came out with the darndest down-home country-like talk you ever heard. By golly, it worked."

Schwartzwalder displayed his genius by making Csonka a linebacker. The plan carried two games into Csonka's sophomore year, then, as Ben recalls, "Fortunately, Ron Oyer, my fullback, got hurt."

New rushing records, by this time no meager achievements, crumbled all over again. For one season, it was Csonka and Little. Then, it was Csonka and anything that got in the way.

"Larry's senior year," says the coach, "we were missing not only a Floyd, but also blocking. With Larry, I could use the term one-man offense without disturbing the morale of the team. In fact, in films, the boys used to sit there and cheer Larry."

Before he left, Csonka carried the ball more than any other back in Syracuse his-

tory, gained the most yards, 2,934, and rushed for over 100 yards 14 times. He wiped out all but Davis's career average per carry record of 6.6 yards.

"The records weren't even in my thinking when I went there," recalls Csonka. "And I don't think the coaching staff was thinking in those terms for me either. It all just kind of happened."

From Jim Brown's varsity debut until Larry Csonka's final game, a span of 14 seasons, Syracuse never had a losing season. It had a combined record of 96-34-1, won one national championship, appeared in six major bowl games, and sent many of its players on to professional football.

Some of the glory has been tarnished in recent years. The racial turmoil of 1970 has left its scars. The university and Schwartzwalder were hurt by the controversial writings of former player Dave Meggyesy, who painted the school as a football factory. School officials now moan the fact that they were not more adamant in fighting back at what they felt were gross misstatements of fact.

Recruiting has never been easy, even during the glory years. For all the great players Syracuse has landed, it has missed with probably just as many. Green Bay Packers running back John Brockington prepped eight miles from the Syracuse campus, but was turned down for admission for a low grade on his transcript. Detroit Lions quarterback Greg Landry also was turned down, but as Ben says with a laugh, "Just as well for the boy, I suppose. I probably would have made him a fullback."

As long as there is a season ahead, Ben Schwartzwalder has never had much time to look back. His office is taken up more with playbooks than mementos. There are a few pictures on the wall, but the most noticeable is one of him and Flip Wilson hamming it up at a banquet. He usually ends conversations having to do with his great backs with, "Yeah, but I've got a boy coming along." In the spring of 1973, he was as excited talking about the prospects for a bruiser out of Vestal, New York, named Chuck Moss as he was recollecting the feats of Larry Csonka.

"I've got one more season to go before I retire, then I'll do my recollecting," he said. "But I already know what my fondest memory is going to be. How many college football coaches make it to retirement age, huh? Well, ol' Ben has been a lucky man. I had some folks who came here and wanted to play. Kept me coaching, those boys did."

by Mickey Herskowitz

Here's Looking Up at You

T his is the story of the Little Quarterback Who Could.

Once upon a time there was a little quarterback who yearned to play with the big boys. But the other players would laugh and say, "You are too small. You must be big to play football."

The Little Quarterback was very sad.

"I know I can," he said, and he practiced every day.

All his life he had been told he couldn't, and he kept repeating, "I know I can, I know I can." And when they let him, he always did.

But it meant nothing if he could not play with the big boys. The pros liked the Little Quarterback. They even gave him a uniform and, standing on the field with the other players, he looked like Johnny of Philip Morris. He was so small that the uniform did not fit and you could only see part of the number on his back.

"I know I can," said the Little Quarterback when everyone laughed, "if they will only give me a chance."

But he wondered if he would ever play football with the varsity boys.

Then came the day of a very important game. The big football players huffed and puffed and banged into each other. But the Little Quarterback only watched. He was too small.

Then, suddenly, the big quarterback was hurt.

The coach looked at the bench and saw only the Little Quarterback. The coach sent him in.

The Little Quarterback ran onto the field thinking, "I know I can, I know I can."

And he did. He became the hero of the game. And the season. And the city.

He thought, "I knew I could if they would let me."

The big football players said, "We will never make fun of you again. You can play football with us whenever you want."

The Little Quarterback only smiled, and practiced that much harder.

And that, fairy tale lovers, is the story, more or less, of Eddie LeBaron. It is also the story, more or less, of people named Buddy Young and Randy Vataha and Tommy McDonald and Charley Tolar and Noland Smith and Essex Johnson and every Napoleon-sized fellow who ever played beyond his inches in the big man's world of professional football.

LeBaron was the Little General of the Washington Redskins for a decade. The quarterback he succeeded was Sammy Baugh, the nonpareil.

It was a long, splendid career and Eddie spent much of it listening to good-natured complaints about his size. In the twilight time, with the expansion Dallas Cowboys, Billy Howton described what it was like catching LeBaron's passes: "You run your deep pattern and look back and nobody's there. You can't see him. And, suddenly, it looks like the ball is coming at you out of a silo."

An All-America at tiny College of the Pacific, Eddie was one of the real miniatures of the National Football League at 5-7 and 160 pounds. For reasons of his own, George Preston Marshall insisted on listing him at 5-9 and 180 in the team's program. It may have been the beginning of all of

Eddie LeBaron

David Boss

51

those credibility problems in Washington.

A popular photograph of the day showed LeBaron standing between two linemen, names now forgotten, one 6-7 and the other 6-8. He looked like a raisinette.

Eddie notes curiously that his size became more of an issue, more of a news item, as the years passed than it was when he reported in 1950. Maybe the players were getting larger. Maybe somebody finally noticed.

Anyhow, the players were getting larger, no question.

In 1956, Eddie quarterbacked the East to a squeaky win over the West in the Pro Bowl, a game that meant $300, cash, to each winner. In 1956, still years before the boom, a player would kill for $300.

As Eddie greeted his wife outside the locker room door, Big Daddy Lipscomb emerged from the other dressing room. "My wife hadn't been around football much," Eddie recalled. "Big Daddy walked over. He was six-nine, three hundred pounds. He had a little beard and he wore a pork pie hat. Sweat was dripping down his goatee. He loomed over me and said, 'You little son of a bitch. I'll get you next year.'

"Hell, my wife wanted me to quit on the spot."

For 11 years LeBaron was the smallest—at least, the lightest—player in the National Football League. Nothing irritated the big boys more than to be done in by a guy you could squash with one thumb, or so they thought.

LeBaron, now a lawyer and part-time television analyst, looks back on his career and concludes, "I made it partly for mechanical reasons. I had a higher release than people like Tittle. I threw completely overhand. I found one thing to be true. They either respect you or they don't. Size doesn't enter into it."

Sadly, he added, "The day of the little quarterback is gone forever. In my prime, twenty-eight to thirty-one, I could play today. But I'd never get a shot at it. I wouldn't in college, either."

The weight of evidence seems clear. In an era when six-footers are considered borderline at best, the ideal man under center is tall enough to peep over transoms—or at least over the upraised arms of those towering defensive linemen who come roaring in like the Bengal Lancers.

But halfback and wide receiver have traditionally been the refuge of the little person, and still are. For our purposes, since the Standard Players' Contract doesn't define such things, those 5-10 and under or less than 190 shall qualify as little persons. Former Jets receiver Don

Maynard is 6-1 and hardly a gnome. But at 170 pounds he looks like the "after" part of a Slenderella ad, and that earns him a spot on our list.

A few years ago, Steve Owen, the old Giants' coach, worked loose a thought on the subject and included it in a book on the game's salad days. We quote:

"The odds are stacked against small men making the major leagues in football, but some have the fiery spirit and the physical toughness to overcome their grave handicap. I recall Two-Bits Homan, of the Frankford Yellow Jackets, who weighed about one-hundred forty pounds but who played halfback as well as a man with another fifty pounds on him. Willis Smith, about one-hundred fifty, was a Giants halfback who had tough fiber in him. Butch Meeker with the Steamrollers was no more than five-seven and one-hundred fifty, but he played in the roughest company and more than held his own. Another Giant, Tut Imlay from the University of California, weighed one-hundred fifty-five pounds but was a genuine first-stringer at halfback. He called our signals, too. How about Buddy Young of the Yanks? And going 'way back, tiny Joey Sternaman, quarterback for the Bears? From Toby Green to the present day, I have never discounted a small man until he has showed me whether he will or won't do. The answer is always on that field with a football in motion and yardage at stake."

Old Steve has laid some heavy history on us, and we regret that honesty requires us to plead ignorance in the case of Two-Bits Homan, or Tut Imlay, and teams like the Frankford Yellow Jackets and the whatever Steamrollers. (Psst, Steve, are we talking about this century? Is this America?)

Thank the Lord, the name Buddy Young sounded familiar.

Buddy Young was a small, black streak out of Illinois who played for teams like the New York Yankees and the original Dallas Texans and the early, pre-Unitas, Baltimore Colts. He has suffered, and he knows prejudice when he sees it. *"I have never discounted a small man until he has showed me whether he will or won't do."* Did you hear what he was really saying?

"The worst discrimination in the world," says Buddy Young, "isn't color. It's size. I could never stop proving myself. I had to work harder, play better, block better than the bigger guys.

"When I came into the league I was five-five and weighed one-hundred sixty-five. I was known as a trackman. At my first camp with the Yanks they acted like I was some kind of sideshow, like I was supposed to go out with the band at halftime."

But the professionals measured Buddy

and accepted him. They found that what weight he had, he did not hesitate to throw around. Early on, he developed an unusual tactic to handle the 250-pound beasts he was required to block in pass protection situations. He would wait until his man had up a full head of steam, then he would leap into the air and propel himself toward the charging lineman's chest.

Instinctively, the fellow would react by catching him. For a moment they would pose there, Buddy cradled in his arms, a tender sight, until the lineman would release him, allowing Buddy to fall on his butt.

It worked often enough for opposing players to grow wary whenever Buddy Young did not have the ball.

By and large, it is possible to draw a few broad conclusions about the little people. They cannot afford to be shy. They are likely to have above average smarts. They have crowd appeal. And often sex appeal. Women find them cute, perhaps taking the logical position that it is better to have loved a short man than never to have loved a'tall.

They must maintain a sense of self in the face of often brazen provocation.

Back when the Houston Oilers were a power in the American Football League —are you old enough, dearie?—their fullback was a small tank of a fellow named Charley Tolar, 5-foot 6-inches, 200 pounds. Charley was an odd sight indeed carrying the ball, as Mel Branch, a Kansas City defensive end, once testified: "When he went by me, he was kneecap high. And do you know, as sawed off as he is, Tolar still ran in a crouch?"

Tolar inspired strange reactions in people. One opposing player said that trying to tackle him was like trying to get a grip on a bowling ball. Another said it was like trying to tackle a manhole cover.

One of Tolar's particular buddies on those early Houston teams was the venerable George Blanda. Once, as luck would have it, the hotel in which the Oilers were quartered was hosting a Little People of America convention. As the players lounged around the lobby, an elevator opened and out poured a group of midgets. "Well," deadpanned Blanda, "It sure looks as though all of Tolar's relatives are here to see him play."

One learns to accept such indignities from so-called "normal sized folk," preferring to answer them in the arena. The pages of vest pocket history are choked with glittering examples.

In 1957, at the All-Star game in Chicago, two All-Americas observed most of the action from the bench. One was Jim Brown, who is another story. The other was

Tommy McDonald, out of Oklahoma, drafted by the Eagles.

"What's wrong with McDonald?" a writer asked the coach who held him out, a man named Otto Graham.

"Too small," snapped Graham. "He won't make it in the pros. He'll be cut."

McDonald reported to Philadelphia, his standing confused by his failure to get into the All-Star game. He was again on the bench when the season began, running at halfback behind Billy Barnes.

Then, against Washington, the split end was hurt and an assistant coach spotted McDonald and sent him in. "I'm going to give you a shot, kid," he said. McDonald caught a touchdown pass from a rookie quarterback named Sonny Jurgensen, and another from Bobby Thomason. He stayed around for 11 years and four teams, and whenever he encountered Graham he had the needle out: "Hey, Otto, do you think I'll make it now?"

Actually, McDonald knew he was headed for stardom from the instant he arrived in Philadelphia. He did not have your ordinary Hollywood introduction. In fact, he got arrested. "They nabbed me when I got off the airplane," he recalled. "The detectives said I looked like pictures of the 'Lonely Hearts Bandit.' Just because he was handsome, educated, cultured, and suave, too. I had to talk my way out of it."

Now, can you picture that happening to Bubba Smith? Of course not.

Going back a little further into our time warp, the case of Bullet Bill Dudley illustrates yet another facet of the little man's game: confidence, breezy, unshakable confidence, and a gift for one-upmanship.

Dudley was 5-9 and 170, one of the truly versatile players the sport has seen: a sidearm passer, with a pendulum kicking style, a fine runner, and a faultless defender. During the war, when service football was the real pro league, Dudley performed for an army squad against a navy team whose stars included Buster Ramsey of the Chicago Cardinals.

The sailors outplayed them all day, but the game was scoreless until Dudley intercepted a pass, wove his way through a broken field and scored the game's only touchdown. He was chased across the goal by Ramsey, who screamed at him, "Bill Dudley, you're the luckiest buzzard who ever played football."

Two seasons later, Dudley, back with the Steelers, returned an interception for a touchdown to beat the Cardinals. Pursuing him, still, was Ramsey.

"Bill Dudley," cried Buster, slamming his helmet to the ground, "I still say you're the luckiest buzzard who ever played football."

Dudley reflected for a moment, then said, "Want to know something, Buster? I'm beginning to think you're right."

In some cases, the largeness of their deeds concealed the size of our heroes. If you suggest to some people that Doak Walker, Red Grange, and Joe Perry, for example, were smaller than life, they are likely to fix you with a look that you could exterminate roaches with.

But they qualified, as do such recent sports models as Mike Garrett, Warren McVea, Jerry LeVias, Mike Adamle, Noland Smith, Robert Holmes, and Nemiah Wilson, all of whom have one thing in common: they're 5-9 or less.

Most of them have one other interesting connection. Call it the Kansas City Connection. Garrett, McVea, Smith, Holmes, and Adamle do now, or did at one time, play for the Chiefs.

In 1969, the Chiefs could have fielded a backfield composed of Garrett, McVea, and Holmes. They had Smith, an elf at 5-6 and 154, running back kicks. Exactly how Kansas City came to corner the shrimp market isn't clear, except that their coach, Hank Stram, is a famous innovator and civil libertarian. He is also 5-7.

"I think shortness helps," Stram once confided. "We get some concealment and we create formations to take advantage of their speed. But it's not something that happened intentionally. I didn't go out to get five-foot-nine backs."

For the record, owner Lamar Hunt, who coined the deathless label, Super Bowl, also hung a nickname on Smith: Supergnat.

One of Supergnat's games was being watched one day on television by 5-year-old Noland Smith, Jr., whose eyes grew wide when the camera picked up his dad standing among the other Chiefs, looking like someone's stuffed toy. "Look, Mommy," blurted Junior. "Look how small Daddy is!"

This is, of course, one of the hazards of standing next to glandular freaks, meaning people over 5-10.

Those 5-10 or under usually become running backs. Mercury Morris of Miami is 5-10. He also gained 1,000 yards in 1972. Denver's Floyd Little, who gained 1,133 yards in 1971, is the same height and so are Altie Taylor of the Lions and Clarence Davis of the Raiders. And Robert Newhouse, the Cowboys' third-year man, also is 5-10.

They have been called elves and gnomes and fleas, but there has been only one legitimate dwarf ever to play in the National Football League. He is Randy Vataha, who at 5-8 and 176 looks less like the star wide receiver for the New England Patriots than something you would see at Disneyland. Which he was.

Growing up loose and cool in California, Randy spent his summer college vacations playing Bashful, one of the Seven Dwarfs (not to be confused with the Seven Blocks of Granite).

It is a fact that Vataha was cut by the Los Angeles Rams after a casual trial, picked up as a free agent by the Patriots, and mistaken for an office boy by the general manager. ("If he's not going to work, get him the hell out of here.")

The staff assistant's answer will forever echo through the corridors of New England lore: "That's no office boy, that's Randy Vataha."

By the end of that rookie season, Vataha had started all but the first of 14 games, caught 51 Jim Plunkett passes, and scored nine touchdowns.

Like Kansas City, the Oilers once recruited enough players under six feet to form a club. And that's exactly what they did. Formed a club. They called it the Dolomite Club, in honor of a mineral found in the Pennsylvania coal country that is reputed to be compact, hard and rough. The idea was Jerry LeVias's, and his clubmates included Woody Campbell, Charlie Joiner, Roy Gerela, and Mike Richardson, who played with LeVias in the smallest backfield SMU ever had. That year SMU, famed for its aerial circuses of old, featured a flea circus.

The Dolomites were a clannish bunch, but they did admit one outsider. George Webster, the 6-5 linebacker from Michigan State, was elected to the ceremonial position of bouncer.

The object of the club, in case you were wondering, was to promote pride and a sense of unity and belonging. It worked fine, except that Jerry got traded to San Diego and, in time, the others were cut or dealt off.

That's the trouble with team spirit. Players always talk about such things —togetherness was last year's operative word—at the start of a new season. But team spirit is the game you won last week. Some say team spirit is what comes in an envelope twice each month.

Yet whatever it is, the little man is more likely than most to believe in it. He tends to get lost in a crowd and therefore can usually be found up front. The fight to get there, and to stay, and to survive, sharpens his competitive instinct.

Jerry LeVias may have said it for all the ungiants: "Each year I get lighter, faster, and more afraid. When you're my size in the pros, fear is a sign that you're not stupid."

Neiman on Namath

December in New York. A cold Wednesday afternoon just after an hour's rain. The streets seem more soiled, the sky seems more gray, the day offers little promise. Inside Shea Stadium, there are puddles of stagnant water large enough to accommodate a naval battle. Discarded newspapers blow like tumbleweed through the upper decks. Empty cans roll down the steps, their clanging and banging an echo against the deserted bleachers. Something left over from Sunday's game is starting to spoil and the smell is everywhere.

Just then, Joe Namath takes the snap from center, retreats those eight graceful strides into the pocket and whips forward that magnificent right arm. The ball sails slightly beyond 40 yards, the laces turning over and over in a perfect spiral, blurred but beautiful. Downfield a long-legged re-ceiver named Richard Caster has made his turn to the sideline. He looks over his shoulder and the ball is there. He swallows it up with his two enormous hands to complete the play. Someone says, "God, wasn't that beautiful?" And, at that moment, in the midst of a dismal winter's day in New York with the trains crashing overhead and the mud creeping up through the bottoms of your shoes, you nod in agreement.

Sure, other quarterbacks in the National Football League can throw a football but, well, Joe Namath *throws* a football. His passes have an elegance, a flair, an esthetic rightness about them. It is the difference between Barbra Streisand and the soprano from the church choir singing the same song, between Jack Nicklaus and the guy who lives next door hitting a golf ball. Class. You don't have to define it...only recognize it. Namath is an original, a work of art. It is only natural, therefore, that a gifted artist such as LeRoy Neiman would be fascinated by the New York Jets' great quarterback.

Neiman is the Jets' artist-in-residence. He sketches in the New York locker room before and after each game. He roams the bench area during a game, sketch pad and pencil in hand, ideas constantly swirling around in his head.

So what is reflected in these four pages are LeRoy Neiman's impressions of a day with Joe Namath. Before the game... during the game ... after the game when the roar of the crowd is replaced by the quiet agony in both knees. Much like its subject, the results are something special.

By now, everyone knows of Joe Namath's knee injuries. They have haunted him since college and he has undergone knee surgery four times. In 1973, he suffered a shoulder separation that sidelined him for most of the season. "When I was younger," Namath said after the shoulder separation, "I used to think that losing was the worst part of football. By now, I've learned to live with the losses. To me, injuries are the biggest downer."

Namath   Ice packs tied to both knees
Dec 29 '68   after Oakland Game

After his Super Bowl triumph in 1969, Namath went on a tour of U.S. military hospitals in the Far East. There he met a teenage Marine who had lost both legs on a Viet Cong mine. "You know what he said to me?" Namath recalled, "He said he wished I had two good legs because if I did, I'd be able to play pro ball for another ten years. Imagine, that kid feeling sorry for me. That left an impression on me. Compared to him, man, I've got no problems at all."

After Boston Game
Oct 26 '69   LeRoy Neiman   Both legs bandaged
Both great toes taped

To many Americans, Joe Namath remains a romantic figure. A swinging New York playboy. Broadway Joe, walking barefoot across his lush llama rugs. But Jets trainer Jeff Snedeker (taping Namath's knee) knows the other side. "He's the greatest man I ever worked with when it comes to accepting pain without complaint," Snedeker said. "I don't think there are many people who could play football in his condition. Nobody really knows what he endures to go on that field every week."

Like dressing the matador Namath before the game SuperBowl Jan 12' 69 Miami

Jeff Snedeker Trainer

by Wells Twombly

Every Day Is Ladies Day in San Francisco

So many years and too many tears ago, there were these two otherwise bright young men who foolishly believed that professional football was the entertainment industry's wave of the future. They were very close to each other. They were half-brothers, because they had the same father. They were also cousins because their mothers were sisters. The elder's mother died and the father sent over to the old country for her sister to come to take care of the motherless child. Love mushroomed. There was a second marriage and another son. It is a classic immigrant's tale.

They were very much alike, Tony and Vic Morabito. Their father had been a seaman on banana boats. His name was Pasquale and he arrived in San Francisco from Reggio di Calabria in the south of Italy just two years before the great earthquake of 1906. He built up a ship's chandlery on the Embarcadero and he taught his two sons one fundamental law: "If it is a matter of principle, a Morabito will go to hell to defend it." And it meant what he said.

The half-brother-cousins were in the lumber business just before World War II when Tony decided that it would be great to own a professional football club in San Francisco. Naturally, Vic would be his partner. The first National Football League owner he approached told him to forget this mad vision.

But Tony Morabito could see the future. He asked for an NFL franchise for San Francisco with the idea that he would be ready to operate three months after the war was over. Both San Francisco and Los Angeles would go into the major leagues because airplanes would greatly reduce travel time. Expansion was inevitable.

Inevitability was not instant, however. The Morabitos were rebuffed in their bid to obtain a pro football franchise. So Tony and Vic waited. Getting a team became an obsession with Tony. When the All-America Football Conference held its first organizational meeting in St. Louis in 1944, both Morabitos were there. They got their franchise and they came rushing home to sign players.

Only Paul Brown of the freshly minted Cleveland club did a finer job of greeting returning servicemen. The Morabitos brought in a number of former NFL players like Len Eshmont, Bruno Banducci, Norm Standlee, Bill Fisk, Parker Hall, and Dutch Elston. They also signed Frankie Albert, the great left-handed quarterback from Stanford.

And so they played professional football in Kezar Stadium, a mass of masonry that slumps like an evil frog on San Francisco's lovely lily-pad of a municipal recreation area, Golden Gate Park. Only then did the city really come to know the Brothers Morabito. There was Tony, outwardly calm to the point of seeming introverted. There was Vic, slightly more lively, but not a public spectacle. This was their public image. Underneath, both of them bucked and heaved like two cans of highly volatile racing fuel. That was their fatal flaw.

Except for a few exciting confrontations with the press, they held their emotions deep inside them, which any doctor can tell you puts a strain on a man's vital or-

Jane (foreground) and Josephine Morabito

Fred Kaplan

gans. There was a ramshackle feud with the *San Francisco Examiner,* whose management got upset when Tony took its annual charity game away from it. There were some notoriously silly incidents when Vic decided that certain writers had been playing fast and loose with the truth and he decided to keep them out of 49ers press conferences and off the team plane. But those were small items, really.

By January, 1950, the San Francisco club had joined the National Football League, the result of the economic collapse of the All-America Football Conference, and the Morabitos were turning down an offer of $375,000 by a Cleveland syndicate, headed by Abe Saperstein, the Harlem Globetrotter-founder, to buy the 49ers. (Tony and Vic said they'd think about it, for $425,000. The deal was angrily refused.)

The half-brother-cousins seemed to be an immortal part of San Francisco, as imperishable as Telegraph Hill or the Golden Gate Bridge or the Ferry Building at the foot of Market Street. In time the Bay might be totally filled in, Mt. Tamalpais might crumble, but the Morabitos were here to stay.

Then the first tragedy happened. It was October 26, 1957, a gilt-edged autumn afternoon in Golden Gate Park. The Chicago Bears were in town and Tony awoke that morning feeling as if he'd had too much to eat the night before the game.

He hated to think what the trouble might be. He was 47 years old and only five years earlier, he had suffered a massive heart attack. But he had survived. He had come to think that he might be well again. It was a fine, courageous piece of self-deception. Deep down, he knew the truth.

"He kept saying how much better he felt and how he probably would live to be quite old," said Vic. "But all the time he was advising me what to do if anything happened to him. He was being courageous."

So Tony Morabito went to Kezar Stadium. He sat down in the front row of the overcrowded press box and he watched the game. The fatal heart attack came early. There was an ambulance waiting in the street outside. The players knew at halftime that something was awfully wrong. By the third quarter, they were told that Tony Morabito was dead. They had kept him alive all the way to Mary's Help Hospital with oxygen and strong stimulants. He died in a hospital bed.

The history books show that the San Francisco 49ers somehow managed to hold on to a 21-17 victory over the Bears. Their dressing room was utterly grotesque. No one talked. Everyone wept. Tony had been a kind, paternal owner.

"Oh, my God, I don't know what to say," said Albert, now the head coach. "I wish we had lost by a hundred points than have this happen. Poor Tony! Oh, my God, poor Tony! This game was tough enough on a healthy man. But poor Tony was living on borrowed time. Oh, hell, I've got to get out of this dressing room. I can't stand being here."

And so Anthony J. Morabito died and his half-brother-cousin-best friend, Victor R. Morabito, succeeded him as president of the San Francisco 49ers. Less than two weeks after Mrs. Josephine Verone Morabito became a widow, her brother-in-law issued a statement:

"The San Francisco 49ers are not for sale. They never will be. They will remain in the ownership of our group."

This was Victor Morabito's public stance. He and his wife, Elizabeth Jane Eddy Morabito, a lady of Welsh descent who may be the only non-Irish, non-Italian in the management group, owned 25 percent of the 49ers' stock. His widowed sister-in-law, Josephine, held 30 percent. Along with general manager Lou Spadia, with five percent, they represented the club's general partners. The limited partners were all either old friends or college roommates or in-laws, like Albert Ruffo, Loretta O'Grady, Franklin Mieuli, Larry Purcell, Jim Ginella, and Frankie Albert.

"The Morabito family did not get into professional football for capital gain," said Vic, whose heart wasn't that strong, either. "I like what I'm doing. We've had chances to sell before and we've turned them all down."

Privately, Victor R. Morabito was advising his wife Jane and his sister-in-law Josie to sell out in the occasion that his heart wasn't any stronger than Tony's. The ladies said that they would take the matter under advisement. Besides, what made Vic think he wasn't going to live well into his 70s?

"We are going to carry on and achieve Tony's dream of winning a championship, no matter what the cost," said Vic.

The headline in the May 11, 1964 edition of the *Examiner* was not much different in wording than the one that preceded it by six years. It said: "San Francisco 49er Boss Victim of Coronary." The warning he had received a year earlier, the one that had placed Vic Morabito in the same hospital his brother died in, for four weeks of rest and observation, had done no good.

The doctors had warned him to take it easy, to hold back on club activities, to delegate authority to others. Vic didn't listen. The San Francisco 49ers had become his passion, just as they had been Tony's. He and Jane had gone to the Bahamas for a vacation just prior to that awful day in 1964.

They had enjoyed themselves in the company of their dear friends, Marie and Vince Lombardi. When they returned, Vic simply forgot the lesson of the previous year.

Jack Christiansen had just been named head coach. A whole new era was opening and Vic was going to take a more active part again. He was 44 years old and the heart attack came while he was at home on a Saturday night. They got him to St. Mary's, just as they did with Tony. But he was dead within minutes after they got him to the hospital.

There was a family conference. Jane and Josie sat and talked. They weren't sisters, they weren't even true sisters-in-law, since that title is reserved for someone who either marries your brother or is your husband's sister. They were simply two women from different backgrounds who had married half-brother-cousins. They had one thing going for them. They were lifelong friends.

When Jane Eddy was a secretary and dating Vic Morabito, a student at Santa Clara University, they used to baby-sit for Tony and Josie's two daughters. Nobody had any money in those days, except Jane, who made $60 a week typing letters. They played poker, mostly so they could spread the wealth, Miss Eddy being poor at cards.

The Morabito ladies met with Lou Spadia. Between them they owned 60 percent of the club's stock. They wanted to know if their general manager would like to become club president and manage their interests for them. Spadia, courtly, wise, emotional, was a logical choice. The offers to buy the 49ers and relieve the widows' minds came pouring in with every jangle of the telephone.

"The 49ers should have San Francisco ownership and they should have Morabito ownership," said Spadia. "There will be no sale to anyone."

The principle was firmly established by Pasquale Morabito—a San Francisco football club should be owned by San Francisco people, preferably Irish-Italian in that largely Irish-Italian city. Even though Jane and Josie were not Morabitos by blood, only by marriage, they understood a principle when they heard one. They did the right thing.

The whole structure of the game is changed but neither Vic nor Tony Morabito would be surprised at its massive scope. There are 26 teams now, nearly all of them turning a sharp profit. The whole nation closes down on Sunday afternoon and watches professional football on television.

Where once the 49ers' mystical inability to win a divisional championship did awful things to their owners' hearts, the San Francisco club was a three-time winner in the NFC West from 1970-72. It is all very grand and very glorious. Surely those ghosts have been at play, watching first at Kezar and then at new, improved, fortified Candlestick Park.

Sitting at lunch are the Morabito Ladies, to use their formal sports page title. They are at the corner table at Julius' Castle, a neo-baroque piece of Victorian architecture clinging precariously to a wind-washed corner of Telegraph Hill. It is there courtesy of the San Andreas Fault. Beyond the window, sailboats glide toward Sausalito and great steamships lumber out of their berths on the Embarcadero, making the first cumbersome move toward Hawaii, Bora-Bora, and all the other ports of paradise.

"We've known each other thirty-one years," says Jane Eddy Morabito. "I don't think we've ever had even a small fight. Why do we get along so well? I look at it this way: I'm extroverted and not too smart. Josie is introverted and very intelligent. It's a perfect combination. I do all the talking and she does all the thinking."

It is a pardonable falsehood and only vaguely accurate. There is nothing wrong with Jane Morabito's intellect. There is nothing dull about Josie Morabito's personality. These are the only women owners in professional football. They keep an exceedingly low profile, trusting in luck, in San Francisco, and in Lou Spadia. Undoubtedly, God enters in there someplace, too.

Sportswriters who rarely meet them have only a misty idea of what they are like. Both are in their 50s. Both are pleasant and pretty. Jane is the younger, livelier, more loquacious one. Josephine is somewhat older, shorter, and seemingly more sedate. Other than that they are largely unknown.

"It is advisable that we stay in the background," says Josephine Morabito. "Lou Spadia does all our negotiating for us. When either of us gets the urge to complain about something, we get together with Lou and we work something out between the three of us. Lou negotiates all the player contracts. We just sit back and shake a lot. There's no question that we couldn't operate the club without Lou."

A long time ago they decided not to attend league meetings. Once upon a time there was another widow who inherited a football club from her husband. Mrs. Olive Bidwell used to represent the Cardinals, but she did not especially enjoy the experience.

"So Larry Purcell, one of the limited partners, speaks for us on matters of the pension fund and club insurance. Marshall Leahy, the club lawyer and an old friend,

represents us on certain legal matters. And Jack White, our general manager, and Lou, the club president, handle the other matters," says Jane. "It works out well, because, frankly, we'd be out of place behind those closed doors. They report back to us as soon as the sessions are over."

There is one small sorrow that both ladies sense. They are remote from the players now. Oh, the athletes are very polite and friendly. Right from the start Tony and Vic always insisted on drafting and signing players with "class." Over the passing years, the 49ers have probably had less problems with personnel than any other professional football club.

"Tony insisted that we draw upon that kind of man for our playing talent," Josephine recalls. "We've always had marvelous people. The trouble is that the club owners and the players find it difficult now to deal with each other on a personal basis. It's a shame. It really is. In the old days, when the 49ers were a fairly shaky outfit financially, we had this crowded office down on Stockton Street. Everybody knew everybody. It was wonderful."

Those were the days, weren't they?

"It used to be a family affair," Jane recalls. "But it has changed. Even the family-owned teams like ours are different. Of course, Josie and I were younger in those Stockton Street days. Frankie Albert was exactly my age. Tony wasn't more than ten years older than the players. He'd hold their hands and he'd help them with their problems. He got Joe Perry straightened out financially by opening a joint checking account with him, so he could guide Joe better."

Those worn-sole and shabby sweater years are wonderfully warm to recollect now. Success always makes sacrifice seem sweeter. Why, do you know that Buck Shaw, the first coach, was offered a part of the team as a reward and he turned it down? Who could blame him then?

"One time we were sitting in Kezar Stadium and the crowd wasn't what you'd call large," says Jane. "Not one of the four of us could think of a thing to say. Finally, Tony broke the silence. 'I hope you're all enjoying this game, because the seats are costing us two thousand dollars each.' Everybody laughed. What else was there to do but laugh?"

The Morabito half-brothers-cousins were openly fretful about what would happen if they died and their widows had to run the club. They would not fly in the same airplane together. Tony and Vic had an agreement, still in force between the widows, that if one wanted to sell, he would first have to offer his stock to the other.

"After Tony's death, Vic would say to us, 'If you two women have any sense, you'll sell out if anything happens to me,'" Josephine recalls. "It thrills me that we've gone as far as we have. I don't think the Morabitos will ever let control of the club pass out of the family's hands. What is the team worth? Who can say? I read offers of sixteen and eighteen million dollars for other teams. That's all I can base our worth on."

When it became obvious that Kezar Stadium was hopelessly antique, the 49ers had three offers from other Northern California communities to relocate. They could have gone across the Golden Gate to Marin County, or down the Peninsula, or even to San Jose. Everyone wanted to build them a stadium.

"Even a rebuilt Candlestick wasn't what we really wanted. Kezar held so many memories for us," says Jane. "But it had to be. Candlestick is within the city limits of San Francisco and the 49ers could never be located anywhere except in San Francisco proper."

Outside the restaurant window, down on the surface of the Bay, the luxury liner gains momentum and churns past the ruins of Alcatraz.

In his elegant cypress-paneled office on the third floor of the Jack Tar Hotel on Van Ness Avenue, the president of the San Francisco 49ers has been talking about his years with the Morabitos. He has lived over half his life in their service. Now he is one of three general partners. Lou Spadia is at the apex of his years on the planet.

"The Morabito Ladies have been wonderful to work for. They know a successful football club can't be operated by committee. They told me there are only two things I can't do without permission—move out of San Francisco and change the team's nickname. It could have been chaos if the Ladies had been even slightly different. But they both have such great common sense.

"Vic's only son, Rick, has been working in the scouting department. I'm sure he's interested in running the club some day. Tony has two daughters. One of them is married to the son of Mr. and Mrs. Jim Ginella. Poor Jim is dead now, but his widow is one of our limited partners. The 49ers will always be a family affair."

A writer wants to know if other club executives ever needle Spadia because he works for ladies. It is a good question, and Lou has a good answer:

"I always say, 'I know my ladies are ladies. I hope you're as sure that the gentlemen you work for are gentlemen.'"

It is a finely-carved piece of old Italian humor and Spadia chuckles softly to himself.

by John Wiebusch

The Nine Lives of Jim Marshall

Tony Tomsic

There was this scene from the movie, "True Grit," in which John Wayne played John Wayne (again) and won an Academy Award. In this scene, a bad old lovable gruff guy with a patch over one eye and the name of Rooster Cogburn is on one side of an open meadow. Rooster Cogburn is mostly bad, mostly old, and mostly gruff. Particularly gruff. But he also is lovable because in actuality Rooster Cogburn has a Heart of Gold.

So, okay, there's John Wayne on one side of the meadow and this group of varmints on the other side. You can tell right off they're varmints because some of them have moustaches and some of them—this is the *real* giveaway—are on black horses. You don't have to remember Saturday afternoon matinees to know that these are guys who obviously are Up To No Good.

And, boy, then it comes (hold on to your popcorn), the varmints riding at John Wayne and John Wayne riding right at the bad guys (all of 'em).

It's really scary. For a second or so. Until the camera flashes back to John Wayne, and he's got the horse's reins between his teeth and he's in there with his six shooter and his rifle blazing.

Well, what happens is a lot of people get shot. A lot of the varmints. John Wayne doesn't ride off into the sunset—not exactly anyway. His horse got shot. He loved that horse. But John Wayne pulls through and, gosh, you almost have to restrain yourself from whistling and clapping and bopping the guy in front of you on the head.

It's something.

Which seems a funny way to start a story on Jim Marshall, the football player. It's not really, though. Marshall's life is a lot like a John Wayne movie.

Both, for example, are unbelievable.

You read some old newspaper clippings. You shake your head.

He almost died of encephalitis. He accidentally shot himself while cleaning a gun. He was the driver in an auto accident in which the driver of the other car was killed. He almost choked to death when a grape became lodged in his windpipe. He had a tonsillectomy and suffered subsequent internal bleeding. He had to battle wind and snow when a Wyoming blizzard ended a snowmobile odyssey in mid-trip. One member of the 16-man expedition froze to death.

You read on. You are ready to believe anything.

He was the defensive end who picked up a fumble and ran 66 yards the wrong way. He was the man who was invited to accept the Bonehead of the Year Award shortly after that in Dallas but who got on the wrong plane (and ended up in Chicago). He was the football player who, as a defensive tackle at Ohio State, scored one touchdown after blocking a punt and another after picking up a fumble. Both touchdowns came in the same game against Purdue and the final score was 14-14. He was the athlete who won the Big Ten discus championship, the athlete who was encouraged to prepare for the decathlon event of the 1960 Olympics in Rome.

And there is (sigh) more.

He sky dives. He scuba dives. He used to model men's clothes. He used to sell

women's wigs. He is an enthusiast of yoga. He skis. He took a test given by a Minneapolis brokerage and the brokerage announced that his score was one of the highest ever achieved by a prospective employee. He has studied Buddhism. He has talked about going after gold in abandoned mines. He has talked about buying a German U-boat (vintage World War II) to search the seas for sunken treasure. He has toured Vietnam. In more than a decade in the National Football League (all but the first with the Minnesota Vikings), he has not missed a regular season game.

You call Jim Marshall in Minneapolis. You tell him you'd like to get together. To talk. He says, fine, that he's free next Thursday morning, and then he asks what you want to talk about. And you say, "You," and he laughs. "What'll we talk about?" he says, and you say you're sure you'll think of something.

Next Thursday morning arrives. Jim Marshall is behind the desk of a telecommunications firm in a suburb of Minneapolis. He is talking about video tape cassettes and how they are going to be the coming thing. He has a full beard. After what you have read, you wonder if maybe he is scared to shave. You wouldn't blame him if he is.

"I am truly excited about the cassette thing," he is saying. "Perhaps more excited about it than any other thing I've been involved in."

You ask how many other things there have been. Besides the wigs and the brokerage. The things you know about.

"Well," he says and he is smiling, "the last job application I had to fill out I needed another piece of paper to list previous jobs held in the past five years."

In the life of Jim Marshall, the constant has been football. The Minnesota Vikings will tell you that it is Jim Marshall who has been the constant.

Norm Van Brocklin, his former coach, said, "Marshall is the fastest defensive lineman I've ever seen."

Bud Grant, his current coach, said, "He just doesn't make many mistakes. And when he does what he does with a minimum of error, well, then there's just no more a coach can ask."

Jim Marshall plays football the same way he lives—reckless but controlled. It is a recklessness in which the snap decisions of the head are proved or disproved by speed and strength.

"I play it loose," says Marshall, "because that's the kind of game football is. The thing about that, though, is that you're bound to goof once in awhile."

Once in awhile. October 26, 1964. Kezar Stadium in San Francisco.

George Mira is back to pass. He throws the ball and Bill Kilmer catches it. Kilmer fumbles. Jim Marshall scoops it up. He runs. Three strides and he is free of traffic. Another stride and he is out in the open. And moving. The pursuers are not the San Francisco 49ers. The pursuers are his Vikings teammates. They are shouting but Jim Marshall does not hear them. He is into the end zone 66 yards later but the end zone he is into is that of the Vikings. He has scored two points for San Francisco instead of six for Minnesota. In the locker room afterwards, he says, "I saw my teammates running down the sidelines. I thought they were cheering for me."

He reviews the incident today and he says, "You can imagine how it was for me then. I have never been so humiliated."

The direction of the football career of Jim Marshall reversed itself after that, however, and in the ensuing years he has twice been named the Vikings' defensive player of the year. The competition for the award included some names you may have heard of—Carl Eller, Alan Page, Gary Larsen, Paul Krause. Jim Marshall has made a name for himself as a football player and he has done it on a team on which mere excellence is not enough.

The honors are testimony to his durability. He played in all 12 games for the Cleveland Browns in his rookie season in 1960 and it did not change when he was traded to the fledgling Vikings in the week before the following season began. He drove nonstop from Cleveland to Minneapolis when he learned he had been traded and he arrived on the Wednesday before the Sunday of the Vikings' first game ever, against the Bears. He was in the lineup that first Sunday and he has been there ever since.

And the marvel of it all is not so much that Jim Marshall has never missed a game. It is that he is able to play at all.

Stationed at Ft. Leonard Wood in Army training in the spring before the 1961 season began, Marshall apparently was bitten by a mosquito that carried the dreaded encephalitis (sleeping sickness). It was the same disease that killed pro basketball's Maurice Stokes. Jim Marshall was more fortunate. Instead of his life, he lost only 40 pounds.

When he reported to the training camp of the Browns in early August he weighed less than 200 pounds. Sapped of strength, he was unimpressive in workouts. The Browns, a contender, could not afford to take a chance on possible rehabilitation. The Vikings could.

Jim Marshall weighed 215 pounds when he reported to the Vikings. He weighed 235 pounds a year later. At 33, he now weighs nearly 250 pounds.

But don't let him kid you. It wasn't easy. And encephalitis is only a part of the story.

In 1963, he was reported to be in serious financial difficulty. The early dreams of financial security turned out to be nightmares. It also was the year he began sky diving and experimenting in yoga. It was the year he first became labeled a kook.

In 1964, the notoriety began early. On January 5, Marshall was cleaning a gun in his car (he said he carried it because he frequently carried large sums of money) when it fired and tore a hole in his left side. He was hospitalized for two weeks. In April, he surfaced as the owner of Chevelure de Paris, a Minneapolis firm that sold highstyle wigs to women. In July, the car he was driving collided with another car that had gone through a red light. The other driver was killed instantly. Marshall was shaken. The year ended with the wrong-way run.

In 1965, the legend expanded. In one year he: was given genius rating in the brokerage test, began skiing avidly, took the wrong flight when he was supposed to go to Dallas to be dishonored for his wrong-way run, became a men's clothing model, was hospitalized with what was feared to be a recurrence of encephalitis (it turned out to be a severe allergy), elevated his rating as a sky diver by increasing his number of jumps to over 100, and was hospitalized in training camp when a grape lodged in his windpipe.

Things were reasonably routine in the three seasons after that. Reasonably routine in his case meaning that not once was he listed in critical condition.

In 1970, there was the appearance in the Super Bowl and an ensuing tour of Vietnam, the report that he and Carl Eller were considering the purchase of an old U-boat "to search for treasure or something," the tonsillectomy in April that resulted in internal hemorrhaging, and the sprained ankle that resulted in him missing his first pro game, a preseason contest.

In 1971, he was in the national headlines again, this time with an incredible story of a fight for survival in the Grand Teton mountains of Wyoming. "It was the toughest thing I've ever encountered in my life," he said later. "I thought we all were going to die."

The journey on snowmobiles began and almost ended when Marshall's vehicle went over a cliff and nearly crushed him. Being crushed would have been incidental to what would have happened after that. Below him was a 2,000-foot drop. After falling 30 feet, however, Marshall grabbed a large rock. He was finally pulled to safety an hour of mental anguish later.

That's how the day began. How it ended was something else. The wind-whipped

snow caused the remaining snowmobiles to stall and the group began a march through the snow to find a place—*any* place—that would provide shelter. The 15 men and one woman (the wife of the man who was the group's guide) were unable to stay together in the blizzard and Marshall became part of a confederation of five (which included Vikings tackle Paul Dickson, the other football player on the trip).

Jim Marshall tells what happened then:

"It got to be dark and we were afraid to stop for fear we'd freeze to death. The snow reached the waist of Dickson and me. The lighter people could walk on the top of the snow and not get stuck but we'd take three or four steps and be exhausted. We passed three or four stages of exhaustion when finally we simply couldn't go any farther.

"Finally, a member of our group, Bob Leiviska, Jr., located a piece of land with a grove of trees and a hill in back of it to block the wind. We decided to stay there for the night. The snow was 10 to 15 feet deep.

"At that point it was sheer desperation. We took everything we had that would burn—one dollar bills, twenty dollar bills, candy wrappers, billfolds, everything—and we made a fire with pine cones and boughs from trees. We burned a hole in the snow six feet deep and eight feet wide. Six feet deep . . . that was kind of symbolic.

"We were afraid if we went to sleep we might freeze to death. We had to work hard to stay awake. It's funny, but there's a strange feeling at a time like that, a kind of serene warmth that makes you want to lie down and forget everything. Fortunately, we were able to conquer the feeling."

The rescue party arrived on the afternoon of the following day. In time for 15 members of the group that had begun in fun and expectation at Beartooth Pass. Not in time for Hugh Galusha, 51, president of the Minneapolis Federal Reserve Bank.

Jim Marshall talks now on a summer day, away from the emotions of the last days of January. He has asked himself the inevitable would-I-do-it-again question many times and he has always come away with the same answer.

He says, "It is my nature to take chances. It is the nature of man. We take chances every day, all of us. When we drive on a freeway we take a chance. When we cross a street we do. To me, if something sounds reasonable then the sky's the limit."

For Jim Marshall, even the sky may not be beyond reach. Do you really think, for example, that Jim Marshall would pass up a chance to ride a dune buggy on the moon?

He'll bet his life he would.

by William Hedgepeth

The Thinking Man's Coach

"DON SHOOOOLA!" The six-year-old boy clutches the wire fence with both hands and tries to shake it down and yells again: "DON SHOOOLA." He is hollering against the sound of wind and constant chatter of birds spiraling in the air or lurking in the palm trees.

"Hey," calls another child not far from the first, "You watchin' Don Shula?"

And then, from somewhere out of sight, comes an older voice bellowing: "TOMMY!"

"Yeh?"

"Get over here!" And at this the six-year-old scampers off. And all is quiet. Which is good, for a solemn athletic contest is underway. But even so, various individuals persist in calling, pointing, waving or whatever. "Hey there! Don Shula!" (This one is a fuzzy-headed hippie-type yet with the glow of purest awe on his face.) "I met you before." Then he passes on and is followed by a honey-tanned bevy of svelte young Miami matrons in short white skirts who smile and give little nods if they happen to catch the coach's eye. Moments later, quite suddenly and for absolutely no reason, a traffic helicopter looms up above the palm treetops and wafts away. It means nothing. Nobody looks.

Here, after all, is Don Shula locked in competition. And he looks adequate to the challenge: A solid chunk of a figure just a shade under six feet; stocky but not disproportionately so; tanned and weathered with light brown hair lightening even more in the Florida sun.

He's radiating great intensity at this crucial moment. It's expected of him. For, as everyone is well aware, here is the Don of Miami, the head coach and guiding light of the world champion Miami Dolphins. He is generalissimo, civic hero, and practically a tourist attraction in these parts. They like him here, as, Lord knows, they should. For according to the seers and elders who adjudge such things, Don Shula is already ranked way on up there alongside the very highest in the uppermost stratospheres of all coachdom. He's done right well.

And here he is: Five-time titleholder as NFL coach of the year...First man in history to win 100 games in the span of a decade...The legendary disciplinarian responsible for steering the Dolphins to the league's first undefeated 17-game season in 53 years and who, in the process, landed on the cover of *TIME* with a story proclaiming him "...perhaps the soundest, best-organized technical mind in pro football today." He is said to have started younger and won more than almost all the rest. He has never coached a losing team. One could go on and on. But I'm sure you've already heard those things; and you've probably known all the rest of this, too.

For me, however, it's all new. Fact is, I know just about next-to-nothing about pro football or anything whatsoever connected with it. I'm sorry, but that's just the way it is. Oh I know I could probably fake it for a while, but eventually you'd catch me up in some dumb blunder of the sort that a real writer of sports could never commit. I feel it's only fair that I should confess this right off so you won't feel cheated or anything. If you want yardage figures, statistics, historical comparisons, and stuff like that, I'm sure they're available on record somewhere. But since these items have so little meaning to me I'm afraid I'd just sound even more foolish trying to drop them in here or there as if I knew what I was talking about. Pro ball is simply one of those particular areas of human activity that I've never before had reason to find the time to pay much of a mind to. This makes things a little awkward, I admit.

Right now, however, everything is just fine. Because right at this moment Don Shula and I are on more or less equal grounds. As it happens, I am here at courtside watching this rising lion of football take on assistant head coach Bill Arnsparger in a bout of *tennis,* and I am delighted to observe that I am not a significantly sorrier player than he is. Tennis is obviously not Shula's game either. Here, at least, we are on equivalent levels of incompetence. That's a relief.

Possibly the coach is mildly relieved, too, in that none of his players are on hand to watch him do this thing. They've all gone to wherever they each go between seasons to rest.

Meanwhile, he—as is usual—is investing virtually every one of his waking hours into some aspect of football: studying stratagems...pondering potentials... calculating contingency plans for every known eventuality after all of which he then commences to meditate on the *un*knowns. He is considered "dedicated." In fact, he is actually, and in the truest sense of the word, a monomaniac if there ever was one. But that's just what you necessarily have to be to do what he's done. Which is this: In their four years as a team B.S. (Before Shula), the rather obscure collection of souls that made up the Miami Dolphins had never won more than two games in a row. In the years since his coming they've become the biggest winners in pro football, as well as record-setters and all-around mind-blowers.

Now all that's quite nice, of course, but the really beguiling feature is that this is to a large degree the same bunch of obscure souls who comprised the Dolphins in the dark years prior to the coming of Shula. "The team has more of a will to win," explained one player. "That's the difference. That's why we're the greatest ever."

Obviously, therefore, this monumental transformation from frogs into virtual princes (as players go) must be the direct result of a coaching talent of the purest and more rarefied form imaginable. In light of the fact that it is so clearly effective, the question seems to be: How, exactly, was such a talent produced, and can the average man make one in his own backyard? That is why I have made this pilgrimage.

Now, according to observations and press reports, Shula's working style expresses itself in a "passion for detail and thoroughness" plus much "meticulous planning." Then, too, he is arrogant and demanding, has a "professorial" attitude, a "disciplinarian's grip" and a weakness for more than occasional lapses into "hollering and screaming."

Probing further into the essence of Shula, you discover that his own mother declared: "He would get furious whenever he lost at anything." You notice where the President himself, the nation's top lawman, wrote him: "You've really come through like gangbusters." And finally you learn about the one particular Dolphin who came forth and disclosed that, "He (Shula) made us into a family."

Taking all this into account, it seems possible to construct a picture of him even before you meet. Don Shula is a potentially explosive madman fanatic slavedriver tyrant. And as if that were not enough, one must note with some alarm his unhealthy similarity to some wild hippie cult leader (what with all that talk of "family" and such).

Hence it is with these anticipations lying in the back of the mind that one must first approach the Dolphins' training center. It is earlier in this same day and here we come upon this low, rambling cinderblock structure that lurks off to the side of the Biscayne College campus in North Miami. Here, like some half-hidden installation, lies the central hatchingplace of plans and repository for all the assorted secrets that Shula's been hoarding up over all of his 44 years.

The preponderance of those years have been spent in football, starting from that point back in Ohio in the ninth grade when he presented the coach with his parents' forged signatures on a required card granting permission to participate. From this he went on to John Carroll University, a Jesuit-run school in Cleveland, where he continued not only playing but also, according to his coach, taking notes, studying and soaking up every nuance of the game. Next followed his life as a pro player—first with the Browns, then the Colts, and finally the Redskins. His teammates recall him as a "scholar of the game" who "seldom made the same mistake twice" and was "always thinking, seeking ways to improve." Shula the player "knew the game and knew he knew the game." He also knew enough to acknowledge himself, at last, as "a marginal player." And so, after seven years of toiling in the fields, he finally laid away his dreams of glory as a player—only to find himself reborn that very next season as an assistant coach in

college, and, after that, as a coaching assistant with the Detroit Lions.

He first registered on the mind of the public in 1963—and at age 33 (which is mighty young, I'm told)—when he was hired as head coach of the Baltimore Colts. During his seven Colts years he ran up the greatest percentage of wins for any coach over a comparable period of time. But things didn't sit quite right with him there particularly after his first failed attempt to win the "Big One," the Super Bowl of 1969. A year later, he severed his roots in Baltimore and promptly reblossomed in Miami as head coach as well as vice-president and part owner of a team whose two most distinguished attributes up 'til then were obscurity and relative ineptitude (or vice-versa). That was in 1970. The rest you know.

Right at this moment the Maximum Coach is closed up in his office here at the training center poring over diagrams and multitudinous notations with his six coaching assistants. He's been engaged in some form of intense concentration all this morning, ever since arriving here following 7 o'clock Mass at the college chapel. But now it's lunchtime which he is obliged to acknowledge by accepting the sandwich his secretary delivers into his office.

On the wall is a poster that asks: "WHO ARE THESE MASKED MEN?"—and here are pictured 11 players all in uniform and wearing black masks—"THE MIAMI DOLPHINS NO-NAME DEFENSE". Another poster crows: "Miami . . . Football Capital of the World."

"We think of ourselves as still in a state of learning," Shula confesses, settling back with his sandwich. "Although we went seventeen and oh in 1972, still we're going through the same routine we've gone through every other off-season. And that means taking everything that we've done and completely analyze it and rewrite our playbooks—throw out, add to—discover new ideas, study other people's films. I think most other coaches do about the same thing. It's hard for me to say because I'm really not aware."

The big black playbook lying there contains diagrams of what must surely be upwards of 8,000 plays, all numerically coded, plus all sorts of training rules, regulations, and reminders as well as a system of monetary fines (for infractions thereof). In addition, there are the actual daily schedules broken down into 10-minute segments. Part of each afternoon is spent studying films. Film, to him, is a great "teaching device." So is just about everything else.

"I know that I'm especially conscious right now of working harder than I have at other off-seasons." The phone rings. Don Shula has an almost Midwestern accent and speaks in a voice that somehow sounds younger and seems older than his actual age. He talks at a sensibly brisk pace and in concise terms, but always in a tone that suggests openness and perhaps even some remote humility.

Certainly he *looks* for all the world the way a coach probably should—what with his physical stoutness, ruddy complexion, a four-times-broken nose, broad forehead, and blue eyes that always appear very much under control. Yet he seems oddly unflamboyant about himself with no apparent inclination toward the kind of self-promotional grandstanding, breast-beating and the making of pithy eye-grabbing statements that one would more-or-less expect from a coach (that *I* would expect from a coach). On top of this, he is extraordinarily receptive to thoughts that have nothing whatever to do with football. But even when the subject is football he tends to de-emphasize his own role in it, other than to observe that he works hard and that he's "still learning." (I must admit at this stage that he is not quite the kind of coach I was expecting. He comes forth as a deceptively sensitive and intelligent and all-around likable fellow. But maybe he'll eventually throw a fit of some sort and roar and babble like a real fanatic. Eventually he'll come clean.)

"My first experience as a player was under Paul Brown," he says in a spirit of total respect. "So I had the opportunity as a player to start under a master. He was the acknowledged master and he's been most influential in pro ball because he brought teaching into coaching. He brought the notebook, the classroom, into pro ball. That puts a teacher-pupil relationship into the aspect of coaching. Whereas before it was more 'All right, let's go out there and kill 'em,' you know? 'Let's out-hit 'em and out-hustle 'em.' There wasn't anything technical about it—that by taking this step first we're gonna get in a better position so that we can execute this type of assignment."

Shula appears to have learned something of value from just about every other coach he's been exposed to in addition to Brown. His working motto, however, is "learn from all, copy none." He even profited from his brief stint as an assistant in college. "If I hadn't done it I think maybe I'd never have had the experience of working with and teaching things step-by-step the way that you have to in college. It makes your presentation more thorough."

Earlier this morning he spent time dictating thoughts and facts about his life into a tape recorder to be transcribed and possibly included in his autobiography. Probably it's on account of this that he's more-than-normally reflective right now.

Though this is a formidable concoction it's still relatively new. "The mystique has to build over a period of time," he contends. "If you continue to beat a team then after a while they start wondering how they're *ever* going to beat you."

Meanwhile—while all the rest are wondering—gentleman Don will be coaxing the Dolphins through practice drills and rigors repeated and repeated past the point that would drive less inspired souls beserk—followed thereupon by going over mistakes and improvements in the classroom. Then more drill. That's the way it goes. "I try to do it with mental preparation and physical preparation and in general with overall preparation to accomplish the ultimate," he says.

The ultimate, one must suppose, is a team that performs together as a flawless unit. But the key element in this is each individual player's realization of his own value and self-worth within the larger organism. What Shula has done in his own way is instill the Dolphins with a sense of group ego whereby each man can operate within the overall pattern without feeling personally diminished. There's absolutely no room for prima donna superstars in this setup.

What this all comes down to is that on the field these players become, in a way, collective extensions of Don Shula's mind. He has expanded their consciousness of the game and of themselves such that he now trusts each team member to know how to flex and cope with unforeseen situations.

And because he trusts them it follows that he treats them strictly as men. He doesn't patronize his players nor act paternal nor dictate their tastes, their praying habits, their preferences in grooming, nor infringe in any other way upon their individuality. "I just don't try to live a man's personal life," he maintains. One obvious outgrowth of this "liberalism" can be seen in the fact that the Dolphins today are probably far and away the hairiest and most moustachioed array of players ever to come down the professional pike.

"I was fortunate that I came up through the ranks myself," Shula recalls, speaking a little slower than before. "I've been exposed to the game in every aspect—as a player, as an assistant coach, and now as a head coach—so I think I can always go back and think about my experiences. There was a time in my career when I was released from a football team. There was a time when I was a starter and then relegated to second string. There was a time

when I was the guy that was frustrated sitting on the bench waiting for the opportunity to play. So I try to relate my experience and give 'em advice. But I don't ever try to mold the thinking of a young man."

"You know," he says, as if thinking out loud, "ten years is a long time to last as a head coach." He has indeed endured longer than is normal for one of his trade and is somewhat fatalistic about it. But at the same time he radiates a distinct sense of liberation. As he explains it, whereas the Colts were an established ball club complete with superstars when he came in as head coach, the Dolphins are a team he's been able to create and shape to his own specifications. Then, too, thanks to his part ownership in the team, he doesn't have to worry about financial security or of being fired—thus affording him the necessary freedom to experiment and develop creatively. "You know," he confides, leaning forward in his chair with the guileless look of one to whom awesome signs have been revealed, "I really do feel now as if I've been reborn!"

Probably the official announcement of his rebirth came to him in the form of the Dolphins' triumph in Super Bowl VII. For one thing, it was a vindication.

After Shula's two previous Super Bowl losses (with the Colts in 1969 and the Dolphins in 1972) all the armchair gurus and miscellaneous pundits who make public declarations about football proclaimed that Shula "can't win the big one."

"You see," he replies when I mention the phrase, "everything else was fine. My winning percentage was better than anyone else's, including Lombardi's. But the *one thing* I wasn't able to do was win the one at the end of the year. That's what Vince did, and that's what put him in the class he was in when he died. So no matter how many *good* things were said, there was always that one negative thing that just kept gnawing."

He pauses, snorts a little chuckle and then announces: "I've been involved in three Super Bowl games. Now I've won one, which is thirty-three and one-third percent. And that's a hell of a lot better than zero percent. Zero and three," he nods, "would have been tough to live with." He laughs at this. "You wouldn't have been here talking with me. And I wouldn't have been invited to many banquets."

More importantly, of course, he's been officially affirmed, at least in his own mind, by that victory. He's finally cut free from the old demons and jinxes of the past and is able now to extend his style and grow in any direction he chooses. His unique approach to the game has been confirmed under fire. Clearly, what he does, works.

And what he does, in a sense, is create the precise atmosphere in which players under pressure can see themselves as individual components of a mutual body. In this state they can actually vibrate, think, and function together as a single disciplined entity, a mobile group brain.

He admits that his temper has been something of a problem in the past, "but I think I've matured a little bit and have better control of my own emotions now. I think that's one of the big things I've learned—becoming more understanding of others. There might be better ways to reach a guy than to blow your stack on the sidelines. Depending on the personality. That *might* be the way to do it, too. But you have to know them individually. That's when I think coaching comes in; understanding each individual. And then, because you understand him, trying to get the most out of each and every man in a pressure situation."

As Shula sees it, "it's not what I know but what the ballplayers know that makes the real difference." This, in fact, is the spirit in which he relates to his team: as a benign headmaster and mentor with the analytical disposition and discipline of a Jesuit priest. Indeed, at certain moments it does seem that he comes across with the intensity of some square-jawed and energetic young clergyman—one whose fundamental shyness is mostly overshadowed by the strength of his convictions and by his obvious open-eyed determination to spread the Good News. It just so happens that this cause occasionally calls for bits of fire and brimstone now and again. But even so, he is not self-righteous and he does not try to be God.

Perhaps this is what inspires his players to speak the name "Don Shula" with an awe bordering on reverence. As one Dolphin vowed quite simply, "He showed us the way."

In truth, the Dolphins have been molded anew under their coach—molded in his image. Like him they are now disciplined from within. Like him they are well-versed in the fundamentals and fine points of sound football. Like him they've come to know the ecstasy of inching toward a vision of perfection. It's the same team as before but infused with new juices, such that, in essence, the Dolphins—again like Shula himself—have been reborn. Together they may well have struck the most effective chemical balance ever formulated between coach and team. And as betwixt them both, you see, they can lick the platter clean.

"Of course," as he confirms, "the name of the game is win. But whatever we've won I feel that's in back of us. The thing I try

to do is, even though we won ball games and played poorly I treat that as a loss. We try to look at all the negative things that happened in the game, and I try to point out to 'em that if we played this way the *next* week there's no chance we'd win. So we try to learn. We try to make corrections the same as you'd make from a defeat, and change the approach a little bit, instead of sayin', 'Oh, we won and that's all that counts.'"

Shula wonders how long the Dolphins can go undefeated, but he doesn't worry about it. "Sooner or later you're going to get beat, you know. And when that happens then you've just got to take that situation and analyze it again and then try to leave it and get back into a winning pattern."

The way he speaks of it, win-or-lose is not a life-or-death matter after all. The goal is to learn the game to such perfection that winning follows as the inevitable result. He gives a slight shrug of his shoulders and leans back. "I don't think you always have to talk about winning. You can talk about maximum performance on the part of the individual. You're trying to motivate that individual toward peak performance. And if you get peak performance here and get it in eight out of the eleven positions—" he shrugs again—"then that's going to equal winning."

The actual competition, to him, is the way you're obliged to measure your team's performance and development. "I think you have to have competition to have motivation. You have to set a goal to be the best, and how else do you know you're the best if you're not into the competition?"

Don has been involved in competition almost from the start—from the near-penniless days when he was one of six kids in a Hungarian-speaking family that suffered out the Depression in an Ohio town called (of all things) *Pain*esville.

"You're involved in competition even from grade school," he exclaims. "I know that competition was in everything that my life revolved around—the playground, the yard, rough-housing with the gang. In grade school when we lost I remember one time going under the stands and refusing to come out, and sobbing and being upset—the frustration, the failure. I guess it's the hard loser. But you learn to live with that and you learn to control it as you get older. I guess it's feeling sorry for yourself and being upset about your inability to perform."

So here we are at these tennis courts late in the afternoon. "Ah, you dog, that was my best shot," Shula snorts when his serve is returned. He is mildly vexed

over his inability to perform as well as he'd like at tennis. He jogs back to the car and muses that if his tennis partner gets much better they just might not compete at this anymore. But he is not entirely serious.

We drive to the posh suburb of Miami Lakes where he lives in a low-slung house on the edge of the 16th hole of a golf course. This house, filled with plaques, trophies, and framed tributes, is considered the training center for another team to whom he's responsible: that is to say his wife, three daughters, two sons, a collie, a pony, and a Palamino.

Don's wife, Dorothy—whose energy might best be described as "relentless"—is currently elated over her new-found skills as a taker of photos. Otherwise, she focuses her full attentions on the sporting life. The rest of the family is equally supportive as well. Even the dog engages in solitary evening walks with the coach while he ponders the imponderable equations of his trade. As it turns out, Shula's entire clan is so immersed in what he does that virtually the entire gamut of his earthly existence revolves around, and keeps getting back to, that selfsame cause: football...and the future.

"Don Shula!"..."Hey, there's Don Shula."..."Hi, Mr. Shula." We are settled at some swank eating spot for a late dinner, but people keep noticing. A waitress brings forth a female fan who works in the kitchen. A gent from San Francisco asks predictions for the upcoming season. And so on. But Shula treats these intrusions with great chivalry and understanding. It is his basic impulse to try to reach people and maybe teach a little something. However, he doesn't indulge in predictions. "You never go into a game with the feeling that you're going to beat a team because they're predictable. You have to be on guard for their doing something a little different...the unexpected."

It's on account of this that he believes the Dolphins can never afford to harden into rigid patterns or ways of being or styles of playing. Besides, "football is a game of game-day adjustments. Things never go the way you expect. We want our people to detach themselves from the game, so to speak, and keep thinking about alternatives and adjustments."

If there are to be no permanent patterns, then it follows that each player, regardless of his position, must necessarily be taught to innovate and to deal with situations no one's yet imagined. What that means is, you simply work harder. By that measure, Shula probably considers his success to be due to nothing more than straight common sense. He came to Miami from Baltimore declaring to one and all, "I'm straightforward. I rely on hard work. I'm no miracle worker."

Indeed, he is NOT a miracle worker, nor magician or anything else remotely supernatural. What Don Shula ultimately boils down to is something quite natural: a genius. (And quite naturally he scoffs at the label.) He is, however, an actual, up-and-about genius calmly engaged in pursuing his calling right before our very eyes. As some sage once propounded, "There are no astonishing ways of doing astonishing things. All astonishing things are done by ordinary materials." To Shula the challenge is always simple: "The thing that you have to do is keep trying to work harder at your job than you've worked." Or, as Thomas Edison put it, "Genius is one percent inspiration and ninety-nine percent perspiration."

Don Shula's career fits the classic pattern. He excelled early; he drilled himself in the fundamentals to the point where he could see the untried potentials more clearly; he accepted the disappointment of his own physical limitations—and realized, as a consequence, that he could still come out on top in the competition by motivating other souls to see and do what he knew could be done. That's what it's all about.

In this light, a victory on the field is further confirmation of his belief that if you merely know what you're doing and can handle it with absolute perfection then winning is something that just comes naturally. A loss, then, is no cause for despair; it just means there's a flaw somewhere in the apparatus, something to analyze, relearn, and try again. The real challenge is purely internal in that what you must forever compete against is imperfection.

The Dolphins have been called forerunners of a "new dynasty." Under Shula, they are in the role of apostles charged with enlarging the dimensions of football by force of their own example, by the imitations they inspire. Dolphins' quarterback Bob Griese even asserts that Don Shula will be the model for coaches of the next decade "because his type of coaching leads to winning."

Once new ways of doing things have been weighed in the balance and found to be successful, the old techniques just don't feel quite the same again. The old tunes won't do for dancing anymore. As football becomes more and more of a mental workout it seems certain that players will henceforth have to be taught not how to follow orders better but how to adapt and think creatively. Shula's own accomplishments stand as proof that these approaches produce results. That in itself is an inspiration. And as if that were not enough, six of his former assistants are now head coaches of other pro teams, thereby extending the Shula system even further into the public domain.

If it happens that this approach to coaching eventually spreads throughout the kingdom the result will naturally be an enlargement of the very scope and meaning of football. For one thing, the Shula system should pave the way for games of greater intricacy involving individual competitors whose perceptions are more fully developed. Certainly that has to be seen as a good thing!

In any event, he has effected some magnitudinous transformations worthy to behold, and has set forth great swirling signs in the sky to be heeded and reckoned with.

Earlier, driving somewhere in his car, it occurred to me to ask Don Shula's description of a coach. "A teacher," he answered with nary a pause nor blink of eye.

The Dolphins have obviously learned from him an entire new way of seeing—a special vision of themselves, and of the joy of being a team, which they will keep from now on. And I believe that my own outlook has been fundamentally altered from now on as well. For suddenly I comprehend my own unfamiliar sensation of fascination and involvement in the whole pro football thing. It comes as a real revelation. I would even go so far as to say that it's much the same sort of insight all the Dolphins reportedly felt after the team won their first four games under Don Shula. "We looked around at each other," one of them recalls, and said, "Hey, maybe this stuff works!"

2003: The O. J. Odyssey

There are records. And there are Records. There are: Most Pinch-Hitters Used, One Inning, By Both Clubs. And there is: Hank Aaron, and Goodbye Babe Ruth.

There are: Most Punt Returns, Lifetime. And there is: O. J. Simpson, and the odyssey of 2,003.

Seymour Siwoff, who heads the Elias Sports Bureau, official performance charters for professional football, knows how it is.

"We love records," he says. "Any kind of records. But mostly we love the big one, the blue chipper. We loved O. J. Simpson in 1973."

The record for most yards gained by rushing in a single season was 1,863 by Jim Brown of the Cleveland Browns in 1963. It was a mountainous figure, an Everest in pro football.

In 1973, O. J. Simpson did his best Edmund Hillary…and then some. In the fourteenth week of the season, on a biting cold day at Shea Stadium, he reached the summit and kept on going. He ended with 2,003 yards. On the following pages is a photographic reflection on that season, along with a week-by-week accounting of the two titans from the shores of Lake Erie, Brown of Cleveland and Simpson of Buffalo.

LEGEND: JIM BROWN 1963 ▓▓ O. J. SIMPSON 1973 ▓▓

Game 1, September 16
Buffalo 31, New England 13
250 yards, 29 carries
Jim Brown: 162 yards

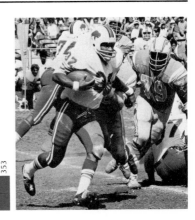

Game 2, September 23
San Diego 34, Buffalo 7
103 yards, 22 carries
Jim Brown: 232 yards

Week One: O. J. opens with a record 250-yard performance against New England.

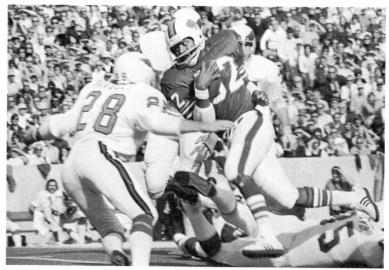

The Juice flowed, and neither the Jets…

…nor the Eagles could control it.

Seven Colts could not corral O. J., who ran for a 78-yard touchdown on this play off left tackle.

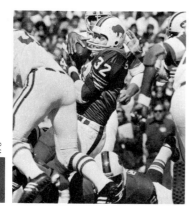

489 476

Game 3, September 30
Buffalo 9, New York Jets 7
123 yards, 24 carries
Jim Brown: 95 yards

664 647

Game 4, October 7
Buffalo 27, Philadelphia 26
171 yards, 27 carries
Jim Brown: 175 yards

787 813

Game 5, October 14
Buffalo 31, Baltimore 13
166 yards, 22 carries
Jim Brown: 123 yards

A stellar Monday night performance: O. J. ran through the Chiefs for 157 yards in 39 carries, a single game record for attempts.

Game 6, October 21
Miami 27, Buffalo 6
55 yards, 14 carries
Jim Brown: 144 yards

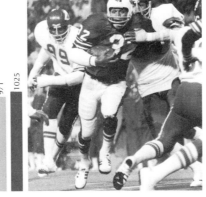

Game 7, October 29
Buffalo 23, Kansas City 14
157 yards, 39 carries
Jim Brown: 40 yards

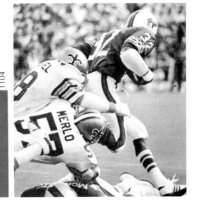

Game 8, November 4
New Orleans 13, Buffalo 0
79 yards, 20 carries
Jim Brown: 223 yards

Simpson's instantaneous acceleration turned a right-side sweep into a 32-yard touchdown vs. Cincinnati.

Game 9, November 10
Cincinnati 16, Buffalo 13
99 yards, 20 carries
Jim Brown: 99 yards

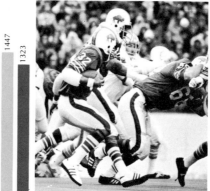

Game 10, November 18
Miami 17, Buffalo 0
120 yards, 20 carries
Jim Brown: 154 yards

Game 11, November 25
Buffalo 24, Baltimore 17
124 yards, 15 carries
Jim Brown: 51 yards

2,003, a number for the ages…and a new standard of excellence.

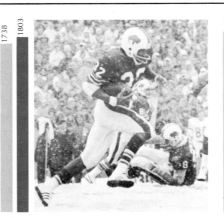

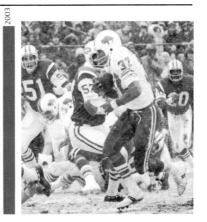

Game 12, December 2
Buffalo 17, Atlanta 6
137 yards, 24 carries
Jim Brown: 179 yards

Game 13, December 9
Buffalo 37, New England 13
219 yards, 22 carries
Jim Brown: 61 yards

Game 14, December 16
Buffalo 34, New York Jets 14
200 yards, 34 carries
Jim Brown: 125 yards

The brutal December cold knifing across the field in Green Bay. Temperature 20 below and falling. Wind boring holes in flesh…A sunny day in Los Angeles Coliseum. Open neck shirt and sleeves rolled up. Temperature nosing toward 90 and not a soda vendor in sight….The great games, the great plays, the sights, smells, and sensations of those football afternoons linger in the mind, needing only a photograph or a name to bring them all rushing back, to make The Memories.

The Memories

BRONKO NAGURSKI the Living Legend

Willardson

by John Wiebusch

Bronko Nagurski: The Living Legend

leg • end (lej'end), n. 1. An unverified popu-lar story handed down from earlier times. 2. A body or collection of such stories. 3. A romanticized or popularized myth of mod-ern times. 4. A person who achieves legen-dary fame.

—AMERICAN HERITAGE DICTIONARY

In the Gordian knot of real and un-real, of happened and might have happened, Bronko Nagurski is all the above, a man bigger than life when he played, a name bigger than life today.

His name. To say it is to say strength and power and hair-on-the-chest maleness. Bronk-o Nag-ur-ski. The sounds are almost chauvinistic. Bronko Nagurski. Treetop tall, able to leap football fields in a single bound, earth mover. Paul Bunyan in the midst of us.

One year when it rained from St. Patrick's Day till the Fourth of July, Paul Bunyan got disgusted because his celebra-tion of the Fourth was spoiled. He dived into Lake Superior and swam to where a solid pillar of water was coming down. He dived under this pillar, swam up into it, and climbed with powerful swimming strokes, was gone about an hour, came splashing down, and as the rain stopped, he ex-plained, "I turned the damn thing off." This is told in the Big North Woods and on the Great Lakes with many particulars.

—CARL SANDBURG

Bronko Nagurski lives in Interna-tional Falls, Minnesota, on the Canadian border. The Rainy River flows through International Falls five months of the year. The other seven months it is fro-zen rock solid. International Falls is called the Icebox of the Nation. Men in plaid wool shirts with ruddy faces smile through their beers there and say, "You got to be hardy to live here."

Bronko Nagurski has been there all his life, for 66 winters and 66 summers. He has been there pumping gas in the station that bore his name until a couple years ago. He has been there answering questions about where the smallmouth bass were hitting. He has been there in the Big North Woods, leading a quiet life while legends grow around him.

Red Grange can't swear the story is true. But he says the man who told it to him swears it was and that's good enough for him.

"A few years ago," says Grange, who played with Bronko Nagurski on the Chicago Bears, "Doc Spears, Bronko's coach at the University of Minnesota, was in Florida visiting me. I asked him how he'd ever come across a guy like Bronko in a place like International Falls. Spears said that he had gone up there from Min-neapolis to see another kid. He thought the kid's name was Smith. Spears told me that just outside of International Falls he saw this young kid pushing a plow. There was no horse or anything else—just this kid pushing a plow! Spears stopped the car and asked the kid just where he might find this Smith fellow. Well, Doc swears the kid with the plow just picked it up and pointed in the direction. Doc knew that Smith or no

Dave Willardson

Smith, he had to have this kid, too. The kid was Bronko Nagurski.''

One bright spring morning Paul Bunyan discovered that the billions of feet of logs that he and his men had cut and dragged down to the banking grounds during the winter were land-locked in a lake in Northern Minnesota. Without blinking an eyelash, Paul ordered Ole, his great Swede blacksmith, to make an enormous shovel. Paul took this shovel one morning before breakfast, and started to dig a canal through to the Gulf of Mexico. He took his direction from the path the wildfowl had cleft in the air during their last migration. He shoveled so fast that soon the sun was darkened as if by total eclipse. The dirt that flew over his right shoulder formed the Rocky Mountains, and what he hurled in the opposite direction (there wasn't any room in the sky, you understand, to throw the dirt one way) became the Appalachians. Paul reached the Gulf at the end of the first day just as the sun was about to set. He flicked a hundred gallons of sweat from his brow with his forefinger, flung his shovel down with a grunt and a smile, and galloped back to camp before the last light was put out for the night.

—JAMES CLOYD BOWMAN

In three years with the University of Minnesota varsity, the teams Bronko Nagurski played with lost only four games, three of them by one point and one by two points.

But it is not the winning or the losing they remember. It is Bronko Nagurski. In three years he played every position except center and quarterback and in his senior year, in 1929, Grantland Rice named only 10 men to the All-America football team. Bronko Nagurski was named at both tackle and fullback.

In a game against Northwestern that year they say Bronko Nagurski scored a touchdown from 12 yards and that during that run every member of the Northwestern defense took a shot at him. When Bronko came down in the end zone it was only because he hit a stack of lumber.

A similar thing had happened the year before, when Minnesota played Wisconsin. Bronko had suffered an injury to his spine but he insisted on playing with a steel brace. It was a game for the Big Ten championship and Wisconsin needed only a tie to win. Late in the game, with both teams scoreless, Minnesota moved close to the Wisconsin goal line. They gave the ball to Bronko Nagurski four consecutive times and on the last effort he took it into the end zone. There were six Wisconsin players on his back when he scored.

Paul Bunyan was very big for his age, of course, but he was never clumsy as many big boys are. Once—the first time he ever went hunting—he sneaked his father's old shotgun out of the house and set forth to see what he could find. He kept his sharp eyes wide open and at last he saw a deer stick its head around a tree four or five miles away. He blazed away at the animal with the old gun, and then was so anxious to see if he had killed it that he started for the spot, lippity-cut. He ran so fast that he outran the load he had fired from the gun, with the result that he got the full charge of the buckshot in the seat of his breeches.

—WALLACE WADSWORTH

He joined the Chicago Bears of the National Football League in 1930, but he was preceded by his reputation. Already he was a folk hero. There was the story about how he ran six miles to and from high school every day in International Falls (even in the winter)…about how he had single-handedly lifted a truck off a dying man…about how he had rescued another man who'd been buried under a pile of logs at a sawmill.

The pros were disbelievers and it is not difficult to see why. They sought softness in the legend early.

In 1930, the Green Bay Packers were the lords of professional football. They had Johnny Blood (McNally) to run the ball and a man-mountain tackle, Cal Hubbard, to clear a path. Hubbard weighed 250 pounds; he was a big man by the standards of any age but four decades ago he was Herculean.

The story is told by Red Grange:

"The Bronk and I were on one side protecting the punter on fourth down plays. Well, the game was getting along and the Packers were beating us and Hubbard passed me after one play and said, 'Next time you guys punt, let me by. I won't block the kick. I just want to get a shot at that Nagurski and see if he's as tough as they say he is.' So the next time we went into punt formation I let Hubbard get past me and I turned around to watch. I'm telling you, Hubbard socked the Bronk a good one, but the guy who went down was Hubbard himself. Hubbard caught up with me as we left the field. He said, 'The kid is as hard as they said he was.'"

I will endeavor to give you an idea of the size of the real Paul Bunyan, something no other man has been able to give the public without resorting to untruths.

From the soles of his feet to the roots of his hair he split the atmosphere exactly 16 feet 11 inches. His weight, he told me, was 888 pounds.

But what interested me most was his face. He had the most unusual eyes I ever have seen. The distance between his eyes was 17 inches. They were the size of ordinary saucers. His nose resembled a fresh leg of mutton. When he opened his mouth in one of his prodigious yawns, one could have inserted a ten-quart pail.

—EARL CLIFTON BECK

In 1963, Bronko Nagurski was a charter member of the Pro Football Hall of Fame. He did not receive his Hall of Fame ring until the following year, however. The reason for the delay was that the L. G. Balfour Co. had made a size 19½ ring. Balfour officials still believe the ring is the largest ever made in the United States.

George Halas shakes his head at the memory. "I assure you that you will not see a more remarkable physical specimen anywhere," says the man who coached Bronko as a professional. "He was six feet, two inches and he weighed two hundred thirty-four pounds and it was all—literally all—muscle, skin, and bone. He didn't have an ounce of fat on him. A lot of men have passed in front of me but none with a build like that man."

Beattie Feathers played with Bronko Nagurski. "He had the most incredible natural strength I've ever seen," says Feathers. "One time we were up in Green Bay working out on the Saturday afternoon before the game. We were all just running around and tossing the ball about when Halas called us into the huddle. The starting team gathered around Halas and he told us to line up in formation to run a few plays. I didn't see Bronko and I said to Halas, 'Coach, we don't have a fullback.' I didn't realize it, but Bronko was standing right behind me. Well, Bronko gave me what he thought was a friendly bop on the helmet, and it knocked me down. He was so big and powerful I don't believe even he knew how strong he really was."

Gene Ronzani was the Bears' quarterback for most of the Nagurski years. "Here I was coming out of Marquette," says Ronzani, "and I tell you, just the thought of playing with Bronko Nagurski scared the hell out of me. And when I saw him I became more of a believer. Not only was he as big and strong as advertised and not only was he a humble fellow and an all-around good guy, but he was the second fastest man on the Bears. And his toughness! He had a bad knee and sometimes he would come limping back to the huddle. I'd ask him if he wanted a time out and he'd say, 'Time out? Hell no, let's play football.' Then he would slap his knee on either side with that big hand of his—slapping the cartilage back in place. We'd shake our heads and away we'd go and Bronko would carry the ball."

The epic battles of the day were between Clarke Hinkle, fullback and linebacker for the Packers, and Bronko Nagurski, fullback and linebacker for the Bears. It was survival of the fittest then; it is mutual admiration today.

"I felt I could play football with anyone," says Hinkle, "and I was particularly anxious to go after Bronko because he was the best. The first time I came up against him I made the mistake of letting him come to me before I made the tackle—or tried to make it. I needed seven stitches to close up the cut on my chin. It was murder, but you had to go after him to be effective. If you didn't you were through.

"Once I went over right tackle and cut toward the sidelines and I saw that Bronko had me cornered. I knew that in blocking or tackling he rarely left his feet. Nor did he wrap his arms around a runner in making a tackle. He merely used to block or tackle with his shoulder or hip or forearm—and that got the job done. This one time I pivoted straight toward Bronko before he hit me. I lowered my shoulder and smashed into and over him. He suffered a broken nose and a fractured rib on that play but it didn't keep him out the rest of the game."

In 1936, two members of the Pittsburgh team attempted to stop Bronko Nagurski from reaching the end zone. One man suffered a broken shoulder; the other was knocked out.

And so as the train carried the Pittsburgh team home from Chicago they played cards and talked about the Bears' fullback. Suddenly the train gave an unusually violent lurch and the bodies of football players were strewn in the aisles.

"Run for your lives men," shouted halfback Warren Heller. "It's Nagurski!"

One day Paul Bunyan climbed a tree during a violent windstorm. After he got to the top it started to blow eighteen hurricanes. After a few minutes Paul and the tree went sailing off into space.

After traveling for days in the air, Paul began to drop. When he hit he made a hole over nine hundred miles long and a good many miles wide. Paul was so tired that he fell asleep before investigating his new surroundings. He had a terrible nightmare that caused him to sweat so much that the hole was filled with water. Years later Henry Hudson found this hole and named it Hudson Bay after himself.

—EARL CLIFTON BECK

Maybe truth isn't stranger than fiction (as Lord Byron wrote) but sometimes it's almost a dead heat...

Once in a game against Portsmouth in 1933 Bronko Nagurski went 45 yards for the winning touchdown, sending two linebackers flying in different directions, running over the defensive halfback, straight-arming the safety aside before colliding with the goal post and caroming into the brick wall at Wrigley Field in Chicago. "The last guy hit me awful hard," Bronko said after he was revived.

Once in a game against Green Bay in 1934 Bronko powered through three tacklers into the end zone, crashing head-on into the steel netting protecting the box seats.

Steve Owen was the coach of the New York Giants. He once said of Nagurski, "He's the only man I've ever seen who runs his own interference."

Lest you smile at fond remembrance, consider this from Beattie Feathers: "When we got near the goal line we didn't put any blockers ahead of Bronko. He was fast but he was not a quick starter and we didn't want to take a chance of him getting tripped up by his own blockers. So he'd just blast through the line without any interference."

Gene Ronzani: "He had that strong forearm and those enormous shoulders and he'd just stick his arm out and batter people out of the way."

Mel Hein, center-linebacker for the Giants: "Coaches always told you to tackle a big running back low, so I tried to tackle Bronko low the first time I faced him and he stampeded me. But if you tried to tackle him high, he kept right on going. Actually, we found that the only sure way to bring him down was to have at least two tacklers. And often that didn't work."

Chris Crosshaul was a careless cuss. He took a big drive down the Mississippi for Paul Bunyan and when the logs were delivered in New Orleans it was found that he had driven the wrong ones. It was up to Paul to drive them back upstream.

No one but Paul Bunyan would ever tackle a job like that. To drive logs upstream is impossible, but if you think a little thing like an impossibility could stop him, you don't know Paul Bunyan. He simply fed Babe (the Blue Ox) a good big salt ration and drove him to the upper Mississippi to drink. Babe drank the river dry and sucked all the water upstream. The logs came up river faster than they went down.

—W. B. LAUGHEAD

Bronko Nagurski was more than just another routine Superman.

"He could do it all," said Doc Spears, his college coach. "He could have been an All-America at any position."

Charles Johnson and Dick Cullum are two of the most respected sports journalists of the last century. Both men saw Bronko Nagurski play for the University of Minnesota and for the Bears. Both men wrote about what they saw for Minneapolis newspapers. And their opinions virtually parallel Doc Spears.

"Bronk really could have been the best at anything he tried," says Johnson.

"In many ways, Bronko was the Babe Ruth of football. They both could do it all. The difference was the Bronk did it less flamboyantly because that was his nature. He's a very basic, very simple man who's uncomfortable when he gets a lot of attention."

"The truth is," says Cullum, "that Bronko Nagurski may not even have been the University of Minnesota's finest fullback. That distinction may belong to Herb Joesting (a senior fullback in Bronko's sophomore year). But I don't disparage Bronko's talents as a fullback...hardly. He was an All-America and I think he was the best fullback ever to play in the NFL.

"But the man's versatility was so remarkable. I remember one game at Iowa when Minnesota was severely crippled and had to lose. But Nagurski played tremendously at five positions—end, tackle, guard, halfback, and fullback. When Bronk went to the Chicago Bears he fit immediately into the fullback position and was not tried anywhere else.

"Yet his friends could not help but wish he had tried some other positions, too. They knew he was a better end and a better tackle than he was a fullback, yet he was enough fullback to be called the best in NFL history. That's a measure of greatness."

In the 1930s, Grantland Rice wrote: "Bronko Nagurski was a star end, a great tackle, and a great back—an All-America in any one of these positions."

Paul Bunyan was of tremendous size and strength, the strongest man that ever swung an axe. He had curly black hair which his loving wife used to comb for him every morning with a great crosscut saw, after first parting it nicely with a broadax, and a big, black beard that was as long as it was wide and as wide as it was long. He was rather proud of this beard and took good care of it. Several times every day he would pull up a young pine tree by the roots and use its stiff branches in combing and brushing it smooth.

—WALLACE WADSWORTH

The statistics of the early days of professional football were something less than official and the yardage totals attributed to Bronko Nagurski can only be

approximate. It is certain that he carried the ball over 800 times and gained over 4,000 yards.

But is that the measure of the man? Hardly.

How do you measure his blocking? In the first 27 years of the NFL, only one man, Beattie Feathers, rushed for 1,000 yards in one season. Feathers gained 1,004 yards in 1934 for the Bears and the men who were there claim Nagurski ran interference on almost every play.

How do you measure the 60-minute player? "If I'd played one way," Bronko Nagurski once said, "I could have played another fifteen years."

And isn't it significant that the plays one of the great runners of all time is remembered best for are passing plays?

In 1932, ties didn't count and the Bears (6-1-6) and the Portsmouth Spartans (6-1-4) tied for the NFL title. They played it off in an indoor game in Chicago Stadium and in the fourth quarter of the scoreless tie the Bears threatened. Nagurski carried the ball three consecutive times inside the Portsmouth 10 but on fourth down the Bears were still one yard short. Nagurski got the ball again. He faked a plunge, then drilled a jump pass to Red Grange in the end zone.

"I had slipped in the end zone," says Grange, "and I was flat on my back. Bronko saw me and hit me and that was the game's only touchdown. He wasn't a great passer technically, but he was always on target."

In 1933, the NFL divided into two divisions for the first time. The Bears opposed the New York Giants in the championship game and their knockout punch was the passing arm of Bronko Nagurski. The big fullback passed to Bill Karr for one touchdown, then brought the Bears a 23-21 victory when he passed to Bill Hewitt, who lateraled to Karr to complete a 25-yard touchdown play.

"Bronko would buck up to the line," says Mel Hein of the Giants, "and you'd have to come in to meet him as a linebacker. Then he'd stand straight up and lob a little pass. We all knew it was coming but we couldn't afford to concentrate on it because we couldn't afford to give Bronko any running room."

A favorite lumberjack sport is rolling a log. A man stands on a big log afloat in the water and starts turning it with his feet, keeping his feet going so that he is always on top and standing safely upright, no matter how fast he gets the log to whirling under him. Paul Bunyan could roll a log so fast that it made foam on the water solid enough for him to walk ashore on, and he is

known to have crossed wide rivers in this way. Not all of this foam which he thus caused has disappeared to this day, and occasionally small bits of it may still be seen floating down many streams after a heavy rain.

—WALLACE WADSWORTH

He was the player of his time—perhaps of all time—but his time was not a time of great reward because it was the time of the Great Depression.

In 1965, Bronko Nagurski told Milton Richman of *United Press International:* "The first contract I signed with him (owner George Halas) was for five thousand dollars. Even though I had a good year, my salary was cut to forty-five hundred my second year. The depression was on, the club was losing money and we had to take cuts.

"I got thirty-seven hundred my third year with the Bears and that's where my salary stayed for a number of years. They upped my pay to five-thousand in 1937 when I talked about retiring and when I asked for six-thousand in 1938 they turned me down. I went home figuring they'd call me, but they never did. Not until five years later."

In 1943, World War II had decimated the Bears' talent. Three tackles and two guards were gone from the 1942 team and Ralph Brizzolara, the Bears' interim general manager (Halas also was in the service) called Nagurski, then nearly 35, and asked if he was interested in coming back to play tackle. He was.

"And once he started to play," says Ronzani, "he was the same old Bronk."

In his first game, against the Packers, he was hit by Ted Fritsch, a young fullback. Fritsch was knocked unconscious. The legend was back.

Nagurski remained at tackle for most of the season, until injuries sidelined both of the Bears' fullbacks for the final game of the regular season against the Cardinals. Bronko Nagurski carried the ball 17 times for 84 yards that day, scoring one touchdown and setting up two others. The derring-do helped the Bears turn a 24-14 deficit into a 35-24 victory.

The Bears trounced the Washington Redskins for the NFL championship in the following month, and Nagurski saw action again at fullback. In his farewell to football, he scored a touchdown.

Even when he was an old man, or what would be old for most men, Paul Bunyan was so quick on his feet that he could blow out the light in the bunkhouse at night; and be in bed and asleep before the room got dark.

—W. B. LAUGHEAD

Bronko Nagurski remains a man of basics, a man who does not demand much of life except a square deal. And he doesn't feel he's always gotten that. He feels his career was shorted…he feels that his days as a professional wrestler (he was an enormous attraction in the 1930s and 1940s) were degrading…he feels that he and other early players should be included in the Players Association pension plan (they are not).

In recent years he has had to undergo major surgery on his knees and he has been dogged by arthritis. He no longer grants interviews (and he seldom did, even a decade ago), choosing instead to guard his privacy.

He lives in International Falls with his wife of more than 30 years, Eileen, and one of their six children, Kevin, a high school senior and an outstanding hockey player (there also are five older children, three sons and two daughters, and four grandchildren).

"I have no regrets," he says. "Nothing I could change, anyway. I watch a lot of modern football and I wonder if I could be happy playing it because I could only play half the time. And I wonder what I'd be playing. I like to carry the ball, but I expect that they'd end up using me the same way the Bears do Dick Butkus now. I'd like that, too. I was very much like Butkus—big and mobile. Besides, I guess I liked defense a little better."

Fifty pounds over his playing weight, he is asked to confirm a story about how he used to enter a room holding his wife out at arm's length.

"That's right," he said, "and I can still do it, only Eileen won't let me."

Who made Paul Bunyan, who gave him birth as a myth, who joked him into life as the Master Lumberjack, who fashioned him forth as an apparition easing the hours of men amid axes and trees, saws and lumber? The people, the bookless people, they made Paul and had him alive long before he got into the books for those who read. And some of Paul is as old as the hills, young as the alphabet.

—CARL SANDBURG

by Jerry Izenberg

The Pottsville Maroons

It is hard-rock country, filled with hard-rock people who have known hard-rock times. In 1865 the Molly Maguires rode through the cold Pennsylvania anthracite nights and took the battle to the mine owners for a decade. These are people who work hard and who play hard but who never lose hard. In point they don't lose at all. There are simply long periods of time in which they let the other side think it is winning.

Out on Route 122, the shuttle road that connects Pottsville, Pennsylvania, with U.S. 22, a drive-in theater stands snowbound and empty each winter. The frosty marquee simply says:

"Closed for season...Reason? Freezin'."

Nobody wastes words in the Anthracite Region.

So this is a story for the little people, the underdogs who turn off the alarm clock each morning and who punch the time clock each day and who, deep down in their frustrated hearts, nurture the hidden hope that somehow, somewhere in this world some of their number will rise up and fight City Hall.

Be of good heart. Your time has come. Come? Hell, it's been here for half a century. It's just that you haven't been listening for it. But the Establishment has heard it. Jonah had his whale, Achilles had his tendon, and the National Football League has Joe Zacko, the 75-year-old field marshal of the strangest guerilla army this side of Professor Harold Hill's 76 trombones.

Zacko and Pottsville, Pennsylvania, don't want much from the world. With Christian charity, they are even prepared to let the world go its own way. All they want is to retrieve the world championship they insist was stolen from them in 1925.

So this is the story of rugged little Pottsville (Pop: 19,210) and Joe Zacko, a retired sporting goods salesman, and their private war with the Establishment. They have been fighting the goliaths of New York and St. Louis and Chicago and Detroit and points north, south, east, and west. They have fought them with phone calls and telegrams; with pep rallies and press conferences.

"Justice," says Zacko, "demands that Pottsville be heard. Pottsville will be heard. We are few in number but stout of heart."

The questions a man in search of "justice"has to ask himself are: Who were the Pottsville Maroons? Who is Joe Zacko? And what the hell is this all about in the first place?

To understand the trigger for this incredible chain of events you have to throw away your television set, forget everything you know about the way professional football is played today, and think back to a world long gone—a world in which the only bonus a college kid received on the day he signed his contract was the grudging consent of management to replace the teeth he would certainly have kicked out of his mouth that fall.

Pro football was sport's step child in 1925 and the localities which dotted the NFL standings included such crossroads of America as Hammond, Indiana, Rock Island, Illinois, and Frankford, Pennsylvania. The game was a weekly exercise in barely restrained violence that drew its

greatest support from America's mill town and mining areas, where Sunday's hangover after the long Saturday nights was far more endurable when you knew there were at least 22 people who would wake up feeling that way on Monday morning. It was a savagely played game and when Pottsville joined the league in 1925 it was already axiomatic that the three levels of football then played in America in ascending order were: college football, professional football, and coal-region football.

In 1924, the Maroons sent Dr. John G. Striegel to Chicago to go after an NFL franchise, while Joe Zacko, who was the team's equipment source, went around town trying to collect funds. Dr. Striegel went directly from the meeting room to the telephone.

"We got it, Joe," the doctor said. "I just wrote them a check."

"You will be happy to know," Joe Zacko told him, "that we finally got up enough money to cover your check."

And so the Pottsville Maroons marched off to conquer a world that included New York, Chicago, and Green Bay, Wisconsin. It began not with a whimper and not with a bang but with a dead heat at the bank. Of such timing is greatness often born.

This, then, was the background from which the Pottsville Maroons—outfitted by Joe Zacko's Sport Shop and coached by Dick Rauch—were catapulted into the National Football League. There were just 16 men on this team. They played football on the outskirts of town each Sunday at Minersville Ball Park, a wooden-bleachered hub of the community (adults, one buck; kids small enough to get under the gate, 50 cents; kids small enough to get under the gate and not be detected by either Zacko or Striegel, the price of the torn seat of their pants.) A supermarket now stands on the playing site. People who remember the reckless violence of the Pottsville defense insist that someday a Frankford halfback may be discovered beneath the frozen food locker.

In 12 games that season, the Maroons won 10 times, lost twice, and scored 325 points to 45 for the opposition. The title-clincher was the 21-7 victory at Chicago over the Cardinals. "Nobody in that league could touch us," Charlie Berry once explained to a war correspondent at Zacko's command post. For one thing, the Maroons of 1925 had a magnificently illegal screen pass. Of course, it was legal in those days. Today's rules would penalize them right out of the ball park.

In any event, Charlie Berry and the boys won the championship of the world in Joe Zacko's shoes and shoulder pads. They held it for exactly eight days.

The biggest name in American football in 1925 was Notre Dame. It was generally assumed that the professional players hadn't been born yet and their parents hadn't even been introduced to each other who could handle Notre Dame in head-to-head combat. Pottsville, which then as now did not take such arguments lightly, immediately challenged a Notre Dame all-star team, featuring the Four Horsemen, to "an extra" world title match at Shibe Park in Philadelphia.

What happened next should have been set to music by Gilbert and Sullivan. The Frankford Yellow Jackets (a rival NFL team that had been defeated 49-0 by the Maroons earlier in the year) protested that the game was a clear violation of their territory—and their box office. Frankford was, after all, on the outskirts of Philadelphia although the Frankford front office generally felt that Philadelphia was on the outskirts of Frankford. It was that kind of world.

The league told Pottsville it was forbidden to play. Would Pottsville withdraw?

In 1865, as every Pottsville schoolboy knows, coal miners from Pottsville, as members of a Union Army division of volunteers called "The First Defenders," broke the siege of Petersburg, Virginia, by digging a tunnel under the barricaded city. Pottsville could lick the Confederacy...Pottsville could lick the Cardinals...Pottsville was going to lick Notre Dame...Pottsville sure as hell wasn't going to run away from the Frankford Yellow Jackets.

The Maroons went down to Philadelphia and played the game in defiance of the league ban. They beat the All-Stars 9-7 on a 30-yard field goal by Charlie Berry and the league promptly stripped Pottsville of its title. The NFL record book today still shows that the Cardinals were the 1925 champions. But the book doesn't have the sense to know when it's licked. It reckons without Joe Zacko's guerrilla army. Who else could put the B'nai B'rith and the Pottsville Rotarians into the field side by side? Who else could get this issue on the NFL agenda so many times that a governor of Pennsylvania once pledged his support in an election year? Who else could battle over a 49-year-old shoe?

In 1962, at a time when the Pro Football Hall of Fame was appealing for memorabilia, Joe Zacko rummaged around in the back room of his old sporting goods store and came up with the shoe Charlie Berry had used to kick the winning field goal against the Notre Dame All Stars. "Give us back the stolen title," Joe Zacko said in a telegram, "and you can have the shoe. No shoe...no deal."

It was Charlie's size-nine that prompted a war correspondent to make his first journey into the guerrilla camp some years ago. On the day he cornered Zacko there, the command post was in full swing. Joe Zacko was holding a strategy meeting with Berry and a man named Walter Farquahr, who died several years ago and who, as a young sportswriter, had covered Pottsville's glory days. It was Farquahr who saluted the 21-7 victory over the Cardinals with an 18-stanza poem that began:

"On to Chicago, win and fight, went the proud little queen of the anthracite..."

Pottsville football was all downhill after that glorious year. By 1928, the league was finished with Pottsville for good. But Pottsville, Joe Zacko made it abundantly clear, is not finished with the league.

"The title was stolen and justice demands its return. Why, we had the greatest football team in America. We had the greatest back, a man named Tony Latone. We had...well, listen. One year we brought in C. C. Pyle's New York Yankees with Red Grange. We had a large crowd so we told Red we'd pay him five-hundred dollars if he'd play the whole game. On the first play he runs into Frankie Racis and Frankie knocks him cold. The next time, Latone hits him and he's out again. When he comes to, he looks up at our boys and you know what he said?"

"I can guess," the visitor replied, "but there's no way it is going to get printed in a family publication."

"No, nothing like that. He just says, 'The hell with the five hundred dollars. It ain't worth it.' And he walks off the field."

Whether it really happened that way or not doesn't matter. What matters is that Pottsville thinks it did. And if the Maroons were tough, Joe Zacko, who outfitted them, has turned to positive granite in his determination to get back his town's championship. During World War II, when the young men of Pottsville went off into foxholes and battleships and got laughed at for their tall stories by the wise guys from New York and Chicago, Joe Zacko went out and mailed every scoffer reprints of the championship team photo and record. It was a beginning.

For a long time after that, nothing much happened. Then a big-mouthed war correspondent told Zacko he wasn't making enough noise.

That was in 1962. "Get them to put it on the agenda at the next meeting. Raise hell." Pottsville did.

That year, Jim Kensil of the NFL called the war correspondent and told him: "Tell Zacko it's on the agenda. Now will you also tell him to stop writing and wiring and having all those people call us."

The NFL did not hear Pottsville's case that year. But it has studied it several times since. Pottsville fights on. Which brings us to the Cardinals of St. Louis, Missouri (Pop: 622,955). Pottsville (Pop: 19,210) is watching and waiting. It wants the title back. A correspondent home from the battle zone tried to mediate with a telephone call.

"Hey," he inquired of a Cardinals' publicist. " Are you going to give the title back to Pottsville?"

"Who is this?"

"Just a man who doesn't want to see a nice city like St. Louis get roughed up."

"Are you in a bar somewhere?"

"Look, all I know is that they aren't kidding around. What's one title more or less? Give it back."

"Listen, we only won two titles in all the years we've been in the league and we're not about to give half of them away."

"All right, but don't say I didn't warn you. Did you ever hear of the Petersburg Mine?"

"Who do they play?"

"It's not a team. It's a tunnel. It was dug by the men of Pottsville under Petersburg, Virginia, during the Civil War. They don't fool around."

Go ahead and laugh, St. Louis. But not long ago Joe Zacko called from the trenches. He is working on a book. "We have new secret inside stuff. We will shock a lot of people. It looks good."

Fight on Pottsville. Honest men everywhere will hear your story and rally to your cause. In the words of the ancient proverb:

"It matters not if you win or lose the game. You are driving the Establishment clean up the walls."

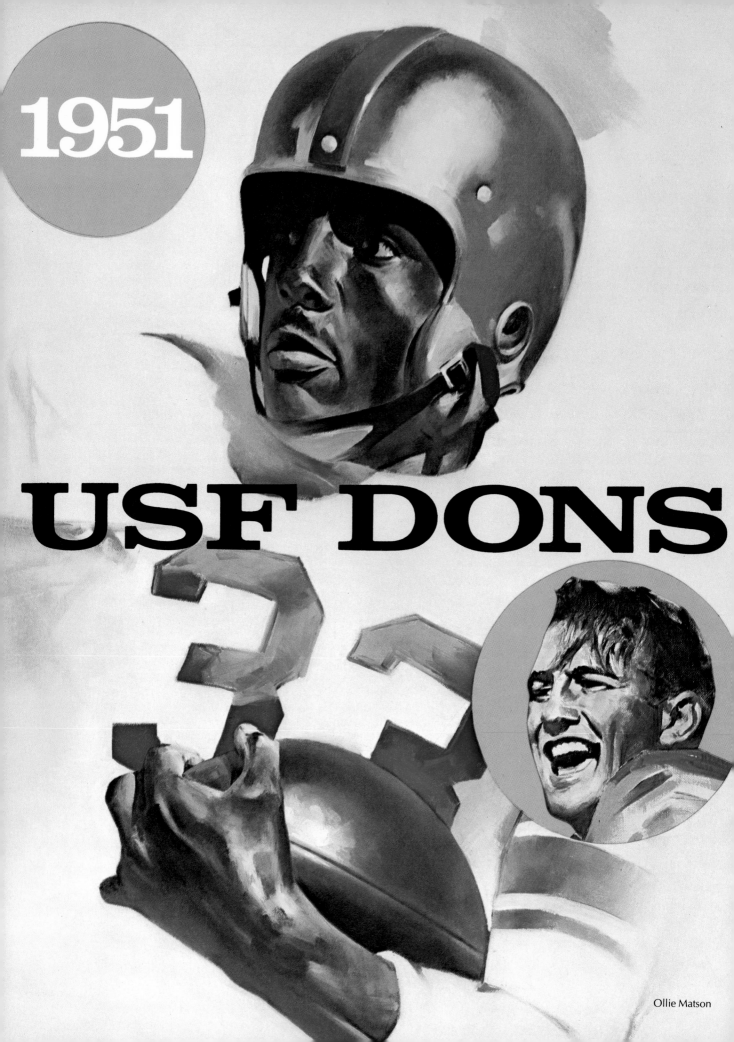

1951

USF DONS

Ollie Matson

by Wells Twombly

Yes, They Were Collegiate!

Lon Keller

In the darkness of early evening, with the first clammy fingers of fog starting to clutch at the light towers, the great stuccoed blob rises out of the trees that surround it. It is an undistinguished structure, a stadium that might have been designed by the workmen building it. It has no redeeming social characteristic. It simply sits there, an ugly frog squatting on that beautiful lily pad that is Golden Gate Park.

Only the high school kids know Kezar Stadium now. Its history is far behind it. There never will be a capacity sports crowd present ever again. The sea gulls wheel in from the ocean and the bay. They decorate seats that used to be filled with patrons of the sweaty arts, people who shared hot dogs and popcorn with them.

Someday the wreckers will arrive and turn the place into a picnic area. The decades will pass and nobody will ever remember that once Kezar Stadium was the home grounds for a professional football team and for what might have been the greatest small-college team ever constructed by a squadron of recruiters who hardly had to leave the neighborhood.

Come back with us now to those thrilling days of yesteryear. There is an unpopular Asian war just grinding down. A President is answering questions about irregularities in his administration. The highways are crowded. Inflation is a popular topic. And Northern California is amazed by the University of San Francisco's incredible varsity. The Dons are mobile, hostile, and agile. They are thoroughly integrated, a rarity for 1951.

Their coach is a fellow named Joe Kuharich. They have at least eight starters whom the professional leagues will draft and sign. Even their sports publicity director shows signs of promise. He is a tall, sparsely settled young man with dark hair and large eyes. He has a tendency to walk into the offices of San Francisco's four metropolitan newspapers and ask, "I don't suppose you'd like to run something about our football team, would you?"

He winces easily. His shoulders twitch and his mouth droops at one corner when he tries to do business. He epitomizes the soft-sell theory even though he doesn't mean to. As he moves from the *Chronicle* to the *Examiner* to the *News* to the *Call-Bulletin*, he evokes sympathy from some of the meanest, toughest sports journalists in the West. His name is Pete Rozelle and he gets his team almost as much publicity as Stanford and California.

Rozelle precedes the Dons into New York one memorable week in October of 1951 and attempts to explain to anyone who will listen that the University of San Francisco has the finest football team in the nation. No one believes him.

There isn't anyone east of the Embarcadero who really knows a thing about Burl Toler, Ollie Matson, Gino Marchetti, Bob St. Clair, Ed Brown, Red Stephens, Mike Mergen, Ralph Thomas, Scooter Scudero, Merrill Peacock. They were not aware that only a year earlier, two other players of note, Dick Stanfel and Roy Barni, had been a part of the same group. This was the time when San Francisco had two professional football teams—the 49ers, who were getting salaries, and the USF Dons, who were to be paid as soon as they had graduated.

"They laughed when I tried to advance the game against Fordham," said Rozelle, who now has a reasonably responsible job in professional football. "I came into the seven newspaper offices and I told them that San Francisco had the best football team in the country. I said that USF was better than anybody they had seen. They didn't ridicule me, but they came close."

Peering back through the shifting mists of time, one can understand the reticence of the New York sporting press. The Dons were, indeed, undefeated. They had beaten San Jose State 39-2. They had utterly destroyed Idaho 28-7. They had crushed Camp Pendleton Marine Base 26-0. Because opponents were scarce they took on San Jose State again and whipped the Spartans 42-7 this time. No one was cruel enough to point out that the only West Coast power not on the USF schedule seemed to be Oakland's McClymonds High School.

There may have been 15,000 spectators in the warm October sunshine at the stadium out on Randalls Island in the East River. Some of them were aware that Ollie Matson had a reputation. Since he wasn't an Eastern football player not too many people may have believed what they had read. Here was an Olympian sprinter with a fullback's physique (6 foot 2 inches and 217 pounds).

He had broken into college football against St. Bonaventure at Kezar with the visiting coach Hugh Devore snorting insults at him. In the final quarter he had gone 92 and 45 yards for two touchdowns that gave USF a 34-21 victory. Afterwards Devore walked into the Dons' dressing room to shake Matson's hand and say: "I'd be pleased if you excused my stupid mouth, Ollie."

Now he was opening in Manhattan halfway through his senior year. Fordham kicked off and Ollie Matson brought the ball 94 yards for a touchdown. Missing only three plays, he carried the ball 29 times for 118 yards. On defense he knocked down seven of Fordham quarterback Roger Franz's passes. In the fourth period he returned another kickoff for a touchdown, moving 90 yards this time. Despite an especially vigorous Fordham team, USF scored a 32-26 victory. Now folks in New York were impressed. Maybe some of them even made a note to believe Pete Rozelle the next time he came around.

"When that USF press agent gets home they'll probably take his sergeant's stripes away for being too conservative," said the *New York Herald Tribune*. "He told writers in advance of the game against Fordham that Ollie Matson was 'considered to be an

All-America candidate by some West Coast experts.' This Ollie Matson is every inch an All-America and not just in the opinion of people living in the West."

Deliriously confident, the Dons shattered their next three opponents, beating San Diego Navy Training Center 26-7, whipping Santa Clara 26-7, and defeating Loyola of Los Angeles 20-2. Despite the fact that they weren't playing California or Stanford or USC, they were gaining a national reputation. They went off to play College of the Pacific in Stockton and the San Joaquin Valley was suddenly filled with football fans.

In those days the College of the Pacific was only a whit beneath the old Pacific Coast Conference in the public's mind. At last there would be a true test of USF's worth as a football team. Some 41,607 citizens showed up at Pacific Memorial Stadium, which Amos Alonzo Stagg had so recently vacated by going into his final retirement.

The Tigers had a number of impressive young men themselves. There was quarterback Doug Scovil, now an assistant with the San Francisco 49ers, and running back Eddie Macon, who played with the Chicago Bears, and tackle Duane Putnam, who later became one of the finest offensive guards in the National Football League with the Los Angeles Rams.

It was judged, in advance, naturally, to be a reasonably even match. It was no sure thing. It was the College of the Pacific's varsity that entered the game with sweaty palms. Blundering badly, the Tigers let the University of San Francisco get ahead 20-0 in the first 20 minutes. Matson gained 178 yards in 29 carries. The defensive line of Bob St. Clair, Burl Toler, Gino Marchetti, and Mike Mergen sacked Scovil eight times and held Macon to 80 yards, much of it in the final quarter.

It was a surgically perfect victory. Matson ran 68 yards for a touchdown in the fourth period and USF had it 47-14. Nobody doubted that if their schedule had been tougher they still would have done extraordinarily well. The year that San Francisco had two professional football teams was coming to a climax and there wasn't any doubt that there would be an invitation from a bowl committee. The newspapers ran such encouraging headlines: "USF High on Orange Bowl List," and "Dons in Running for Cotton Bowl."

Chauvinism ran rampant, if not to say amuck. Writing in the *San Francisco Chronicle* Dick Friendlich said: "The finest football team in USF history stood in the front rank of the nation's powerhouses yesterday, shoulder to shoulder with Stanford, Tennessee, and Princeton, undefeated and

untied. By dealing a fine College of the Pacific team a 47-14 licking Saturday night, the worst Tiger defeat since the Stockton college took on major football responsibilities, coach Joe Kuharich's Dons dispelled all doubts about their real strength."

The chairman of the Orange Bowl committee was so garish in his remarks about the Dons that many of the players actually made plans to be away from home during the holidays. Matson told his mother that it was a foregone conclusion. Oh, the committee was going to look at Baylor, Rice, Texas, and Oklahoma. But that was a formality. Those schools always had high voltage teams and some courtesy had to be paid to them in return for future considerations.

"I am personally very partial to a California team," said the chairman, Van Kusserow. "I've been pulling for the University of San Francisco all season long. The visit of Santa Clara and its great victory in the 1950 Orange Bowl game left a great impression on me. Further, the game brought more publicity to California and Florida than any other Orange Bowl contest. Several committee members feel that the Dons are the ones to face Kentucky in this year's game."

The winter rains struck the San Francisco peninsula, as they always do, and the Dons stayed inside, watching the films of their victory over College of the Pacific and waiting for the telephone operator to ring from Miami. They waited and they waited. They stayed in shape. They planned and they schemed. They saw pictures of the University of Kentucky's team. They dreamed gaudy dreams. No call ever came. No explanation was ever given.

"I firmly believe, even now, that we had the finest college football team in the nation that year," said Matson, now offensive backfield coach at San Diego State. "I think they were afraid of us. They didn't know how good we were. So they ignored us after all that big talk. But we got our revenge in the National Football League. No one team ever put so many guys in the big league. If Burl (Toler) hadn't been hurt he would have been fantastic. Even our publicity man was an immortal. Think about that."

Matson finished his undergraduate career with two important national records. He averaged 174 yards in every game he played in and he carried the ball 245 times his senior year. His lesser statistics were equally as attractive. He scored 41 touchdowns and gained 3,166 yards. He was so good that hardly anybody realized that Scooter Scudero was also a brilliant ball carrier.

Football perished at the University of San Francisco the following year. Small Jesuit colleges all over the nation were examining their budgets and they seemed to come to the conclusion that shoulder pads and game jerseys were a lower priority than books for the library.

The 1951 USF varsity was the last to turn the professionals on. In addition to Rozelle and Kuharich, the National Football League came in and got Matson, St. Clair, Marchetti, Ed Brown, Mike Mergen, Ralph Thomas, Merrill Peacock, and Burl Toler. Ironically, Toler was rated far ahead of Marchetti or St. Clair as a prospect. His shattered knee, suffered in the College All-Star game, took care of that. Instead, he made it to the NFL another way, joining the officiating staff as a line judge in 1965.

All St. Clair could do was last 12 years with the 49ers, play in five Pro Bowls and make all-pro six times. Brown played with the Chicago Bears and the Pittsburgh Steelers for 15 years and if he didn't become the great professional everyone expected him to be, he at least had a great time trying. In between parties he went to the Pro Bowl twice and, once, in 1954, he came back to San Francisco to throw a 60-yard touchdown pass to Harlon Hill with seconds remaining that pushed the 49ers out of the playoffs.

Guard Lou Stephens and kick returner-defensive back Scooter Scudero both played with distinction for six years with the Washington Redskins. Guard Mike Mergen, receiver Ralph Thomas, and receiver Merrill Peacock spent two years each with the Chicago Cardinals.

"There were some other players on the team who might have made it in the NFL now that there are more teams all looking for talent," said Kuharich not long ago. "There were only a dozen clubs then and they could afford to be more picky. We had a tough group of guys. Our facilities were nothing. The team had a surplus quonset hut for a locker room. Our spring practices lasted four months. The drills were four hours a day for a six-day week.

"Those fellows were superbly conditioned. They went both ways, you know. Ollie Matson was probably the best defensive end. Toler could play tackle on offense or linebacker on defense, with equal skill. He was an outstanding center, too, when we used him there. Those fellows hated to come out of the game. I never removed one of them without getting a terrible argument.

"At USF we had what we called the Blood Pit. It was one-on-one, something that a lot of teams don't bother with anymore. A defensive man practiced his techniques on an offensive man and vice-versa.

The better player had to force his way around. You needed strength, quickness, and intelligence. Almost every one of the San Francisco Dons had just that. For speed, we'd give Marchetti a five-yard sprinting start on Matson and goad Gino into not letting Ollie catch him. If Matson did, we'd up the margin to eight yards. It was fun."

The years have slipped past silently and the city of San Francisco has not produced a football player to match Ollie Matson. He still holds a place close to Joe DiMaggio as a local folk hero. Athletes graduate from the school system every spring and go off to play at schools all over the nation. The best of them leave with an asterisk next to their names. (*) Might be almost as good as Ollie Matson.

Here was a self-confessed mother's boy. But Mrs. Gertrude Matson was an extraordinary mother. A school teacher, she had graduated from Texas Southern University in Houston and done advanced work at Sam Houston State. When Ollie was 13, she decided that California was a better place for a black teenager to mature.

"Whatever I was or whatever I am today I owe to her," said Matson. "She kept me moving in the right direction. I'd want to take a detour down a dark alley and she'd be right there telling me to smarten up. She kept a close touch with sports. She used to remind me when I was at USF that I should publicly thank my linemen for blocking. She used to say, 'Son, you'd look fairly stupid without those people.' She was right."

One evening in 1972 there was a short, but fascinating footnote to history. Gino Marchetti and Ollie Matson became the first two college teammates ever to be inducted into the Professional Football Hall of Fame in Canton, Ohio. There are 81 men whose faces have been cast in bronze and then bolted to the wall. Only Gino and Ollie played on the same college team at the same time.

"No one will ever convince me that the 1951 University of San Francisco Dons weren't the best," said Marchetti. "Ollie led the nation in scoring. Hugh McElhenny was second. We played our best when things were toughest. If we had been at Notre Dame they'd still be writing books about us. It was a privilege to play with those guys."

Now only the high school kids play at Kezar. The place belongs to the bats and the owls at night time and to sea gulls in the afternoon. Gone are the professionals and gone are the college kids. Only a few old settlers remember the year when San Francisco had two professional teams, one of which got paid.

1972 Hall of Fame inductees:
Ace Parker, Ollie Matson, Gino Marchetti

by Jim Murray

One Man's Image

They came from the Old Country and they had names like "Anton" and "Stefan" and "Josip" and "Stanislaus" and they had a big edge on people who needed to rest.

Their icon was work. They harnessed up to it like Percherons at birth and they died in the traces. They were born with a silver shovel in their mouths. Sunup to sundown was their idea of a work day until the electric light came in. Then, they worked till they fell asleep.

They carried their money in their belts where it got as sweat-stained as they were. They didn't trust banks, people, governments, or each other. "Heaven" was a place where you got a lunch hour.

They had short powerful arms, squat immovable legs. God (or environment) built them to shovel, haul, cut, pull, and push. They weren't much on dancing. They were long on reality and short on imagination. An open hearth furnace is no place for fairy tales. The company store does not sell costume novels.

They came to America and they disappeared into the steel mills where they hauled the molten ingots or pounded sledges or laid track. They put human as well as processed steel into the backbone of the country.

They farmed the barren fields everyone else quit on. They grew tobacco under gauze. They put tunnels under rivers, beams on buildings. They had rings around their heads from hard hats.

When they went to college, they took courses that meant money. English Lit was safe from them. The *Lives of the Minor Poets* would not get Papa out of the coal mines. Daydreams weren't something you paid good money for. They learned how to build bridges with a pencil or build a machine that could dig ore and let Uncle Louie up from the mine shaft.

Their god was steel and iron and gold. Their god was a man who minded the store. Vacations were for the rich. They all ended up with backaches. So they feared an open window more than an open hearth. Better a hundred-degree heat in the foundry than a few days off at no pay because you couldn't straighten your back.

In football, they were in the line. In war, they were in the infantry. In life, they were in the pits. On a ship, they were down in the hold.

They bit coins and held paper money up to the light. They never took checks. The part of Europe their people came from, they didn't trust their neighbor all that much. He brought flowers one day, a bayonet the next.

George Stanley Halas came from a long line of these people. He came from a craggy land known as "Bohemia" in the old Austro-Hungarian Empire and it's the heart and lungs of Czechoslovakia now. It's funny that "Bohemian" should come to symbolize a kind of unwashed, frivolous, violin-playing gypsy, because the real Bohemians were the craggy types outlined above, fools for work who sowed the barren sides of the Carpathian Mountains or produced the best mechanics in Europe in the airless factories of the Industrial Revolution. They lived by their backs, not their wits.

George Gellatley

George Halas's father was a tailor in America. When he cut you a graduation suit, you could expect to be buried in it. He paid his bills, he was on time with the rent, and you could take his handshake to any bank in Chicago and get a loan on it. He didn't put out the "Closed" sign on the shop until the whole street was empty and the street cars stopped running.

Son George got a chance to go to the University of Illinois and escape a lifetime of needles in the mouth or coal lamp in the hat, and, when he wasn't playing football, baseball, basketball, or soccer, he was washing windows, cutting grass, sweeping floors, or selling sandwiches.

When he left college, his first job was playing right field for the New York Yankees and he was good enough that it took a hip injury for Babe Ruth to take the job away from him. But he considered two hours of baseball a day to be loafing. So he played football and worked in a stock brokerage on the side.

When he couldn't get his job back from Babe Ruth, George went to work for the Decatur Staleys football team.

The Chicago Bears, you see, started life as an 11-man advertisement for a shirt-starching compound. George worked so hard keeping the team together and successful, that he actually felt guilty taking Sunday afternoons off to block and tackle.

Owner A. N. Staley gave George $5,000 to take the team out of town in 1921. George got a $25 million franchise literally for less than nothing. All Staley wanted was that they keep the name "Staleys" for a year.

When he sank the five grand in pro football, lots of people thought he would be better off throwing it off rooftops or spending it on chorus girls. His mother wondered why he had bothered to learn to build bridges.

Pro football was started by six guys sitting around on Huppmobile running boards in Canton, Ohio, one afternoon in 1920. The only survivor of that group is George Halas. One of the reasons pro football survived is George Halas.

George Halas not only played end, he sold tickets, swept floors, shovelled snow, ushered patrons, coached, counted, flacked, worried, wet-nursed, and evangelized. He spent Staley's get away money on uniforms and the first 20 bucks that came through the till, he ran down to the drugstore and bought iodine and tape.

When not a single Chicago newspaperman showed up to cover the game, George hired a press agent. Not even baseball had thought of that. Today, a team would as soon take the field without a quarterback as without a public relations man. A former one is

National Football League commissioner.

A felicitous nickname, pinned on a trackman-halfback at the University of Illinois, the "Galloping Ghost," turned Red Grange into a million-dollar property and pro football into a billion-dollar one.

George Halas went into partnership with Red Grange. Which is to say, Red got 50 percent of the take from a Bears-Grange tie-up. When Halas saw a line around the block the next morning, queued up to get tickets, he knew pro football was here to stay. Grange had under priced himself. Over 65,000 people showed up at the Polo Grounds to see him. The rest of the Bears were just $100-a-day spear carriers. In Philly, 40,000 sat in the rain. Coral Gables built a stadium just for him and charged $18 a head.

That the promoters quickly caught on may be seen from George's wry joke that, in St. Louis, a mortician fielded an All-Star team to face Grange and, after Grange ran wild, the press suggested they should have checked the All-Stars for a pulse.

If all the man hours George Halas put into his Chicago Bears, and, inferentially, into pro football over the past 50 years were to be totalled up, they would probably be found to be running neck-and-neck with those put in by the United Auto Workers over that period.

He is tireless, termagant, contentious, cantankerous; if he were in government, there'd be a stamp out on him by now. Yoked to pro football, he has worked for it on his knees like a charlady, at a desk like a clerk, with a rake like a gardener, at a blackboard like a teacher, with his hat in his hand or a clench in his fists, when he made $56 as he did in 1922 or lost $18,000 as he did in 1932.

Of course, if all there was to George Halas was the 16-hour day and the seven-day week, pro football would still be in its pass-the-hat stage. Halas schemed, raged, plotted, conspired for his foundling sport. He had such uncanny ability to spot motivation in a football player that he got a quarterback (Sid Luckman) out of the Ivy League, ends from obscure campuses (Harlon Hill from Florence State) and fullbacks (Bronko Nagurski) from such frozen north country that they didn't thaw out till the third week of summer practice.

He wrote and rewrote the rules himself but this didn't stop him from chasing referees up and down the sidelines abusively for enforcing them. He took a kick at a fan once when he was a mere 67 or so. "I knew it was time to retire when I missed," he admitted. He lectured at a clinic once. "People think I invented the game of football," he began, thought a minute, then added: "And I did."

He changed the rules to put the goal posts on the goal line (then got the best placekicker in the business), was the first to see the wisdom of permitting a forward pass anywhere behind the line of scrimmage. If he spent 16 hours a day *working* for pro football, he spent the whole 24 *thinking* for it.

He tested ideas by disagreeing with them. He was the first to see that mating with television would be like marrying an heiress. He built the greatest teams the game has ever seen and would have cheerfully poured it on a rival team consisting wholly of his grandparents, maternal aunts, uncles, and infants. What some people thought was his biggest blunder of all time, defeating Washington 73-0 in the 1940 title game, actually was a showman's stroke. That dramatic score demonstrated two things: pro football's proficiency and honesty.

The Halas act is hardboiled but old friends know the right ventricle is full of fudge. The crust is hard but it's meringue. He cries at sad movies, is as sentimental as a Carrie Jacobs Bond lyric.

What Ford was to autos, Rockefeller to oil, Vanderbilt to railroads, or Morgan to money, Halas was to football. It must give a man great satisfaction to see an enterprise he was given $5,000 to take off somebody's hands grow into an industry with a waiting list of millionaires and cities waving blank checks and bidding to be let in.

On the other hand, satisfaction is time-consuming. And for the old Bohemian workhorse, he finds he can squeeze it in about 1976. You see, that's a Leap Year and he can give it five minutes on February 29. While he's shaving.

Frank Rippon

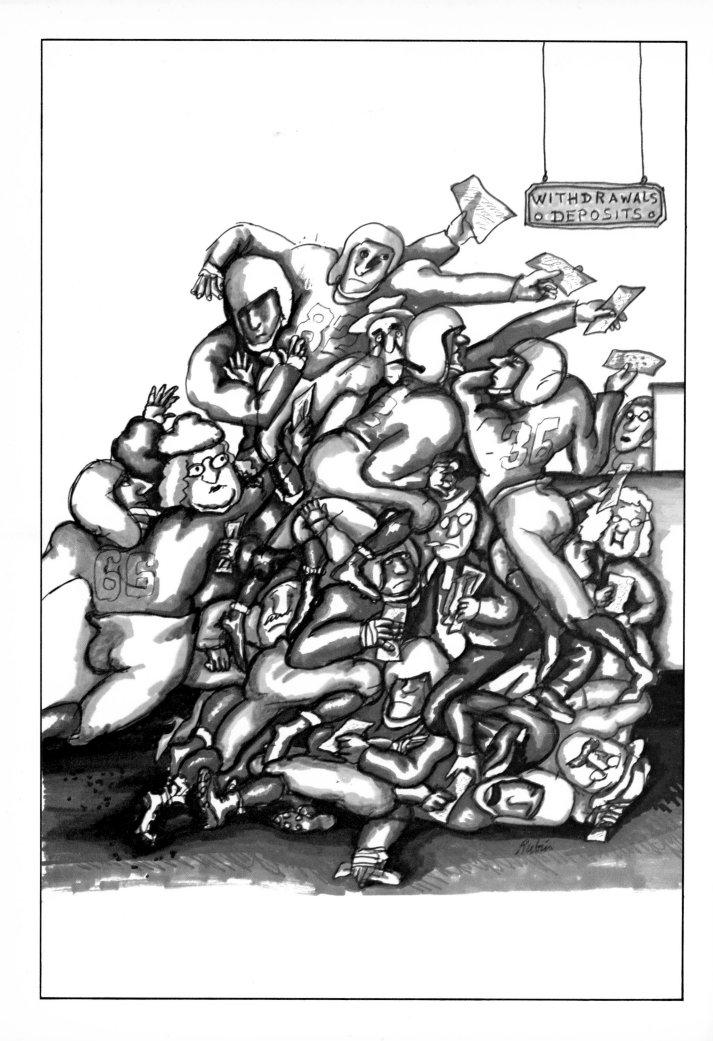

by Mickey Herskowitz

Once Upon a Time in Dallas

Marv Rubin

It convulsed them in Dallas, in 1960 when Lamar Hunt decided to call his pro football team the Texans. He could have called them the Aardvarks, or the Zombies, or any of 10,000 splendid names in between. But he chose the Texans. Possibly he was trying to cash in on the success of the last team to own that name.

The original Dallas Texans were so successful they did not even finish the season. They lost 11 out of 12 games and established what was, to that time, a world record for returning kickoffs, 67. The Texans—we think of them as the first, or vintage Texans—folded up like an old road map at midyear and were left in the lap of the National Football League. It was a team without a flag, living on the league's purse, playing its last five games on the road.

This was 1952. And you know that we are in a cycle, that we are indeed belly surfing across a wave of nostalgia, when people resurrect the memory of the '52 Dallas Texans. They were the product of a curiously mixed decade, one that gave us Elvis Presley, hula hoops, the bop, duck tail haircuts, and the soda fountain as a center for the American youth culture.

Has it been more than 20 years? It has. And today, in the city where the Texans failed so utterly, the Dallas Cowboys now hang their headgear. The Texans are to the Cowboys what Wallis Warfield Simpson is to the British monarchy. Related if not by blood, at least by legend.

It is surprising how few people are aware that there existed in 1952 a team called the Texans. On the other hand, maybe it isn't. The Texans did not leave much of a foot-print on the sands of professional football. Yet it was not a team bereft of talent. It had Buddy Young, an exciting little runner who could move like a wisp of smoke at his peak. There were soon-to-be stars in Gino Marchetti at end and Art Donovan at tackle. And a few tough, willing pros such as Dick Hoerner and Tom Keane, part of a carload of 11 players obtained from the Rams in a sensational trade for Les Richter. But the Texans were a team in between.

When they lost, which was nearly always, they did so with regret. Once Frankie Albert offended them, by faking a punt and passing deep, looking for a quick one with the 49ers ahead by 30 points. "When the ref wasn't watching," recalls Art Donovan, "one of our guys cold cocked him. He tells Albert, 'If you get up I'll kill ya.' He didn't get up."

The owners, the city, the team suffered separately but equally. "It was," decided Tex Maule of *Sports Illustrated,* "a screwed up operation from the beginning."

It isn't widely known, and he does not go out of his way to enlighten people, but Maule served as publicity man for the old Texans. To get a break like that he had to walk away from the same job with the Rams, world champions the year before.

"I was convinced the Texans couldn't miss," reflects Maule, today pro football's best known historian. "I was hired by Frank Fitzgerald, Ted Collins's son-in-law. When I got to Dallas I asked for Fitzgerald. He had been fired the day before. I was off to a great start."

The new owners of the team were the Miller brothers, Giles and Connell, heirs to a textile fortune. They were men of the cloth, so to speak, but they were quite unprepared to lose their shirts in a game that was not yet our national mania.

Formerly the New York Yanks, the team had made a large dent in the bankroll of Ted Collins, who made his pile managing Kate Smith. In 1952, larger crowds were turning out to hear Kate Smith sing "God Bless America" than to see the Texans play.

By the end of the season pro football was a dead issue in Dallas. As a prospect for any kind of future revival, it looked about as appealing as the Los Alamos Testing Grounds. In January, 1953, Al Ennis, who had been dispatched from the home office of commissioner Bert Bell to help organize the franchise, wrote a sad, bitter letter to the club's executive secretary, Marilyn Cunningham:

"It is almost certain that Baltimore will receive the franchise so nonchalantly thrown overboard by the Texas millionaires. They have already sold over fifteen thousand season tickets and are still going strong—a most amazing performance, and one that indicates tremendous civic pride. This is the sort of civic interest which all of us in the league confidently expected Dallas to exhibit—but we were wrong…it will be a long time, if ever, before anyone outside of Texas will believe that any group of Texans would not quit *cold* if the going got rough."

Still, the team might have been saved for Dallas. The wealthy Clint Murchison, Jr. had indicated an interest in bailing out the Millers. But when the crunch came Murchison was in South America, and Bert Bell declined to give the team's management time to contact him.

The ominous signs were present in training camp—an uncertain coaching staff, a team composed of strangers. And a city that hadn't really asked for this blessing wasn't tuned up for it.

The team trained in Kerrville, where after practice one day Maule discovered a solitary Buddy Young still on the field, doing situps. Taking in the deserted landscape, Maule grinned and said, "What's the matter with you, Buddy?"

Between grunts Young replied, "Tex, a man is going to have to be in peak physical condition this year just to survive."

Young was, and he did. A black man playing in a city then still largely segregated, Buddy became the team's most popular player. Whatever else, the Texans quietly struck a blow for social justice. "There was talk of segregated seating at the Cotton Bowl," says Young. "But the Texans knocked out Jim Crow. I think that was a breakthrough."

As the season wore on, few of the players shared Buddy Young's intensity. During its final days on the road the Texans bivouacked in Hershey, Pennsylvania, the league taking the position that everyone has to be someplace.

The five-week sentence in Hershey was an exercise in playing out the clock. Most of their practice time was spent playing volleyball over the goal posts. They were as restless as sailors waiting to be discharged.

The Texans were a mixed collection of styles and temper. "We had some characters," recalls Young. "Chubby Grigg, we got him in the Weldon Humble trade. Chub was mean as a snake, fat as a hog, on the downside of his pro career. His whole disposition was mean."

Once, when Buddy tried to break up a fight, Grigg picked him up and threw him into the phonograph, around which the team would gather and listen to Kay Starr sing "Wheel of Fortune," night after night. "We sure hated to lose that record player," said Donovan.

Young remembers the starting quarterback, Bob Celeri, as "almost uncoachable. It wasn't the Age of Aquarius, but he was the first guy I knew to do his own thing and he was doing it in 1952. He liked to throw in situations like fourth and twenty."

The purest character of all, the one around whom the deeds of the season unwound like a fire hose, was the head coach, Jimmy Phelan, a handsome, whimsical Irishman.

"We had a good time in spite of everything," insists Donovan, "mostly because of Phelan. He had a great line of bull. It was a picnic just being around him. One day we were working out at a field near the Rose Bowl, getting ready for the Rams, and we ran off a couple of plays without fouling up. Phelan stopped practice, loaded everybody on a bus and took us to the racetrack. Jimmy loved the races."

Donovan was out of Holy Cross, in his third year as a pro and on his way to greatness with Baltimore teams still to come.

He was Phelan's favorite and, in the sight of his coach, in the midst of a season where little went right, he could do no wrong. "Phelan went to Mass every morning. I'd be dragging in around six o'clock and he'd be waiting there for me with a cab, and he'd take me to church with him.

"He cared about the game. If he thought you were laying down, he wouldn't stand for it. But football had passed him by. He was one of the only coaches I ever knew who hated practices more than their players did."

It was a season of continuing bumps and bruises, a season without pity. "I hurt my leg against the Rams in the Coliseum,"

Donovan went on. "A guy fell into the back of it. It was killing me, but I stayed on the sideline and watched the rest of the game. When it was over everybody runs off and leaves me on the bench. I can't walk! I have to crawl all the way off the field, up the ramp and into the dressing room. The team doctor checks me over and starts looking for some crutches.

"Phelan stops him. He screams, 'That son of a bitch is an IRISHMAN. He don't need no crutches!' Jimmy, he loved me. It turns out I got a broken knee. I was back playing three weeks later."

As an organizer, Phelan's idea of planning was the kind that made Pearl Harbor famous. His assistants, Cecil Isbell, Will Walls, and Alex Agase, did most of the coaching, and he sent them to Kerrville for a week of early practice with the quarterbacks. At the time, the Texans had neither an offense nor a defense.

"What the hell will we work on for a full week?" asked Isbell.

"Work on the cadence," said Phelan. "One-and-two-and-three."

When Phelan arrived in camp a week later, the first thing he did was change the cadence.

Later in the training period the Texans acquired Don Klosterman from the Browns. Klosterman had led the nation's passers at Loyola in 1950.

He joined the team in San Antonio, where the Texans were to play the Redskins that night in a preseason game. "I went to the Saint Anthony Hotel to meet Phelan and go over the plays and terminology. When I got there he told me we'd do it before the game. All I had to do was punt and placekick.

"Now, I had come from Cleveland, where Paul Brown ran a super organized camp. With Brown, you go into a game knowing the first three plays—what to look for, where the kickoff will go, who will run it out.

"In the Texans' locker room, the first thing they did was give me the shoulder pads that belonged to Mike McCormack, a big tackle. Finally, Phelan quiets the team and says, 'Okay, hit somebody and we'll win the game.' That was it. The players went by me so fast I thought a deluge of dysentery had hit the team."

The Texans made their Dallas debut on September 28, 1952, against the New York Giants in the Cotton Bowl. A crowd of 17,000—it was to be their largest home audience—turned out to see the return of SMU heroes Kyle Rote and Fred Benners.

The Giants won 24-6, and the only Texans' touchdown was set up on a punt fumbled by a New York halfback named Tom Landry.

Don Klosterman missed a 33-yard field goal attempt and was released by Phelan the next day. He was dumbfounded, a condition he had been in steadily since his first day on the job.

"Hell, I was a quarterback, not a kicking specialist," he fumed. "The ball hit the uprights and bounced back. And the next day I got cut. I was mad as hell. I couldn't believe it." Hurt, angry, disappointed, Klosterman left after exchanging a few X-rated words with Phelan.

Weeks later, preparing for their second date against the Giants, the Texans were viewing the film of their first encounter when Phelan stood up and cried, "Stop the camera. Run that back." The film spun backwards until there, again, was Klosterman's kick hitting the uprights and bouncing away.

Phelan sat down, folded his arms and looked smugly around the room. "Now," he demanded, "who says I didn't give him a chance?"

Anyone connected with the Texans can recite verbatim two stories that have become classics of the pro football gender. It is a ritual so automatic as to leave no variation in the retelling. It is like asking Francis Scott Key to sing a medley of his hit songs.

A conversation with Tex Maule begins with a half-sentence: "Tex, every ex-Texan tells the same two…"

And Maule interrupts: "…stories. The one about Phelan calling off practice so the players could cash their checks, and the one at Akron, where the crowd was so small Phelan told them they should shake hands with each fan."

"Yeah, that's it."

"Well, after a while, the whole thing got to be a comedy."

It wasn't easy to keep up with either the team or the front office. The owners decked them out in cowboy hats and colorful shirts, which the players refused to wear. Donovan gave his to a truck driver. At one point, Bob Celeri was released and hired back at a lower salary. One lineman was suspected of being paranoid. When Phelan tried to send him into a game he refused. "Why me?" he said. "I went in last time." He thought people were out to get him.

The team's only win, over the Bears 27-23, came after the club had tapped out in Dallas. That was the game played at Akron before a crowd of around 3,000, where in his pregame pep talk Phelan suggested that "we dispense with the customary introductions, and the players go into the stands and shake hands with each fan." It loosened them up, or something, and they played the hell out of the Bears ("George Halas," says Donovan, "nearly croaked.").

In no other game that season did the Texans come within 17 points of a tie.

The week of what turned out to be their last game in Dallas, the Texans picked up Frank Tripucka, the former Notre Dame quarterback, from the Cardinals. When it was announced that Tripucka would start that Sunday against the Rams, Maxwell Stiles, a Los Angeles columnist, asked Maule how he could be ready on such scant practice time.

Maule, who was not your typical press agent, sighed heavily. "Well, hell," he said, "it only took Phelan thirty minutes to give him the offense, and it wouldn't have taken that long except Jimmy went over it twice."

The game was played in a blinding rainstorm. From the press box it was impossible to see any fans at all. Those who did attend had taken shelter under the stadium overhang. The Texans tried, and did not play badly, but the Rams outgunned them 27-6.

So the adventure in Dallas ended, almost unobserved, on a day without sunshine.

The Texans had moved to Dallas to drumrolls of optimism. They were pioneers, bringing the blossoming sport of pro football into the lusty southwest. The city meant jobs, futures, riches. The players had also heard that that the American Airlines stewardess school was based there, and they were excited.

The day the franchise folded, Phelan announced it to the squad by canceling that afternoon's practice. "Boys," he said, "the league has decided to make us orphans. We're through in Dallas. Here are your checks. It is my opinion that you should get to the banks with all due haste."

Some had money coming they would never collect. One of them was Alex Agase, the assistant coach, who was in charge of the film projector during their last five weeks on the road. Alex had designs on that piece of equipment. It was worth $250 and he planned to hock it. "I had just been married," he recalled, "hadn't been paid in months and really needed the money. I was sure Phelan had forgotten about the projector. The day before the season ended Jimmy walked into my hotel room, opened the closet door and walked out with it."

Cecil Isbell, who had been on the wagon for years, tumbled off it the team's last night in Dallas. He placed one phone call, to a depressed Giles Miller, and what he told him will never be printed on a Hallmark card.

A building team, a town with a college tradition, weak management…those were not the ingredients to inspire the fainthearted. But when the team took its leave of Dallas, the Miller brothers showed up at the airport to see them off. Giles was crying.

There were several neat, human twists and turns to the legend of pro football's Lost Battalion:

Murchison, who was out of town when the Texans lost their lease, became the owner of the Dallas Cowboys, who kept theirs.

Don Klosterman, who as a young quarterback lasted one week under Phelan, is today the general manager at Los Angeles.

The second Texans, owned by Lamar Hunt and raised in the new American Football League, also fled Dallas and now reside happily and successfully in Kansas City.

Buddy Young retired in 1955 and is a member of the commissioner's staff, working in player relations.

Maule, who quit a job with the Rams to return to Texas, was succeeded in Los Angeles by a fellow named Pete Rozelle.

There is, of course, a remaining touch of irony that demands expression. I asked Tex Maule what would have happened if…the Millers had shown the staying power to see it through, or if…Clint Murchison had been allowed to save the 1952 Texans.

"That's easy," said Maule. "Today they would be the Baltimore Colts."

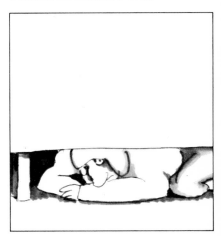

by Jim Klobuchar

Believe Everything You Hear

"A psychiatrist told my mother I should have been an actor. It never occurred to me, but there might have been a thread of logic to that. My earliest memory is standing on the windowsill of my nursery, pulling up my nightie for the benefit of a small audience across the street. Without knowing it, I might have pioneered a new art form."

— JOHNNY BLOOD (McNALLY),
reflecting on his narrow escape
from orthodoxy.

The tyranny of time eventually ruins our illusions. About the reindeer and Robin Hood and the called home run.

Time cannot touch Johnny Blood. He is no illusion. If you wish you may call him Johnny Blood Past. He has the corporeal form of John V. McNally Present, who moves among us performing a kind of droll and graceful penance at the age of 70 by advancing causes and modestly curtailing his poetic eruptions.

It is a grand attempt, but it should not be taken seriously as an act of contrition. The world will pardon much in its folk heroes but it will not allow them to abdicate, and John McNally therefore yields gently to the will of Johnny Blood's public.

So strum no minstrel's mandolin for the departed spirit of Johnny Blood nor consign it to the floating pantheons. Johnny Blood McNally performed such mind-bending deeds and so adroitly sidestepped adversaries like logic, deputies, and linebackers he must rise above mere mythology. You do Johnny Blood no favors by making him a legend. Instead, cherish him. He was authentic, as much as the swashing of the bathtub gin of the era that spawned him, or the moody-whistling trains on which he hoboed.

And if you are a football fan who would like to flash back to the bare-knuckled adolescence of professional football, when the players shouted bets across the line of scrimmage and slugged and cursed and laughed at each other for $100 a game, congratulate yourself that there was no television to glamorize Johnny Blood.

It would have been unbearable to watch the rail-riding vagabond curled in front of a fireplace, reciting "To a Skylark" with a popcorn popper in one hand and a flapper in the other.

How much better to experience Johnny Blood at leisure. Certainly you can sing your ballads, about his transcontinental motorcycle rides with hot-breathed maid—no, make that hot-breathed young women, for the sake of accuracy; about his eighth-floor leap onto Curly Lambeau's window ledge to collect an advance; playing a football game with a punctured kidney; doing a midfield jig to a chorus of Piccolo Pete during a time out; stalling his car broadside to stop the Packers' train, which he had missed owing to the late-rising habits of a blonde.

His football was the football of joy, the expression of an impish Achilles. He was lavishly endowed with ability and nerve and a gift for the improbable play, when nothing else would rescue his team from catastrophe. But the total weight of these qualities never smothered his renegade tilt and usually got no better than a draw. He won football games for the Packers with extraordinary catches and runs, scored 37 pro touchdowns, and played on four championship teams. But he contrived to strike a redeeming balance with these achievements by getting fired by the Packers for reporting groggily to practice one day and falling on his rump attempting to punt.

They voted him into the Pro Football Hall of Fame lustily and deservedly. But it was never clear which Johnny fascinated the selectors more persuasively, Blood the champion or Blood the happy heretic.

The dilemma in singing ballads about Johnny Blood's 22 years in pro football is that you have trouble separating the stanzas, the ones in which the truth is merely outlandish from the ones in which the truth is plain horrendous.

"In some ways," Johnny Blood McNally admits, "I was a horrendous character. Maybe the zodiac had it right. I was born under Sagittarius. As I understand it, this made me part philosopher, part stud by decree of the stars. It is a helluva burden for a man to carry and practically impossible to live up to, although I don't deny making the attempt for a couple of years.

"When I look back on it, I can see that some of my unorthodox behavior came out of my upbringing in Wisconsin and had nothing to do with the zodiac. Some of the Blood stories you hear talk of me as though I were some kind of society football player. I did get money from my family later, but they never trusted me with it until I was fifty-five. My mother was a school teacher who got hold of me early and pumped a lot of myths into me, Grecian myths, Irish myths, King Arthur stuff. That part of me was going to be adventure. My father was a small town businessman and athletic fan, but a left-handed, curly-haired Irishman, which explains a lot.

"My mother was born on a farm in St. Croix County, Wisconsin. Her favorite activity was breaking horses. Maybe she looked on me as another kind of colt. I loved her, but I just didn't cooperate very well and so one day she handed me a poem entitled, 'The Bronco That Wouldn't Be Broken.' Remember that one from your school days? Anyhow, she smiled when she did it. I suppose she was making some kind of statement."

The punctuation for it could have been furnished in ensuing years by professors, railroad dicks, sea captains, Nevada pit bosses, defensive ends, and football coaches, all of whom in some form failed to saddle the obstinate bronco. John McNally was a multi-directional prodigy, a high school graduate at 14, a teenaged economist capable of launching a book on the subject, a dedicated college dropout, and a mirthful revolutionary in general.

The straight arrows of John McNally's youth were the authorities at St. John's in Collegeville, Minnesota, the earnest fathers at Notre Dame, the worried fathers of his girl friends, and that collection of ringing social principles we call Rules.

McNally defied them impartially, including the one against amateur athletes accepting coin for their labors. To spare the feelings of his coach at St. John's, John decided to function incognito for a Minneapolis semipro club. He covered his tracks by selecting the name of Johnny Blood, borrowed from the marquee of a theater where Rudolph Valentino's "Blood and Sand" was playing. The choice was so good it seemed to have providential help, which may not have been a coincidence. "People have told me," John McNally said, "that I'm really a frustrated priest."

The priesthood is one of the more novel other-lives proposed for Johnny Blood McNally by his admirers and biographers, and one of the very few he has not actually attempted. He is the kind of man, with his history and his still-lean and courtly carriage of today, that impels otherwise non-psychic types into rambling notions about reincarnation. Nobody, the theory goes, could possibly pack that much living into one lifetime without some prior experience.

So how will you have it with Johnny Blood? Did he duel against the baron's cutthroats with D'Artagnan? Race the chariots for the hand, or whatever available, of the senator's daughter? Did he sail with Captain Kidd or ride with Zorro?

"Reincarnation," John granted, "is an intriguing concept. Who am I to say no? I don't believe in it, but I never considered many things impossible. I think I would have been a lousy swordsman, although a good pirate because of certain skills I cultivated at quick escape in my earlier years. I've been a lecturer, miner, dockhand, gambler, seaman, coach, and farm hand. I don't know who else I might have been. If I had any relatives in other lives, it might have been some combination of John L. Sullivan and Errol Flynn. At least that would have been my preference."

Johnny Blood needs no hypnotic regression to make it as a bona fide sage. His life has been filled with a Decameron menagerie of characters, symbolic questings, odd triumphs, and hilarious defeats. It is a kind of pilgrim's progress from the reckless appetites of the warrior-nomad to his sense of duty in a pensive old age.

He has never blushed for the urges of his prime. Yet he does regret 10 years of his middle age in which "I didn't really do a damned thing except to go around obliging people who wanted to dredge up skeletons

of another time. I would join them in having one more happy wake for the career of Johnny Blood."

In this he may be making a needlessly hard judgment. Nobody has ever provided aging folk heroes with a manual on how to repudiate the fiction gracefully without spoiling the larger fun generated by the truth. So John has suffered the blarney without protest, fully recognizing that the genuine Blood stories are better. He is also a practical man. It wouldn't do him any good to deny any part of it, including the fairy tales.

Which is another reason John has been welcomed in the newspaper offices across the land with that special kind of hospitality accorded the arrival of an ice cream cart at a kindergarten picnic. Thus his recent public lobbying, first a McNally-inspired campaign to draft Supreme Court Justice Byron R. White for President and later an appeal for pensions to oldtime pros, encountered little resistance breaking into print.

The experience has jarred him somewhat. "I'd want to talk all about why Whizzer White (whom he coached with the Pittsburgh Steelers) would be so qualified to serve as President in case of a deadlock at the Democratic convention," he said, "and the sports columnist would nod and then ask me if it were true that I once stole a cab in St. Louis in an emergency to protect the reputation of a young lady."

The story, naturally, was true, which sort of consigned Whizzer White to the subterranean sections of the story, to John's mortification.

He is having to battle a similar conflict of interest between John McNally, maverick knight, and John McNally, advocate, in his current mission to extend pro football's pension benefits to the men of the game's formative years. About this he comes as close as he is capable to real anger. "I think," he said, "the lawyers are waiting until the old guys are all dead."

It should not be neglected that among the several lives of John McNally was a promising career as a feed salesman. It ended under provocative circumstances but John concedes himself some gifts of persuasion.

It was such power that enabled him to draw out a book on Basic English from a college library in the thirties while he was touring with the Packers. "It was Ogden and Richards," he remembers. "They invented 'Basic English.' It was all the rage among the young scholars in those years. The incident took place during one of my interludes of intellectual curiosity. I checked out the book from the librarian and then just forgot about it. A couple of months later somebody from the team office called me and said, "Another first, John. According to this letter from Palo Alto you're the first pro football player who ever stole a book from the Stanford Library."

John made immediate restitution, out of his abiding fondness for the academic groves. This affection, if ever doubted, was reinforced in the 1950s when John McNally, a pro football player for two decades and onetime international roustabout, returned to St. John's as a lecturer in economics.

His scholarship was dimmed in the 1920s, however, when he got kicked out of Notre Dame for violating curfew and refusing to identify his accomplices.

Like his contemporary in the fields of arts and letters, the first Thomas Wolfe, Johnny Blood McNally was bewitched by trains. They were his Arabian carpets of adventure, his deliverance from drudgery and the sites of his random showdowns with the forces of calm and order. He bummed his way around the country on trains, ran across their roofs, challenged the Chicago Bears on a train, and once nearly derailed his own team.

"It was simply an obligation I had to a young woman," he explained of this latter feat. "She was a late riser, which put great demands on chivalry. Anyhow, the Packer train was leaving at ten A.M. for the West Coast, from where we were going to sail to Hawaii for some exhibitions.

"I got a late start for the depot and discovered the train had left without me. There was really no choice. Either I stopped the train, which was then just pulling out of the yard, or I got fined for missing it."

His priorities clear, McNally floor-boarded his touring car for three blocks and swung it across the tracks a couple of hundred feet in front of the advancing train.

"I couldn't imagine that the engineer was a callous man and would run the engine through the car," McNally relates, "especially since the lady and I were still in it."

Sensitivity triumphed. The engineer stopped the train, McNally valorously turned over the wheel to the young woman, kissed her auf wiedersehen, and boarded the train.

"Would you believe this?" he asked. "A few months ago, in the spring of 1974, I was visiting in Palm Springs, California. The late Arthur Daley of the *New York Times,* a really lovable person, had written a column about some of my experiences. One of the girl's relatives saw Daley's column and forwarded it to her, asking whether I was the guy she had talked about years ago. A copy of the letter was sent to Arthur, who sent it to me, and on this day in

California I met the girl-on-the-tracks, forty years after the incident. She's a widow living in San Bernardino, and remembers the whole thing very clearly."

One wouldn't wonder. Nor should one be surprised that McNally waited 30 years to avenge another small railroad crisis involving a less hazardous gamble.

It wasn't uncommon for the pro footballers of the 1920s and 1930s to wager against each other on the quirk of the moment before games. Such indiscretion today would invoke immediate thunder and damnation from the league office. But in those days the athletes considered it a legitimate source of walking-around money. No big sums were involved, nor were they available, in view of the relative penury of the shoulder-padded bettors. Ten dollars was standard. "We never looked on it as immoral in any way because you always bet on yourself," McNally explained. "Of course, if I were with management I can see how it would have a different complexion. I had a ten dollar bet on this game with Carl Brumbaugh, the Bears' quarterback. We won the game and afterwards I went on the Bears' train to collect the bet.

"All hell broke loose. Somebody got the idea I came on board to challenge the whole Bears' team, which wouldn't have been very bright considering the few escape routes open. I barely got out of there in one piece, and I didn't collect the money from Brumbaugh.

"A couple of years ago they got all of the old Bears and Packers players together for the one-hundredth anniversary Green Bay-Chicago game. I spotted Brumbaugh and said, 'You bastard, you still haven't paid the ten dollars.' He almost keeled over laughing and he paid me the ten dollars. I hate to think what inflation did to the original ten bucks."

It is hard to suppress the notion that it would have made a rare exhibit for the Hall of Fame.

Yet in a substantial way the Blood legendry has inflicted a disservice on the Blood artistry. Players of that era concede there were one or two better runners and one or two better receivers and defensive backs, but none with Johnny Blood's diversity, speed, or gift for climatic play.

"I don't know what my speed was," John acknowledges. "Nobody timed you scientifically. I do know that every now and then we'd get a guy in camp who was supposed to have run the hundred in nine-six. It was nine-six in those days, not nine-one. They must have lost a few decimal points on the train because I could always outrun them when we put the shoes on.

"It's pointless to compare the players of then with the ones today. Sizes are different

and the game is different. But yes, I could play in the pros today. I'm sure I'd be a wide receiver. I'd go about one-ninety or so and I know I'd be able to get downfield fast enough. But you see the crucial difference is the sixty-minute business. We played the whole game. Well, if I played the whole game today I wouldn't have to worry about getting mauled by two-hundred-eighty-pound defensive ends because the same guy would have to play offense and you're not going to have flankers weighing two-hundred-eighty pounds running hitch-outs.

"A lot of people today have the impression we played the game in those years with bums and unemployed muleskinners. Listen, there were people in our lineups who became doctors and lawyers or became successful in a dozen other ways. We had a Ph.D in the lineup once. Duke Slater played, one of the great blacks, who became a judge. And of course Whizzer White, who now sits on the Supreme Court bench and should be President.

"We didn't have the outer space equipment they play with today and sometimes we went without a helmet. All they were in those days were flimsy pieces of leather that were okay for the morale but weren't worth much to the skull.

"The games get a little fuzzy in your memory. Still, I can remember a couple of plays as vividly as though they were on the television screen in front of me right now. I remember lining up on our two-yard line after I went to Pittsburgh as player-coach, and the Bears were going for a touchdown. You *know* the ball is going to Nagurski. He's squatting down there with his big wide nostrils, ready to run through the wall. The only thing you know about it is you've got to get in front of him and hit him before he starts rolling. He's already knocked three of our guys out of the game—one with a broken leg, one with a broken arm, and, Lord knows what happened to the third. I don't say Nagurski was the strongest runner of all time but I do know he was the best fullback—I mean offense, defense, blocking, and power when he had momentum. So I still have this picture of the two-yard line, of Nagurski hunkering down ready to get the ball, and here he comes!"

John's voice softened as the story progressed, and he halted his recitation to allow the leprechaun's latent smile to frolic beneath his still-clear blue eyes.

"Yes, and then, John," his companion prodded.

"I honestly can't tell you how it ended. I don't know whether I stopped Nagurski or if he scored. The only memory I have is that big son of a bitch coming into the line so incredibly huge he took up all the daylight."

The more philosophic of today's professionals, when away from their accountants, sometimes impute qualities of spiritual fulfillment to the game. They talk solemnly and unapologetically about the fraternal love it creates among players who share the grime and sweat and fears.

"I think we had that bond," John said, "but it was never expressed as love, and I think they beat that word to death nowadays. I'm not going to quibble over words. Football had more spontaneity on the field in our years, which could have meant more fun, I suppose. But I remember the exhilaration they talk about. I remember it from a play where I caught a pass near the goal line. I don't know who we were playing. I think Herber threw it. I just remember going up for it with another guy, and I jumped a little higher. It was an important game, and I knew I had the touchdown when I caught the ball. I was floating, really. It was like the slow motion you see in the television highlights today. I could hear the crowd roaring and it seemed like I'd never come down. The goal posts were in front of me but this is the God's truth: I actually believed I could have jumped over the cross bar. I just felt elevated, all through me. No matter what the ball player tells you, he just doesn't feel that very often."

And when he felt it no more, Johnny Blood went seeking, for a new respectability in a time and society where rebels were not so quickly indulged. He went back to St. John's in the early 1950s to teach and to coach, with passable success, but even in a place so sequestered he was fundamentally a curiosity. The rakehell becalmed. He looked professional and sometimes he sounded that way, but he was more the pastured bronco then he was the serious intellectual of his fugitive imaginings. He attended graduate school at the University of Minnesota at the age of 50, half-hoping that would launch him into scholastic excitements. But he confessed to himself before he did to others that his spirit was an imposter when confined by blackboard and brick walls. Intellectualism and poetry recitals were fun, easy, and even impressive when the philosopher had a swaying audience of nonpoetic listeners to enchant, and with whom he could sway in unison.

He became a traveling ornament on the pro football circuit, a figure stately and commanding because of his appearance and past, also endearing because of his musty flights into philosophy.

To some of the regulars at Packers or championship games, the middle-aged surrogate of Johnny Blood was tedious and sometimes a simple pain in the rear.

I looked on John McNally then as a lonely man but a very captivating man, honestly searching and struggling but too much the creature Johnny Blood Past to make any permanent break with Johnny Blood of any age.

He married, commuted between St. Paul and New Richmond, Wisconsin, ran a couple of small businesses and acquired money from the legacy of his mother's publishing family. He divorced after 10 years with expressions of surprise that it endured that long, remarrying several years later. The union is doing well.

And Johnny Blood, 70, is a healthier man spiritually. He gave himself to his Whizzer White cause and the old players' cause because it was ruinous to a man's self-respect to turn his life into a tired puppet show in which new audiences smiled and gaped and appreciated while the well-meaning puppeteer-biographers asked Johnny Blood to re enact it, one more time.

His carriage is straight, the shoulders unbending, and the hair a virile mottled gray. Sometimes he has shortness of breath and he may ask you—no, he will *tell* you—he does not hear as well. He is not a sad or solemn man, understand. He will talk about the old years if you wish, and he will do so with animation and obvious affection. But he has more peace now.

"You humble me, John," his companion said. "I have known a lot of people who have striven for all the points on the compass that are available to the curious man. Adventurers and seekers. Some of them are good people, but most of them are roleplayers in some fashion. You may have been a character, but you were a helluva character and a very honest character."

John accepted this as a reasonable judgment.

"I've always seen myself as an outrider," he said. "You've seen the movies where a guy goes out by himself and hits the bush, a little away from the crowd. Well, I think that was me. I think everybody has regrets of some kind.

"I read. Sometimes I meditate. I wrote some poetry but I don't think it was very good, except for one, which I do remember and can recite, but no more in public. It's too bad about classic poetry, I mean the kind Wordsworth and Keats wrote. It was beautiful and the language was enduring. I regret they don't write poetry like that any more."

There is one truth about youth. It can be overwhelmed by the seasons and taunted by a tremor in the lips, but when it is the youth of Johnny Blood, it is never really destroyed.

They do not write poems any more like John Keats wrote, nor play football like Johnny Blood.

by Jack Murphy

Has Compassion, Will Travel

He is the prototype of a well-adjusted man. A successful orthopedic surgeon, a man who finds happiness in the company of his wife and six children, a man who is buoyed by his faith in God.

To get the essence of Bill McColl, you make a good start by hearing him describe his oldest son, Duncan.

"Here," he says, "you've got a guy who is six-four and two-hundred fifty-five and fast. He wears his hair short, he's an Eagle Scout, and he's kind of a square, disciplined kid. I can see a lot of myself in Duncan."

Duncan McColl's father is a formidable person, both intellectually and physically. He is so big he fills a room. We were chatting in the master bedroom of Clan McColl's recreation retreat at Canyon Lake in Southern California, and it soon became evident Dr. William McColl requires a lot of body space.

He frequently crossed and uncrossed his long legs and I moved my chair backward to avoid infringing on his terrain. As a football player of distinction with Stanford University and the Chicago Bears, he had worn size 14-D shoes. Now, in his mid-forties, he's lost a step or two of his speed but he still leaves a large footprint.

When I proposed an interview, Bill invited me to Canyon Lake during a long holiday weekend because his work days are filled with his medical practice in West Covina, California, and his family, religious, and political activities. He is an activist in the best sense of the word.

The McColls chose Canyon Lake as a place for family fun because it is geographically convenient for Bill, his brother, John, and his sister, Marilyn. Canyon Lake, a man-made reservoir near the community of Elsinore in Riverside County, is about an hour away from Bill in Covina, John in San Diego, and Mrs. Marilyn McGaffey in Whittier.

They're a close bunch, the McColls, and they practice togetherness in a relaxed way.

"Twenty people slept here last night, ten kids on the living room floor," noted the doctor as we entered the McColls' three-bedroom cottage. Now the place was empty except for Bill's mother, who was busy with a vacuum cleaner.

"I'll shut this thing off," she said.

"Don't bother, grandma," said Bill, "we'll talk in the bedroom."

The living room area being vacuumed by Grandma McColl was bare except for chairs placed around a card table. A chess set was on the table. When the kids come in from water skiing and swimming, they sit or lie on the floor.

"No television sets here," said the house physician. "Everybody plays chess."

A remarkable family, the McColls. They go back in history to a Scottish chieftain, Angus McColl, who attracted the attention of Sir Walter Scott by slaying a dozen warriors of the MacPherson clan with his singing broadsword. In recent times they have been drawn to medicine; there have been as many as 18 McColls healing the sick in Southern California. One of the tribe, Dr. Campbell Laidlaw, was personal physician to the late MacKenzie King, premier of Canada.

Don Weller

"We've always been a close-knit family," said Bill. "We still make it to the Christmas party in San Diego every year, about a hundred of us. And the Angus McColl name is still around. My brother's oldest son is Angus."

The children of Bill and Barbara McColl are six in number: Duncan, 19; twins Bonnie and Carrie, 17; John, 16; Milton, 15; and Jennifer, 13. Bill is reliving his boyhood through Duncan, the family's star athlete.

Like his famous father, Duncan had a wide choice of schools and scholarships when he graduated from high school. And, like his father, he chose Stanford. Duncan is a student there now, an offensive lineman of high promise.

Bill seems surprised by Duncan's athletic skills.

"I had kind of written him off as an athlete. I was very careful never to push him or encourage him too much or to make him feel pressure. All of a sudden, I see a guy who is a big-time athlete."

A chip off the Auld Scot. Bill had been a versatile athlete acclaimed as an all-star in three sports at Hoover High School in San Diego, and here was his son carrying on the tradition.

"He was a scholar athlete of the National Football Foundation," recited Bill, "the president of his school church group, a starter on the basketball team, a hurdler and sprinter with the track team, and a tackle on a winning team who was recruited very hard by UCLA, the Air Force Academy, and Stanford."

It isn't necessary to ask what this means to Bill McColl, who never believed football was the most important part of his life but who cherished the experience.

"Today," he reflected, "a lot of young people have turned away from athletics but I'm awful glad my kids see it differently. It's fine that my sons and daughters think that playing on the varsity teams and going out for three sports, getting straight A's, and going to church are good values.

"Within the total complex, varsity football in college is very worthwhile. It is one of the great unifying forces of college life. Take my own school, Stanford. The kids raised hell up there for awhile and then they got a Rose Bowl team. The campus quieted down, everybody got behind the team, and there has been a tremendous change in the total college atmosphere."

Such is the perspective of a man who scarcely can be described as one-dimensional. Old-fashioned, maybe. Square, sure. But not a jock living on memories.

When Jerry Kramer retired from pro football, he worried about losing his iden-tity. "Giving up football," he reflected, "is giving up the hero's role. I wonder how much I'll miss being recognized, being congratulated, being idolized."

Nobody ever made the transition more graciously than Bill McColl. In the first place, he always had twin careers: football and medicine. But football was supportive to medicine. Football enabled Bill and Barbara to have a family while he completed his medical requirements.

By the time he volunteered for two years as a medical missionary in North Korea, the McColls had six children ranging in age from 11 months to 6 years. And the same spirit of adventure still possesses the man.

Twice in recent years he has sought a seat in Congress, losing the Republican nomination in primaries to an apostle of the John Birch Society, John Rousselot, by only 57 votes, and being badly beaten by a Republican moderate, Carlos Morehead. Yet he is tempted to try again.

Why? Can't he better serve others as an orthopedic surgeon? This is not a happy time for his party. Doesn't his family deserve better than Washington?

The questions are familiar to Bill McColl; he is prepared with answers which reveal both a healthy ego and a strong commitment to society.

"There is still a certain amount of idealism that hangs around. I kind of figure that, with the problems America has today, there is a question of survival. We need the best man in public service. I think I'm one of the best America has to offer; it's my responsibility to run.

"There are many good reasons not to be in Washington, particularly at this time. But if you are asked to go, then, by God, I think you ought to go. Now is the time we need guys trying to come along and pick up the pieces.

"It's like when there's a war and there's a front line. Some of us feel you ought to be up there."

The cynical might say McColl is still seeking identity, clinging to the role of hero. Indeed, perhaps this is a factor. McColl says he enjoys campaigning and admits he likes being among people who believe in him and share his views.

"I like campaigning. It's hard work but you meet an awful lot of good people. You'd be surprised at the people who will work and support you. And you'd be surprised at the number of people who won't stand up and be counted.

"Whether it's athletics or politics or anything else, I think you want to be surrounded by people who like you and tell you how good you are. That's important. When you're feeling good, you're powerful and strong."

The doctor smiled. "This is a little bit tongue in cheek because that's been Nixon's problem. He was surrounded by people who overly protected him and they went a little bit overboard. Still, Abraham Lincoln said he didn't ever want to hear bad news; he shut off criticism because it really doesn't do that much good. Maybe certain people can tell you specific things, but in general it's just bad mouthing."

If McColl holds strong views, he's entitled. He's not the sort to avoid a brawl lest he get his nose bloodied. He knows that if criticism could kill, the lowly skunk would have perished long ago. He'll risk being contaminated by politics—or the touch of a leper.

In 1962 young Dr. McColl had put football behind him and was preparing to begin the practice of medicine when he volunteered to go to Korea as a missionary at the Presbyterian hospital in Taegu. He made his decision while attending a church camp at Saugatuck, Michigan.

"I decided I was only living as a second-hand Christian," he explained. "I asked myself, 'What does God really want me to do with my life?'"

The role of a medical missionary fit his personal philosophy and his need for a fresh challenge. He preferred a church mission to a government-sponsored program such as the Peace Corps.

"It appealed to our spirit of adventure. We were sure it would be beneficial to us in learning to understand both people and our faith."

So he bundled up Barbara and the six McColl siblings and went off to Korea for what he now describes as one of the "mountaintop experiences" of his life. Working among those afflicted by leprosy, tuberculosis, and other diseases, the big (6 foot 5 inch, 240 pounds) American doctor was both enriched and humbled by people and events.

He went to Taegu to teach orthopedic surgery to young Korean doctors, but became a pupil instead. He learned about the treatment of leprosy, about life, about himself.

When Dr. McColl reflects on his two years in Korea, he has the manner of one fulfilled.

He speaks of the "opportunity to live as a minority group in a culture far less tolerant than our own, to be among a few whites in an Oriental culture." And he became much more sophisticated about leprosy, the dread disease which has made outcasts of its victims down through history.

There are an estimated 100,000 lepers in Korea, including 30,000 in the province where McColl labored among them. Now he describes leprosy medicine as "one of my main side interests." He's a director of the American Leprosy Missions and attended the International Congress on Leprosy in Norway last year.

"We treat leprosy with respect," McColl has said, "but not very much. We wash our hands after visiting patients."

Now he speaks of misconceptions about leprosy. "For people who don't understand, it is a terrifying disease. Actually, leprosy is the least contagious of all contagious diseases.

"It requires long, intimate contact with a susceptible individual, such as a mother-child relationship. We have statistics which show that among spouses married to leprosy patients less than ten percent become infected."

He estimates there are about 2,000 leprosy cases in America, half in the city of New York, 50 in Los Angeles.

"It's a great disease to study if you want to learn about the human body," McColl suggested.

The most agreeable part of McColl's Korean experience was the closeness of his family.

"We lived right in the hospital compound and I was able to have breakfast and dinner at home with the family. When the kids were off at school, I could have lunch with my wife. There aren't many jobs in America where you can have your family together in that manner. In two years you learn a lot about each other and it's pretty nice."

In the years since his Korean adventure, McColl has had to budget his time carefully to know the pleasure of being with his family. In addition to his medical practice in West Covina (the McColls reside in nearby Covina), he's been into politics, he's been a trustee of the California State College system, and he's on the Board of Deacons of a Presbyterian church in Covina.

Typically, son Duncan's success as a high school football player involved the entire family. Two of the McColl daughters are song leaders and everybody pitched in to help before the big games, and there were no little games.

"The girls were making posters the night before the game and the next morning here's a big banner in front of the house: 'Go Get 'Em, Duncan.' It's grand that the corny old high school spirit is still alive. When everbody is involved with high school athletics, it's just the greatest thing there is."

This from a man who for eight years performed so splendidly as an end for the Chicago Bears, balancing football and medical studies, and verifying the judgment of his coach, George Halas.

Today he says of Halas, "He was one of the great men of my life all the way through."

It was Halas who persuaded McColl he could combine pro football and the study of medicine.

McColl came to the Bears as a third draft choice for the 1952 season, and Halas accommodated himself to McColl's busy schedule. Often it was necessary for Bill to miss the Bears' workouts and one year he was absent for most of the club's preseason training exercises. But he completed his medical studies at the University of Chicago in three years.

McColl became a doctor of medicine in 1955, then interned for two years at the Stanford Medical School before beginning residency at the University of Illinois Research and Education Hospital. He obtained his credentials as an orthopedic surgeon in 1962.

McColl's regard for Halas combines affection with respect. "If I were on a desert island and in need of help," he has said, "and could get out only one message, it would be to George Halas."

It is more likely that Bill McColl would build a raft and one day come ashore at Waikiki Beach. He's always been resourceful and precocious.

As an athlete-scholar in high school in San Diego he attracted so much attention at one awards banquet it was said the lobby of the U.S. Grant Hotel resembled a college coaches' convention. He was the first athlete since Glenn Davis to be honored as an all-California Interscholastic Federation selection in three sports (football, basketball, and track). There has been only one other since McColl: Marty Keough of Pomona.

The college coaches soon learned McColl was unapproachable. He had resolved to attend Stanford on an academic scholarship and he declined the usual tour of college campuses available to athletic prodigies. That would have been inconsistent with the values he learned from his late, beloved father, Dr. William Frazer McColl.

Yet Bill McColl's son now attends Stanford on an athletic scholarship because, after all, thrift is a tradition of the Scots—thrift and pragmatism.

"I went on an academic scholarship because it paid more than the athletic scholarship," explained McColl. "If I were going now I would go on an athletic scholarship because I probably couldn't qualify for an academic scholarship."

McColl's years at Stanford were a happy time. There he found the girl—attractive, vivacious Barbara Bird—who became his wife. And there, despite the grind of such heavy subjects as biochemistry and microscopic anatomy, he blossomed as a football celebrity.

This was a big man who did things in a big way. At various times he played seven positions. Once he threw a touchdown pass measured at 70 yards before it dropped into the hands of a receiver. He caught anything he could touch, he was denied a 53-yard field goal only by tricky wind currents, he averaged almost 12 yards running with the ball on end-around plays. His strength was legend.

During a rugby contest he crashed into 230-pound Les Richter of California, a rugged character who relished contact. The impact knocked both parties backward 10 feet. Richter left the field. McColl arose, shook his head until the mist cleared, and continued.

On another occasion, serving as a linebacker, McColl slammed into California's Johnny Olszewski, a running back of considerable reputation. McColl hit Johnny O so hard he became Cal's first satellite. "What zoo did that guy escape from?" asked Olszewski groggily.

Later in life McColl would give the same energy to medicine, to the California State College Board of Trustees, to the California State Board of Public Health, to his church, to the American Leprosy Missions, to his large, active family, and to the California Republican State Central Committee.

Obviously, his gifts are many. The man even knows how to relax. He seemed a man at peace with himself as we chatted in his cottage at Canyon Lake, the place the McColls purchased with funds from their father's estate.

"We thought it would be one of the nice things we could do with the money." said Bill. "We thought it would be good to have a place where all the kids could be together."

The oncoming generation of McColls are bright, attractive, spirited. And they stay busy with a variety of activities in the family tradition.

"I like to see young people into anything that requires group discipline," said Dr. Bill. "If a kid doesn't play football or basketball, I'd like to see him in a band, glee club, or orchestra. Or a gymnastics team. It's tremendous to be on a Rose Bowl team; twenty years later you can get together and retell the old stories.

"But you get exactly the same thing from other group activities. I know guys who were in glee clubs which toured the Orient. They embrace each other and relive the old times just like football players. It's the same camaraderie, and it's beautiful."

If you have the qualities of Dr. Bill McColl, it is no trick to know the beauty of life.

by John Wiebusch

On the Homefront

Across the Dnieper they came, reclaiming Kiev and Smolensk and Vitebsk and freezing to do it. The hunter now the hunted, the pursuer become the pursued. The wind and the snow and the Russians driving the Germans west. Turning it around on the tundra.

The lake was quiet that December and the big snows did not come from out of the prairies. The wind can be a savage in Chicago but it was silent in the last month of 1943. Christmas seemed to come in unnoticed and snow that should have been white was flecked with black.

It was not a good time but it was a better time than it had been. The news from overseas was full of hope. And sorrow. In war that is inevitable.

And in Chicago they prepared for a football game. The Bears were to play the Washington Redskins for the championship of the National Football League and for one afternoon at least, men would be able to forget.

In the year before, Franklin Roosevelt had said, "Sport is the very fiber of all we stand for. It keeps our spirits alive."

The struggle in Africa had ended in the summer and in the fall the pincers had turned in on Italy. Now the Allies drove on Rome, at Cassino and Anzio. The arteries were being cut off.

The pro football season of 1943 was a strange mixture of unpredictable conclusion.

The Bears against the Redskins was no surprise. In three of the previous six seasons they had faced each other for the championship.

In 1937 the rookie quarterback, Sammy Baugh, had thrown three touchdown passes and the Redskins were supreme 28-21.

In 1940 they were matched again—to use the verb loosely. In a score unmatched in the 20 pro football seasons that preceded it and the 34 that followed it, the Bears got off to a fast start and the Redskins never stopped running. At the finish it was Chicago 73-0.

In 1941 the Bears won the championship again, this time defeating the Giants (the Redskins had placed third in the East), and in 1942 they sought a third consecutive title. Once more, their opponent was the team from Washington. Two years before, in the season of the 73-0 debacle, the Redskins had defeated the Bears during the regular season; Washington had been favored in the championship game. This time it was different. It was the Bears who had won during the season; it was the Bears who were supposed to win in the game that meant everything. And it was the Redskins who won 14-6. It was sweet revenge. It had become a rivalry to capture the hearts of escapists.

And in 1943 there was to be still more.

The planes found Hamburg in the summer and they reduced ashes to ashes. Now, in the winter, they turned the skies black over Berlin. The sounds of Christmas were the sounds of air raid sirens and buzz bombs. The Germans were taking it on the chin.

Sammy Baugh, weeping

109

There had been 10 professional football teams in 1942 but the manpower was draining away. In April, 1943, Dan Reeves, who owned the Cleveland Rams, asked if his team might suspend operations for the year. In June, the owners of the Steelers (Art Rooney and Bert Bell) and the Eagles (Alexis Thompson) asked if they might merge franchises to create one respectable team.

And so they began the season with only eight franchises and with the player limit reduced to 27. They held a lottery to divide the remaining members of the Cleveland team and they went searching for able bodies who knew how to play the game.

In 1937, at the age of 29, Bronko Nagurski had taken his battered and bruised body back to International Falls, Minnesota. After seven years of playing 60 minutes a game—at fullback and at tackle—he said he was tired. And in the five years after that he rested. Until the Bears came around with an offer he really couldn't refuse.

In 1943, at the age of 35, Bronko Nagurski came back, a little slower, perhaps, but no less strong and wearing that same stone face. There was glamour in pro football with names like Hutson and Hinkle and Baugh and Luckman. But there was only one Nagurski. Only one Bronk. And there were few bigger stories in sport that year than his return to the Bears.

The Japanese came out of the jungles of Burma, pouring across the Irrawaddy River in a last gasp at supremacy in the corner of Asia. They fought in a tropical sauna, the Japanese against the Chinese and their American commander, General Stilwell. The counterattack was awful, a test of body and mind and will and desire and guts. The Chinese had a little more of all of them.

In the Western Division, there were the Chicago Bears, the Green Bay Packers, the Detroit Lions, and the Chicago Cardinals.

In the Eastern Division, there were the Washington Redskins, the New York Giants, the Phil-Pitt Steagles, and the Brooklyn Dodgers.

It was a league of barely 200 football players, a league struggling to survive in a world of turmoil. Says Art Rooney, the co-owner of the Pitt half of the Phil-Pitt team: "It was tough then but it was fun, too. Everybody had common problems. And maybe winning and losing weren't quite as important either."

The fire in the South Pacific was over Bougainville, an oasis of white sand and lush green in the Solomon Islands. The

planes of the Japanese met the planes of the Americans and the winner would control the ocean south of the Equator. The Japanese fought long enough to lose 3,000 planes. Then they fled to the north.

The schedule was 10 games long in 1943. You played home-and-home games with the three other teams in your division; you played each of the other teams in the division once. Simple? Not quite. Because of the difficulties of scheduling, the season became a crazy-quilt of early dates, byes, and late dates.

The Bears, for example, opened the season two weeks ahead of most teams. The Redskins finished it two weeks after most other teams.

When the Bears met the Redskins on November 21, it was Chicago's ninth game and Washington's seventh. One thing was unmistakable: Neither team had lost a game (although each had been tied once). This was the regular season game of the year, a preview of the coming attraction of the championship game. No one doubted that, and no one felt differently after Sammy Baugh had thrown two touchdown passes and helped the Redskins to a 21-7 win over the Bears. After all, to win its divisional title, Washington had only to capture one of its three remaining games; and Chicago had clinched at least a tie in its division even before it met the Redskins.

For the Bears there was no problem. On November 28 they defeated the Cardinals and then they sat back and waited to meet the Redskins. The game was scheduled for December 19 in Chicago.

On December 19 the Redskins were not playing in Chicago. They were playing in New York, breaking the tie for first place that existed in the Eastern Division.

The last three games of the regular season were a disaster for the Redskins. They lost to Phil-Pitt 27-14 on November 28. It was their first loss of the season but they still carried a two-game lead over the Giants going into the two season-ending games with the Giants. The first game was in New York. The Giants won 14-10. The second game was in Washington. Thoroughly demoralized, the Redskins lost again, 31-7.

The impossible had happened. The Redskins and the Giants were both 6-3-1 and a tie-breaker was scheduled.

In the first seven games of the season, the Redskins had outscored seven opponents 198-65. In the last three games the Redskins were on the short end of a 31-72 game ratio.

"We knew we had to take it to the Giants," says Sammy Baugh. "We had to get 'em early."

The bomb came early. Baugh to end Joe Aguirre. Suddenly the confidence was back. The Redskins went on to win 28-0.

Now the dream game that had almost turned out to be a pipe dream—the Redskins versus the Bears—was all set. They would meet on the day after Christmas in Chicago.

The German battleship Scharnhorst sailed out of the Alta Fjord on Christmas Eve. She moved north and west toward the Arctic Circle, escorted by five destroyers, advancing on the ambush of the Duke of York. The Germans met the British on December 26. When the battle was over, the Scharnhorst was at the bottom of the sea and more than 2,000 men were with her.

It was easy to get an argument no matter which way you felt. The Bears had not played a game for nearly a month. Was that too much inactivity? The Redskins had played pressure games on each of the previous three Sundays. Would those efforts leave them emotionally and physically depleted?

And the players. In 1943, you thought the greatest quarterback was either Sid Luckman of Chicago or Sammy Baugh of Washington (although under the Redskins' single wing, Baugh technically was listed as "left halfback"). There was no in between, no alternative. And no matter who you chose you had the numbers to back you. Luckman set records that year for most yards gained passing (2,194) and most touchdown passes (28). He averaged 11 yards a pass attempt and in one game against the Giants he broke another record by throwing for seven touchdowns (four men have since equalled that record but no one has broken it). Baugh's statistics were equally dazzling. He led Luckman in passing efficiency and ranked number one in the league in completions (133) and percentage of completions (55.7). And he also led the league in punting (45.9 average) and in interceptions (a safety on defense, he had a record 11).

On this day, the hot hand was to belong to the kid from Brooklyn, the Ivy League quarterback five seasons out of Columbia, Sidney Luckman.

"I want this one," he said, "more than I've ever wanted anything in my life."

In the championship game of the year before, the Redskins had intercepted three passes by Sid Luckman. Interceptions led to both Washington touchdowns and in the end the Bears had lost 14-6.

And it did not change when Chicago played in Washington in November, 1943. The Redskins intercepted two Luckman passes and won by two touchdowns.

Sid Luckman had four weeks to think about the pressure, four weeks to digest the earlier humiliations, four weeks to add psychological fuel to the fire in his cold war with Sammy Baugh.

On December 26 Sid Luckman was ready to play a football game.

So was Bronko Nagurski. But with Bronko it was different. For Bronko there was no psychology. That was for someone who could pronounce it. For Bronko Nagurski, being ready was simply a matter of being there.

"It's a game," he said. "It's a tough game. Tough on the body. But it's a living, too, and when you do something for a living you should be ready all the time. Doesn't matter who you are, either."

Nagurski weighed 235 pounds, and in the 10 games that had gone before he was used primarily as a tackle and a blocking back. The regular running backs had averages of 6.1 (Dante Magnani) and 4.6 (Harry Clark) and Clark said of the Bronko: "Anybody in the world could run behind him. All you have to do is step over the bodies."

Clark spoke in exaggerated jest but in the game in Wrigley Field on the day after Christmas there was no humor. There was only carnage.

"I never saw a game in which so many people were hurt," said Baugh. "A lot of people took some terrible licks out there."

Sammy Baugh was one of them. The first one of them. And there was irony in his injury. In retrospect, that one single play epitomizes this game more than any other.

On the opening series, the Redskins began from their own 30. Three runs lost two yards and Baugh was back to punt. It was a high spiral and Sid Luckman fielded it on his own 28. Luckman went nowhere with the ball. Baugh went to the sidelines—and he did not walk a straight line. No one is really sure what happened, least of all Baugh. All they know is that while in pursuit of the ball and Luckman, Baugh fell and was kicked in the head. The preliminary diagnosis was a minor concussion. It kept him out of the game's next 35 minutes. And by then it was all over.

Baugh's replacement was George Cafego, a second-year thrower out of Tennessee. For a time—for a short time —Cafego seemed to be enough.

After a bitter first quarter in which both teams were unable to sustain an offense, Cafego and the Redskins began from their own 40. On third-and-nine, Cafego hit Wilbur Moore for 34 yards. Two runs netted nothing and Cafego looked for Moore again, at the goal line. Moore did not catch the ball but he did catch it from Magnani, a defensive back. The Bears' defender was called for pass interference and Washing-

ton had a first down at the 2. Andy Farkas needed two plunges to get the touchdown.

The Redskins had the lead but the fire was in the eyes of the Bears. Luckman needed just five plays to get the tying touchdown. Three of the plays were runs that netted seven yards. Two of the plays were passes that netted 60. The first was a 29-yard pass to Ray McLean on a third-and-eight from the Bears' 35. The second was a 31-yard screen pass collaboration with Clark that gave Chicago its first score.

Luckman had begun to put it together and on this day he was not about to let it come apart. Later in the second quarter he directed another drive, a drive that was climaxed by the touchdown of Bronko Nagurski. Three plays—two of them Luckman passes—pushed the Bears past midfield. It was all Luckman and Nagurski then. Luckman took the ball 24 yards on a sneak and Nagurski carried it across with two runs that totaled 21 yards. The touchdown was scored from the 3.

At halftime the Bears had the lead (14-7) and the momentum. It seemed that only the return of Baugh could turn this one around. The Redskins knew that. And so did Sid Luckman.

In this game Luckman played both ways and the derring-do of the second half began with an interception. Luckman picked off a pass by Cafego and returned it 21 yards to the Washington 36. On the next play the interceptor turned quarterback and threw a touchdown pass to Magnani.

Down by two touchdowns, the Redskins turned to Sammy Baugh. They asked him to make a miracle, and there was a moment when it seemed possible. Baugh drove the Redskins to the Bears' 18. It was first down. A touchdown here might reverse the momentum. Baugh was back to pass again...he was looking for Wilbur Moore...he found him...he threw...and Sid Luckman intercepted.

The Redskins were reeling and Luckman followed with a knockout punch. On third and 12, he hit Magnani in the flat and the Bears' halfback took the screen pass 66 yards to a touchdown.

Baugh gave the Redskins one last, faint hope with a touchdown in the final minutes of the third quarter. But then Luckman had the ball back again...and he was throwing a 29-yard touchdown pass to Jim Benton. The Bears followed by recovering an onside kick...and Luckman had the ball back once more...and he was throwing a 16-yard touchdown pass to Harry Clark.

Chicago held the ball for the first 11½ minutes of the fourth quarter. Only at the final gun was there mercy for the Redskins. The final score was Chicago 41, Washington 21.

In the locker room, Luckman accepted the congratulations and the handshakes. He held the game ball and said, "I guess we showed them how it should be played."

On one winter afternoon, Sid Luckman had attempted 24 passes and completed 14 for 276 yards. Five of the completions went for touchdowns, a championship game record. He also rushed eight times for 64 yards and his 340-yard total was more than 100 better than the combined output of the Redskins. And he intercepted two passes.

"You can't have a better day than Sid had out there," said Hunk Anderson, one of the Bears' coaching triumvirate. With George Halas in the navy, Anderson shared coaching duties with Paddy Driscoll and Luke Johnsos.

Lt. Comdr. Halas was there as a spectator, though, and he pushed his way through the crowd to give Luckman a pat on the back. "A great game," he said.

In another corner of the room, Bronko Nagurski pulled yards of tape off his body. "Well," he said, "I'm retiring again. It's not a game for a thirty-five-year-old. And besides, I can't listen to George Halas's songs all my life."

Nagurski's farewell to football was a heroic one. He rushed seven times for 44 yards and caught two passes from Luckman for 14 yards.

The game ball belonged to Luckman but Nagurski, a sentimentalist under the harsh exterior, asked the quarterback if he might have it because it was his last game. "This was my last game, too," said Luckman, "and I want this one to put among my souvenirs. I'll buy you a dozen footballs to have around the house but this one I keep."

Luckman was due to report for active duty with the Merchant Marines in New York in eight days. But he would return in the following year and in every ensuing season through 1950. In 1946 he helped the Bears to another NFL championship.

Down the hall, Sammy Baugh did not talk with the press.

"He's still woozy," said Dutch Bergman, the coach. "Let him be."

Later, Baugh would say, "They beat the tar out of us. They played their game very well."

General Eisenhower and Field Marshall Montgomery were huddled in London. It looked good in the south and in the east. It seemed as if it would only be a matter of time. There were rumors that Eisenhower and Montgomery were plotting a western front...maybe an invasion. After two days of conferences they issued a joint statement. It said there would be no comment.

by Heywood Hale Broun

Farewell the Gods of Instant Legend

In the dim yesterday when athletes traveled on trains, the back platform of the observation car was the framework in which many Americans saw their sports heroes for the only time in their lives.

When the train stopped at a crossroads town to drop mail or pick up water, the whole population would be waiting for the magic moment when the great man, up to then a smudgy newspaper picture, appeared in the round, in the flesh, in that nearness which was just short of the bliss suggested by the old line "Shake the hand that shook the hand of John L. Sullivan."

When my father was a baseball writer traveling through spring training with the New York Giants it used to amuse Ring Lardner to take him onto the back platform and introduce him to the circle of sport worshippers as Jess Willard, a man my father resembled only in weight. The fake Willard would say a few modest words, clasp his hands in the traditional fighter's gesture and withdraw, leaving a knot of excited Floridians discussing their unexpected celebrity bonus.

There are probably still old folks down there who remember seeing Willard when they were kids, a Willard whom even today they remember as appearing shockingly out of shape for a fighter, but a jolly good fellow for all of that.

This is, in a sense, a perfect example of an old time sports memory. It is vivid, exciting, highly personal, and wildly inaccurate. Of course, lots of other people saw the actual Jess Willard but if you were to ask for a description they would strain the reality through so many layers of subsequent ex-

perience that they might well come up with a picture of my father.

So great was the hunger in those old days for a look, a touch, a close view of the gods of games that when it happened, excitement and near hysteria vibrated the eye and the ear and turned the memory into the broad and golden outline of instant legend.

When George Halas announced that he had signed Red Grange to play with the Chicago Bears, the lines began to form next morning outside the Spalding store where tickets were announced as available, and stretched four abreast, around and around the block. Later that year people paid twelve and a half Coolidge dollars per ticket to see him play a Florida exhibition.

If now, fifty-odd years later you asked those ticket buyers to tell you about the Grange they saw, they would take out a memory as loved and polished as old ivory and give you a description of something no human being could ever have accomplished. They would describe to you the flight of a bird in a football suit and they would tell you that nobody they see nowadays on the television has ever come close.

Television has, of course, given us a closer and more accurate view of what goes on. By the use of instant replays, it permits us to see exactly what happened in the detached atmosphere of hindsight so that we are infinitely more knowledgeable, and our memories are a great deal more accurate. What it has taken from us in exchange for this is the moment of mad immediacy when adrenalin has blinded us to the true picture and given us a myth disguised as an observation.

My own first memories of professional football go back to a man I remember as being approximately three feet high, Davey O'Brien, quarterback of the Philadelphia Eagles. In my mind's eye —and the mind is that of a frenzied college freshman now somewhat tattered through being stored in the head of a middle-aged man—O'Brien is a tiny creature who has to reach up to take the ball from the center and who then fades desperately back like someone from one of Charles Schulz's Peanuts teams lost in a nightmare of ill-intentioned monsters. Somehow the little O'Brien escapes the huge linemen and passes the ball 100 yards through the air and we are all cheering and crying and dealing to each other almost as much punishment as the players are managing on the field.

Some factual researches have revealed to me that O'Brien, though small for a football player, actually weighed 160 pounds at the time, and is a person whom I, at 163 pounds, am not entitled to regard as spectacularly undersized. My factual researches have no impact on the vivid picture I project on my personal screen when I summon up that impossibly sunny Sunday in the Middle Jurassic Age, however.

Neither is it true—or rather can it be true that the head of Bill Hewitt, who never wore a helmet, actually changed shape like a squeezed melon as he dove in for a tackle? It seems medically unlikely, but that is the way I remember it.

"There were giants walking the earth in those days!" cry all we middle-aged and more than middle-aged rememberers of the sports figures of our childhoods and youths, and there are no tapes or films or objective views of a small glass square to say us nay.

It is, of course, the refuge of all of us to feel, when youth is far enough behind us, that it was the world's last age of innocence. The medieval adventurers who went on the First Crusade used to shake their heads over the sad lot who marched off to the Second, as my father thought my 1930s idols, Carl Hubbell, Tuffy Leemans, and Davey O'Brien to be pale shadows of such demi gods as Christy Mathewson or Charley Brickley, who drop-kicked five field goals against Yale—a feat mysterious to me because I never saw anybody drop-kick anything against anybody.

The young of my son's generation and those who came after, are, and will be, so impressively informed that one wonders if they will have the chance to make or hold those larger-than-life images which are such stuff as dreams are made on.

Split screens, isolated cameras, and slow motion replays will give a heretofore impossible dimension to watching. As the astronauts know far more about the moon than is contained in all the poets' speculations, so tomorrow's fans will see more than did the wisest of coaches and scouts twenty years ago. Also, in the new trend to absorb sports heroes into the worlds of commerce and entertainment, there is inherent a more extensive acquaintance with Olympus than was possible to those who waited in the depot for the glimpse of Jess Willard waving from the observation car.

Of course, the facts and photos brought back from the moon have the immediacy and excitement that goes with authenticity, but the poetry and fantasy tend to fade and the pale-faced moon from which we hoped to plunk bright honor is no longer a ghostly galleon tossed upon cloudy seas.

There will still, naturally, be the special excitement of being actually on the scene, but even then the following day's delayed tape will show what really happened, thus fixing and clarifying the memory. It is a remarkable prospect and as the techniques are refined, it may be possible to check through, at will, an electronic box of great moments which can be mixed according to the whim of the viewer.

It is going to be remarkable and I am sorry that I am not going to be around for much of it. I have a consolation, however. I have a recollection, uncontradicted by any earthbound film, of Davey O'Brien, no taller than my knee, throwing a football the length of the field on the fly.

Lon Keller

by Lee Hutson

The Train Don't Stop Here Anymore

S ammy Baugh would meet the train in Amarillo. Slingin' Sam, the superlative passer, the man who played for 16 years in the National Football League, would saunter out onto the station's wooden platform in well-worn cowboy boots, carrying a cardboard suitcase. Squinting into the Texas-hot July sun, he'd see the Santa Fe pulling in, fussin' and steamin', and he'd smile and wave to familiar faces. The last four cars on the train were for the Washington Redskins.

Sam would still be shaking hands and saying "howdy" and looking for a place to sit when the conductor would call "All aboard," and the Redskins would be off again and on their way to Los Angeles.

That was in 1938 and 1939 and 1940 and 1941, and after the war it was that way again for a while. The Washington Redskins were going to California, and they were going by train.

In the middle years of professional football's so-called "modern era," that is post-1930, the Washington Redskins were pro football's most traveled team. It was something they came by honestly enough, since it was more or less an inherited characteristic.

The Redskins are direct descendents of the Duluth Eskimos. Ernie Nevers's Eskimos. The traveling Eskimos of the early 1920s. During the formative years of the NFL, the Eskimos were principally a road show. The stadium in Duluth, Minnesota, was small, the attendance was sparse, the weather bitter, and no one much wanted to play there. One year the Eskimos played 27 games, all on the road.

Finally, they were sold, moved to Boston, became the Braves, were sold again, this time to George Preston Marshall. Ultimately, they moved to Washington.

George Preston Marshall was a man of enormous imagination, one of sports' true innovators, and possibly professional football's greatest promoter. He was a flamboyant man with an uncanny facility for drawing attention to both himself and his team.

It was Marshall's idea for the Redskins to hold their training camp on the West Coast. California was not nearly as accessible then, of course, and moving a football team, with 40 or 50 players, equipment and all, was no simple undertaking. But Marshall enjoyed the summer weather there, and he also saw the train trip West as a matchless publicity device.

It was an era, now dead, in which Zephyrs, Comets, Meadow Larks, Meteors, Super Chiefs, and Flying Yankees carried Americans over more than a half-million miles of track winding, crossing, and stretching long and flat across the land.

***When we got married
back in 1944
We'd board that silver
liner below Baltimore
Trip to Virginia
on a sunny honeymoon
Nobody cares about
the railroads anymore**

*Nobody Cares About the Railroads Anymore by Nilsson. Copyright 1969 by Dunbar Music, Inc., 1133 Avenue of the Americas, New York, New York 10036. Reprinted by permission.

Sammy Baugh (left), Dick Todd
Nate Fine

For the Washington Redskins the trip to California began in Washington in early July. A private car would be attached to a Baltimore & Ohio train, and club officials, press, and players living in the area would board for the ride to Chicago.

Chicago served as the single largest player pickup location. Players from throughout the Midwest received their carefully arranged itineraries well in advance, and they could depend on the train being on time. Trains moved with such regularity that farmers, hearing a distant whistle, would set their clocks.

From Chicago, a gleaming 4,000 horsepower diesel-electric locomotive would pull away, heading west.

The Santa Fe would stop in Kansas City, in Amarillo, and in Albuquerque, picking up players at each stop. After four days and three nights, the "Redskins' Special" would arrive in California. A couple of seasons, they arrived in San Diego, and trained at Brown Military Academy. But usually it was into Los Angeles, and then a bus ride to Occidental College.

But when, in 1946, the Rams moved to Los Angeles from Cleveland, the tone and the tempo began to change. Within two years a preseason charity game was arranged between the two teams. Training camp became a period of earnest preparation. No longer were the Redskins playing the Hollywood Bears before a couple of hundred curious spectators. They were playing the Rams before nearly 100,000 people.

In Washington, as in most of the country during that time, the press took scant notice of professional football during the late weeks of summer. Football camps were open, and even some nonleague games were being played, but it was still baseball season and the nation's sports pages were almost entirely devoted to baseball's pennant races. It was a situation that frustrated Marshall, who understood the value of early publicity, particularly in terms of advance ticket sales. It was a precedent that he set out to break.

Marshall correctly surmised that if he invited sportswriters along for an all-expense paid trip to California, they would hardly be able to resist. And he also calculated that, once aboard the train and traveling with the team, they would be obliged to file football stories in order to justify the trip. It was an arrangement that worked out well for everyone involved. The writers had a working vacation, and the Redskins began making the sports pages in July. Marshall delighted in what he saw as a master stroke, and no man who ever lived could more fully enjoy a *coup de theatre*.

But there was a curious irony in the makeup of the Redskins' president, who was nevertheless frightened of speed despite his outward flamboyance and zestful life style. He never in his life drove an automobile or flew in an airplane. But he loved trains.

There was a time in this country not so long ago when no man was considered to be a well-traveled American unless he had crossed the Great Plains and the Rockies in a stream of train cars. Marshall had.

He knew the railroad's routes, its depots, and its schedules. He knew the small towns and the flat lands and the mountains. He could look out at acres of wheat fields from the window of his Pullman car and tell you how the farmers were going to do that year. In even the smallest town he could put you on to the best place to eat, and he knew when the Rocky Mountain trout was at its most delicious. He knew when and where he could get off the train and pick up ripe casaba melons, which he loved, and he believed that the dining cars on America's trains served the best corned beef hash and poached eggs in the country.

The predictable, inevitable, inexorable coming of the airplane as a means of mass travel must have distressed Marshall, who died in 1969 after a long illness. He was a man of another time, a time when travel across this country was a shared experience, an adventure choreographed by the clicking-clacking metallic sounds of steel wheels on iron rails.

The *Los Angeles Times'* Rams-Redskins charity game became a huge success. It marked the beginning of the pro football season on the West Coast. There was prestige to be won, or lost, and the gate receipts became indispensable in helping to defray the growing costs of transporting the Redskins to the Coast.

The *Times* game would culminate the Redskins' five-week stay in California. The morning after the game, the team would once again board the Santa Fe and head east. But going east by way of perhaps Denver and San Antonio and Dallas and maybe Mobile or Charleston or almost anywhere if there was a football game to be played. In some years, the trip home included stops in Oregon, Idaho, and Montana.

The Redskins, traveling by train, played the Green Bay Packers in Birmingham and the New York Giants in Raleigh. They played the San Francisco 49ers in Portland and the Pittsburgh Steelers in Baltimore before that Maryland city had a professional football team. They played the Chicago Bears in Memphis and Little Rock and Shreveport, and the Detroit Lions in Amarillo. They played the Chicago Cardinals in Denver, and the Dallas Texans in San Antonio.

They would be on the road for weeks, sometimes months, stopping for a couple of days practice and a game, then getting back on the train and heading for the next city or town. Each year it was five preseason games and then off to a league city for the season opener. Sometimes they opened at home, and that meant they would get home sooner. But sometimes they opened on the road. In 1952, the Redskins left Washington on July 5, and they didn't return home until October 6. That year their first two league games were away, opening the season in Chicago against the Cardinals and then going to Milwaukee to play the Packers.

On the road, traveling by train back and forth across the West, the South and the Southwest, treating fans to the delights of men, traveling together.

We'd tip that porter for
a place of our own
Then send a postcard to your
Mom and Dad back home
Did somethin' to ya
when you'd hear that "all aboard"
Nobody cares
about the railroads anymore

David Slattery is an executive assistant with the Washington Redskins. He has worked for the team since 1960. Before that he was a Washington sportswriter —one of those men whom George Preston Marshall lured into writing summer football stories. Slattery began traveling with the team as a writer in 1948. He and Marshall became close personal friends. It was a friendship that lasted until Marshall died. Slattery traveled with the team every year. And when the team began to take its long trips by plane in the mid-fifties, he and Marshall continued to travel by train.

Slattery is a man of robust humor. He loved the old train days, and he has an Irishman's knack for relating story after story, recreating a time when people and events moved to a different beat than the one played by today's drummer.

Slattery is especially fond of his memories of his boss. "He was a fascinating man to travel with," Slattery recalls. "He was a real historian, a student of America. Everywhere we went, everything we saw, Mr. Marshall would point out some historical fact. He knew the damnedest things…especially about the railroads."

Marshall enjoyed gathering around him players, writers, porters—anyone who would listen—and "holding court" in his private sleeping car. Thus surrounded, and plainly comfortable in his green and gold striped pajamas, Marshall would put forth questions and when the answers weren't quickly forthcoming, he would begin to share with the assembled a selected portion of his cumulative knowledge.

He'd ask, for example, if anyone knew what the standard gauge was for most railroads in the country, knowing full well that no one did know, and knowing but dismissing the fact that no one cared. He'd then say that it is 4 feet, 8½ inches, adding, as a tease, that it was that width because that was the distance between the wheels of a Roman chariot. Now who could resist asking what the Roman chariot has to do with the American railroad?

The question would of course be asked, and Marshall would look around the room with his expression of I'm-glad-you-asked-that-question, and he'd continue. When the Romans occupied the British Isles a couple of thousand years ago, they of course brought along their chariots, and the chariot wheels were indeed set 4 feet, 8½ inches apart. After a time (the Romans stayed for about 200 years) the wheels wore ruts in the roads, and any Briton who wanted a ride with the minimum number of neck-breaking jolts per mile, was wise to build his wagon or cart with wheels that coincided with the ruts. When, centuries later, the British built the first railroads, they laid the rails along the paths of existing roads and the ruts were a convenient place to lay the track. And since the earliest American steam locomotives were manufactured in England, the wheels were set apart the same distance as those on the ancient Roman chariots.

We had a daughter
   and you oughta' see her now
She has a boyfriend
   who looks just like My Gal Sal
And when they're married
   they won't need us anymore
They'll board an aeroplane
   and fly away from Baltimore

"With fifty or sixty men traveling together for weeks at a time, some funny things happened," Slattery recalls. "I remember once in Amarillo. We had played a game there, and it was hotter than a pistol. We slept on the train that night after the game, but we weren't leaving until morning. It would have been all right, but the air conditioning broke down. It got so hot that it was almost impossible to sleep. We had this big guard on our team then named Gene Pepper, from the University of Missouri. Well, poor Gene just couldn't sleep so he took his mattress and went outside. The whole yard is full of freight cars with flat tops, so he puts his mattress on one and goes to sleep. When the rest of us get up that morning, there isn't a single flat car in the yard except the one Pepper is on—and he's still sound asleep.

"Then there was the time when we went off and left Nate Fine."

Nate Fine is the Redskins' photographer. He's been with the team for more than 25 years. He is one of the finest sports photographers in the country, and he is one of those men who are always on time. In all his years with the team, he has never missed a team bus, train, or plane. Not in 25 years. But he'll never live down that night in Birmingham.

"We were in Birmingham," Slattery begins, obviously enjoying what must be the ten-millionth telling of the Nate Fine Story, "and for some reason that I forget now we were overcrowded. So the conductor asked Nate if he would mind moving to another car just for the night. Nate is always obliging, and so he went. He just walked up there, maybe two or three cars, and he was just wearing his pajamas and his robe, and goes to bed. Next thing we know, there we are parked very nicely off to the side and the rest of the train, with Nate aboard, is pulling off for Chattanooga. Well, Nate felt the train moving and he was out of bed in a hurry but it was too late. There he was standing on the rear platform waving and hollering. Away he went, with no clothes, no identification, no nothing. We got him back on another train."

Slattery has many memories. He can still picture Sammy Baugh and his backup quarterback, Harry Gilmer, sitting at a dining car table and diagnosing plays with salt and pepper shakers as players. And on the rides through Texas, when it seemed as though the state would never end, Baugh would periodically look up and drawl, "I told you fellas Texas is big."

And there was the time in 1948 when John Stanshefsky was waiting for the train at Johnson City just outside Pittsburgh. He was there with all his relatives and half his friends and it was a big crowd and they were all there to see big John off to camp. "I don't to this day know why it happened," says Slattery. "The train slowed down almost to a stop in Johnson City and Stanshefsky is smiling and kissing everyone goodbye and picking up his suitcases and all the time the train hasn't stopped yet. Pretty soon John is sort of trotting after us…still trying to look cool and composed before the folks you know, but the panic is beginning to spread. And when the train begins to pick up speed, well, there's John, who never was the fastest man in the league, running for all he's got with suitcases in both hands. And the crowd that had come down to send him off began to cheer and shout 'go John, go!' Well, he never caught the train, but he gave it a helluva try. We picked him up later in Chicago."

For every funny story, there must have been a hundred card games. Slattery remembers that he and Bones Taylor and Bill Dudley and Jim Peebles had a running bridge game that lasted for several years. "I don't think we ever paid off."

But they were good times as Slattery recalls them. "There was something special about it," Slattery says, "and it'll never happen again. Everyone really got to know each other on those trips, and there was a sense of camaraderie or team spirit…and I know how corny that sounds. But there was, and it brought everyone together—players, coaches, management, and even the writers.

"There are a lot of advantages to plane travel, that's pretty obvious. You have to have it today. The schedule is built around it. We still take a train up to Philadelphia for our game with the Eagles, but that might as well be a plane ride. That train zips along at over a hundred miles per hour and we're in Philadelphia in less than two hours. Still it's a chance to look at some of the countryside. We pass through some good farm land and cross a couple of rivers…it's a lot better than looking out at the tops of clouds."

Did somethin' to 'ya
   when you'd hear that
   "all aboard"
Nobody cares
   about the railroads anymore.

The railroads did do much to build America. From the first transcontinental train trip from Boston to San Francisco in 1870, the railroads grew and sprawled to a peak in the mid-forties when, quite literally, the country moved on rails. There were more than 500,000 miles of track across the land, traveled by 24,000 freight trains, 17,500 passenger trains and operated by more than one million men and women.

The railroads have inspired ballads, songs, and drama, and they have left behind a uniquely American folklore. There is, somehow, romance to be found in those huge metal giants that once chugged and whooshed and whistled their way across the country.

"The case has been made," Slattery says, "that things are better today than they have ever been. And who knows, maybe they are. I'm not knocking what goes on today. I'm only saying that I'm glad that I was around for the days of the train rides because, for better or for worse, one thing is sure: It'll never be like that again."

117

by Paul Zimmerman

It Was Pro Football and It Was New York

A few months ago they had a football game in New York's Randalls Island, an old stadium in the shadow of the Triborough Bridge.

About 2,000 fans showed up to watch the New York Fillies lose to the Midwest Cowgirls. Girls football. A flaky night, but it brought back memories.

"It reminded me," said a fan with a past, "of watching the old Titans play."

The old Titans. Just mention the name and you're bound to get a laugh. Larry Grantham and Don Maynard, who were Titans from the beginning, can laugh, too, but it's a laughter born of sadness.

"Well, it was pretty rough in those days, particularly the financial aspect of it," Grantham said. "You know, you're twenty-two years old...first time in the big city...trying to raise a family...and you're not sure your paycheck's going to clear.

"Sometimes Don and I hear these kids moaning about one thing or another, and we just look at each other and smile."

Grantham was a 210-pound linebacker of ordinary build but finely tuned football instincts. He played 13 seasons and in his twelfth, 1971, he was voted the Jets' most valuable player.

Maynard was a Giants' reject, by way of Canada. They didn't like his sideburns or cowboy boots, a decade ahead of their time in 1958. He lasted 13 memorable seasons, too.

"I'll never forget the first time I ever laid eyes on Don," Grantham said. "It was at our first training camp in 1960—Durham, New Hampshire. I got to camp late, as usual, and the first guy I saw was Don, sit-ting on one of those old New England-style stone fences.

"He was sitting there with a big hat on, and cowboy boots. He looked like he was waiting for the rodeo to start. He had blue jeans on, and a belt with a big brass buckle that had number thirteen on both sides. And written across the face of it was 'Shine.' That was his nickname in college.

"I'll never forget that 'Shine' belt as long as I live."

For three seasons, 1960 through 1962, the Titans bore the image of one man, Harry Wismer. Harry's sportscasting had become legendary. "He announces a foot-ball game," Jimmy Cannon once wrote, "like a holdup victim hollering for a cop."

Harry once announced a runner going from the 45...to the 50...to the 55-yard line. For a couple of seasons he did the com-mentary for the day-old taped replays of Notre Dame games. His trick was to an-nounce, "Neil Worden is now in the Notre Dame backfield," and sure enough, Wor-den would carry the ball on the next play. Of course he'd been in the backfield all along, and Wismer had already reviewed the tape. But it made Harry seem like a prognosticating genius.

The AFL was bankrolled by millionaires in that first season of 1960—oilmen Lamar Hunt in Dallas and Bud Adams in Houston, insurance tycoon Ralph Wilson in Buffalo, hotel man Barron Hilton in Los Angeles —but Harry had hustled his way in by the side door.

He married Henry Ford's niece. Harry knew how to present an idea, but he al-ways operated on the brink of bankruptcy.

Harry Wismer

Peter Green

119

So he cut corners and saved money. Lord how Harry saved money!

"An underfinanced club with a very poor image," was Lamar Hunt's capsule of the old Titans. It was a mild evaluation.

The Los Angeles Chargers once wrote to the Titans for team pictures. The return mail contained 100 head shots of Harry Wismer. The Chargers' public relations man, Bob Burdick, once visited the Titans' office to pick up some tickets. The office was Wismer's apartment at 277 Park Avenue. The actual entrance, though, was on Forty-Eighth Street, and a lot of people never found it.

"When I rang the doorbell, a Swedish cook stopped me and said, 'What you want?'" Burdick recalled. "The ticket office was the bedroom. The coaches' office was the kitchen, and the press agent's office was a butler's pantry on the way to the bathroom. Two people couldn't squeeze by it at the same time.

"When I went into the bedroom, there were thousands of dollars worth of tickets lying all over the bed. No one was there. The two ticket men had been arguing about who'd be the first one to go out for lunch, so they both left. While I was there, a guy came in looking to buy two tickets. He left a ten-dollar bill on the bed, picked up a pair and left."

The Titans' press agent was Ted Emery, who came from Dartmouth. His operating budget was zero. When he asked for stationery for his releases, Wismer told him to visit the stationery stores and request free samples.

A few years later Grantham mentioned that Weeb Ewbank was the first coach to give them a playbook ("A sensible kind of thing for a pro football team to have"). Sammy Baugh, the original Titans' coach, countered with, "Before you can have a playbook you've got to have paper."

But Harry made sure the Titans stayed in the newspapers. He would greet all reporters with, "Congratulations." He would phone them at midnight...2 a.m....4 a.m....with bogus rumors of trades, serious illnesses, even deaths. He would step into a crowded elevator and announce, "Well, they just shot Castro." Sometimes Khrushchev. Just to keep in practice.

Subway posters advertised "Harry Wismer's Titans of New York." When the team took the field the band would play. "I'm Just Wild About Harry." After a while nobody was, but what the hell, it was pro football and it was New York.

The money men in the early AFL were signing a few top drafts away from the NFL, but the Titans got nothing in those drafts. "Drafting means nothing," Harry told his general manager, Steve Sebo. "Watch the other teams' cut lists. You'll do all right."

"There's no way you can win games," Baugh said, "by using people who aren't good enough to make the teams you're trying to beat."

But somehow Sammy Baugh's Titans of 1960 and 1961 managed to go 7-7 each season, which was a minor triumph. It was not until 1967 that the Titans—by then the Jets—were able to win as many as seven again. Baugh had some legitimate stars in those days—the long-range pass-catch threat of Al Dorow to Maynard or Art Powell, plus quality runners in Bill Mathis and Dick Christy. It was a team that could have been developed by adding a few good draft choices.

One thing it did leave, though, was the memory of some indelible characters. There was Hubert Bobo, the crazy linebacker with the two bad knees.

"We were playing cards one night on the plane trip home from a game," Curley Johnson, the punter, once recalled. "Bobo was angry about something, so he was punching every guy who dealt too slowly."

"Didn't you do anything about it?" someone asked Curley.

"Do anything? I was the most nervous guy there. It was my deal next."

The trip they still talk about is the one from Abilene, Texas, to Mobile on a preseason swing in 1960. Wismer decided that the 900-mile trip would be cheaper by overnight train than by plane, since he would also save a dinner bill (Harry used to book 8 P.M. flights for West Coast trips to avoid paying meal money). Harry assured the Titans they'd be in an air-conditioned train all the way.

Of course there was no air conditioning, and the trip through the late-summer Texas oven was a nightmare. There wasn't even any hot water for shaving. By the time they reached Mobile, the team was just about out of clean clothes. In Mobile they learned a parade had been scheduled in their honor.

"Everybody in ties," Sebo ordered. So of course Maynard dutifully knotted a tie over his T-shirt.

Billy Mathis, a 220-pound, crew-cut halfback from Clemson, had just been obtained in a trade, and he met the Titans at the station.

"He looked like the greatest thing we'd ever seen, a real All-America," Grantham said years later. "He was clean.

"I signed with the Titans for what I thought was a fifteen-hundred dollar bonus," Grantham says. "I found out later that it was really an advance against my salary.

"All of us eventually got the back pay coming to us when the league stepped in

and took over the team during the 1962 season. But I think Sammy Baugh took a pretty good beating financially. I know for a fact that if a kid was having problems Sammy would slip him something out of his own pocket.

"In 1960 six of us got together and rented an apartment. Me and my wife, Nick Mumley and his wife, Dick Jamieson and his wife. We found a place in New Rochelle, but the lady wanted two hundred dollars security. We pooled our money and came up short. I went to Sammy and asked him for four hundred dollars. Three other couples needed two hundred dollars for another apartment, and I was borrowing for all of us.

"Our apartment had a bedroom and a living room. We had the lady put in extra beds. Thank God we were all good friends. I remember we had a system worked out about raincoats. If anyone had to get up in the middle of the night, he or she grabbed a raincoat and put it on.

"Anyway, when I went back to Sam to pay him his four hundred dollars, he looked at me and said, 'I never loaned you but two hundred dollars.' I told him, 'No, Sam, it was four hundred dollars—honest.' That's the way he was. He never kept any records, just gave people money when they needed it."

The lessons of those early days aren't forgotten. A few days before Super Bowl III, some writers asked Weeb Ewbank about Maynard.

"I think Don's got every penny he ever made," the coach said. "They say that he checks into a hotel with two empty suit cases, but they're full when he leaves. Soap, toilet paper, towels...you name it."

"Isn't that terrible, what they said about Don stuffing his suitcase with toilet paper?" someone said to his wife, Marilyn, the next day.

"It's worse for me," she said. "I've got to unpack those suitcases. It isn't easy, smoothing out all those crumpled toilet tissues."

In 1963, though, Sonny Werblin took over. He brought backers—and money.

"I remember one practice we had at our Peekskill camp," said Paul Rochester, a defensive tackle.

"Sonny was up there that day, with his big car with the bar set up in back. I knew practice was going to be something special—to impress the boss. Sure enough, it started raining—then hailing. Hailstones as big as golf balls.

"We kept practicing, though. There we were, taking our stances with hailstones bouncing off our rear ends, and Sonny watching the whole thing from his car."

The old Titans were officially dead.

Whatever Happened to Old Whatshisname?

Don Maynard

Where have you gone Sidney Youngelman? And Pasquale Lamberti? And Lowe Wren? (Or was it Wren Lowe?) And Thomas Tharp? And Wayne Fontes? And Frank D'Agostino? and Frederick Julian? (Or was it Julian Frederick?) And Dewey Bohling? And Americo Sapienza? And Blanche Martin? And Thurlow Cooper? And Hall Whitley (Or was it Whitley Hall?) And Gerhard Schwedes? And Moses Gray? And John Klotz? And Hubert Bobo? (Or was it Bobo Hubert?)

Ah, names…but then maybe the name of the game is all wrong. Maybe it is not "where have they gone?" and "where are they now?" but "who were they then?"

Surely Blanche Martin is a character in Tennessee Williams' new play…

Surely Gerhard Schwedes is a member of Willy Brandt's cabinet…

Surely Frank D'Agostino is singing in a lounge in Las Vegas…

Surely Sidney Youngelman can tell you why seersucker wears better than gabardine…

Surely Americo Sapienza discovered football…

Surely none of those things are right.

All of them—Blanche Martin, Hall Whitley, Hubert Bobo, Sidney Youngelman, Americo Sapienza…and ad infinitum—were members of the New York Titans (circa 1960-62).

A total of 91 men wore the uniform of the Titans…and some of them (though not a lot of them) will admit it today.

One ex-Titan with a long memory is Bill Atkins, now the defensive backfield coach of the Buffalo Bills. Bill checked into New York in 1962, when the Titans' ship was sinking.

"Bulldog Turner, our head coach [Turner replaced Sammy Baugh as coach before the '62 season], really made a sincere effort to improve the team," said Atkins, "so he was constantly shuffling players, bringing in new ones, getting rid of those who weren't helping the team. But he had competition from Harry Wismer [the Titans' owner], who kept players he *liked* rather than those who might help the club.

"So when Bulldog cut a guy, the fellow would have to go to Harry and see if it was true or not."

Sometimes it wasn't. One player, Ed Kovac, was cut and rehired five times.

Turner was something of a character himself. Alex Kroll, one of the few draft choices the Titans signed, is now a vice-president with Young and Rubicam, Inc., an advertising agency. Kroll recalls the final game of the 1962 season. Wismer had been unable to meet his payroll, the AFL had taken over operation of the club, and Bulldog was readying his team to play the Houston Oilers.

"He gathered us together," says Kroll, "and reminded us that this was the last game of the season. 'There probably won't even be any New York Titans next year,' he told us. 'So most of you are playing in your last pro game. Most of you aren't good enough to play anywhere else.'"

The statement was only a half-truth. Larry Grantham and Don Maynard are proof of that.

Grantham came to the Titans as a receiver but he was moved to linebacker not long after he arrived. He has been a linebacker for the Jets (nee Titans) ever since—although the longevity did not seem apparent at the time. In the 1961 edition of *All-Pro Football,* Murray Olderman wrote: "Grantham is a scrapper but the Mississippian only weighs one ninety-five, which is hardly keeper size."

Maynard, who teamed with Art Powell to give the Titans an awesome one-two receiving punch (in three years they combined to catch 375 passes), holds the all-time NFL record for most yards gained receiving (11,834).

Success also has followed other ex-Titans. Bob Mischak, one of the co-captains, is plebe football coach at Army. Lee Grosscup, who quarterbacked the '62 club, is a sportscaster with ABC. Safetyman Dainard Paulson is a high school coach in his home state of Oregon. Running back Bill Mathis, who went on to several productive years and climaxed them by playing in Super Bowl III, is an investment broker in Manhattan. Al Dorow, the quarterback who threw 26 touchdown passes in 1960, coached in Canada the last couple of seasons. And Sammy Baugh, the kind man who shepherded the Titans through their first two seasons, lives a life of leisure on his ranch near Rotan, Texas.

Three years. The New York Titans lasted three years before the end came. Before it ended (of course) with a whimper not a bang.

In a first-person story written for *Sports Illustrated* three years ago, Kroll wrote:

"The final day of Titans football ended with the score 44-10 favor Oilers and 50 to 75 onlookers present, not including the two teams. Still there seemed to be a small personal consolation for coming to the park that day. The game had been billed as the last ever in the Polo Grounds. Shea Stadium was supposed to be ready for the Mets' opening day in April. So I had seen the end of a historic ball park. The Polo Grounds, where John McGraw and Bill Terry, Tuffy Leemans and Charlie Conerly had built legends, had seen its last legend. Us. And for myself, I would be the last man ever carried out of the Polo Grounds on a stretcher. It was a record of sorts.

"But the completion of Shea Stadium was delayed a whole year. Early the next spring the Mets' Rod Kanehl ran into the outfield wall and had to be carried out. So even this consolation for playing with the Titans was not to be granted. It came later. To Grantham, Maynard and Mathis in the Super Bowl. To the rest of us in the secure knowledge that we had been the last major league team to play almost entirely for laughs."

Most of the Titans are gone…but they are hardly forgotten. Still, some questions remain unanswered.

Like…where *have* you gone Sidney Youngelman?

by John Wiebusch

A Long Winter's Day

On this morning Bill John did not need an alarm and when he awoke he stretched his arm up behind the lamp on the nightstand, found the clock and pushed the button in.

"Time?" said Gloria John. She was awake, too.

"Time," said Bill John and he swung his legs out over the edge and onto the cold wood floor. "Damn," he muttered as he pulled back white lace curtains and looked out into the night, seeing moonlight on frozen snow and nothing else.

"On Christmas morning it would be beautiful," he said.

Gloria John laughed softly and nodded her head in the dark. "It's not what you'd call football weather," she said.

The business manager of the Cleveland Rams let the curtain fall and he rubbed his hands together, moving in front of the warmth of a register.

The dawn was still four hours away and it was more than six hours beyond that to the football game, the one between the Rams and the Washington Redskins, the one for the championship of the National Football League.

It was 3:30 a.m. in Cleveland on December 16, 1945. The temperature was eight degrees below zero.

Emil Bossard was the first to arrive at the stadium, parking his Chevy in a corner of the unplowed lot and hurdling snowdrifts to get to a side gate. The wind was coming up from Lake Erie, out of the north.

Inside, Emil Bossard opened an office door and switched on an electric heater. He put a thermos full of coffee on the desk and he stood and watched the black coils turn pink and then red.

It would be a day Emil Bossard would never forget. He had known that for a long time but the meaning was underlined in the five days before, when the temperature dropped along with the snow. The groundskeeper looked at his watch. The hired hands should be along shortly, he thought.

It was 6:20 a.m.

Bob Waterfield's alarm went off at 6:30 and he turned on the light and reached for the playbook on the floor. The rookie quarterback had turned the pages a thousand times and still he did not feel totally sure. He would spend nearly two hours studying it this time.

The field at Municipal Stadium was coming to life. Emil Bossard and Bill John walked atop the snow that covered the tarp that covered the straw that covered the grass.

"I don't know if we can do it," said Bossard. "I hope we can but I don't know."

"We can do it," said John. He kicked at a chunk of ice and snow. "We can do it but it won't be easy."

The problems involved more than just clearing the field. Or opening a spot in the snow and straw where the field should be. The problems involved cleaning up the stands, too. Over 40,000 tickets had been sold for this game—although it would have been more, maybe 80,000, if the weather

123

had not turned. The snows of Saturday night and Sunday morning had blanketed the seats and aisles.

"What we need is some organization," said John. "We've got a lot of guys who are willing to work."

He had hired over 300 men, some of them servicemen back from the war that had ended in the summer before, most of them drifters and vagrants who would be on the next train south.

At 7:30 a.m., Emil Bossard stood under the goal posts and addressed a gathering of huddled stormcoats. "Men," he said, "we need your help."

Nate Wallack opened the press box, removing his right glove to sift through a ring of cold keys. "Damn," he said aloud, to no one.

Inside the press box there was room for only 50 reporters, far less than the space that was needed. A lot of them would have to sit outside with makeshift planks as writing tables and no shelter from the harsh winds.

Nate Wallack knew what it would be like, about the abuse he would have to take. He knew that there was not a sportswriter alive who would not complain about such working conditions.

The Rams' public relations director looked through the glass that had Jack Frost all over it, at a rusty thermometer outside. It was one degree below zero. It was 10:15 a.m.

Bob Waterfield arrived at Municipal Stadium at 10:30, his teeth chattering and his playbook under his arm. He was to duel Sammy Baugh, the man the writers called Slingin' Sam and of whom it was written, "He is a legend in his own time."

Waterfield hung his parka in the back of his locker and went in to talk to Adam Walsh, the coach.

"We can't let this weather stop us from playing our game," said Walsh. Waterfield said that the weather would not be a factor. "Good," said Walsh. "Get dressed and then we'll talk."

In front of his locker, Bob Waterfield took off one of the three sweaters he had put on an hour before. He was thinking about his college days at UCLA and how it was never like this.

Bill John knew he was in the middle of a living, breathing miracle. In less than four hours the center of the field had been opened up and the rest of the playing area was almost uncovered. In the previous 10 days he had supervised the laying of nearly 9,000 bales of straw on the field and he had wondered then how they would move

them when it was time to play. A lot of people, he thought, we'll need a lot of people. The young owner of the team, Dan Reeves, had given him money to work with. "As much as you need to make the field first class," Reeves had said.

But it had not been easy. First there was the matter of finding enough straw to cover the field. And not just pitchforks of straw but bales of straw, enough to make a four-foot layer of insulation. Bill John had taken out ads in papers all over Ohio and western Pennsylvania. He pleaded for farmers to volunteer straw, looking for a surge of charitable Rams loyalists. When that failed, he offered to buy it. Not a lot of farmers could afford to part with winter straw and hay, though, and the bales trickled slowly into Cleveland.

Bill John surveyed the bustle around him and he was proud.

It was five minutes into the afternoon.

Nate Wallack finished passing out the statistics and the facts sheets inside the press box and then he moved outside, a box of thumbtacks in his pocket. He would use the thumbtacks to fasten the papers to the assigned outside spots.

A few writers were there already, moaning about what it was like. "You guys will be lucky if your typewriters don't freeze up," said Wallack. "The hell with my typewriter," someone said, "how about my hands and my nose?"

Nate Wallack's hands and nose were cold, but it was his feet that were freezing. He decided not to say anything.

It was 1 p.m. on December 16, 1945, in Cleveland, Ohio. The kickoff was an hour away. The temperature was three degrees above zero.

Sammy Baugh's ribs ached with pain and there was added discomfort from all the tape that ringed his body. He had suffered the injury a week before, against the Giants, but there was no public announcement to indicate that his condition was anything but perfect.

"We can't help ourselves by saying anything," said Dudley DeGroot, the head coach. "So let's keep our traps shut."

Now, only minutes away from the opening kickoff, DeGroot had to make a decision. He summoned Sammy Baugh and Frankie Filchock, the second-string quarterback, for a conference. Baugh had led the National Football League in passing during the regular season, completing an incredible 70 percent of his passes, but Filchock had been the league leader in 1944 and there was no team around that had such strength in reserve.

"The minute your ribs start to bother

you, you let us know," Dudley DeGroot said to Sammy Baugh.

Sammy Baugh said he would.

Emil Bossard was talking and Bill John was shaking his head. "There's nothing could have been done about it," said Bossard. "Nothing at all. The field just up and froze on us, pure and simple."

The insulation had proved to be only temporary. With the tarp and the straw removed, the field had frozen like a bullet. The only blessing was that the skies were beginning to clear. It did not look as if there would be more snow.

"Emil," said Bill John, "you did the best job a man could do. We all did." John opened a gate that led up into the stands. There were not many people there but then in a stadium that seats over 80,000 a crowd a third or fourth of that can appear lost.

At the box office, Bill John stopped to see how things were going. The Rams' business manager was told that only a dozen or so tickets had been sold over the counter.

"The weather," said Bill John, and there were nods of agreement.

The game would begin in 10 minutes.

Harry Wismer was the man behind the microphone in the broadcasting booth. Harry Wismer under the double overcoats and scarves and stocking cap.

"I must remember not to get too close to the mike," he had told some cronies the night before. "If my tongue hits the metal, it could be all over." He got a big laugh with that one.

Now, the engineer counted down and when he dropped his hand, Harry Wismer leaned in toward the mike. "Good afternoon, ladies and gentlemen," he said. "It is cold in Cleveland. With the kickoff of the thirteenth championship game of the National Football League just five minutes away, it is six degrees."

It was miserable on the sidelines, where the wind whistled through all the open spaces and there was no hiding place. Before the game began, players from each team tore open bundles and scattered straw along the sidelines, where they would sit. Some of them burrowed down into it.

The Rams' first series sputtered on the Washington 5 when a fourth-down run fell inches short. In came Sammy Baugh and the Redskins.

On first down, Baugh fumbled the snap from center and had to scramble after the ball in the end zone. When he retrieved it he threw wildly, far out of bounds. The call was intentional grounding and Washington was penalized back to its 2-yard line.

On second down, Baugh dropped back to pass again. But the attempt caromed off the arm of the goal post and fell back into the end zone for an automatic safety.

The two points seemed insignificant at the time. Later, they would be the margin of victory.

The look of agony on Sammy Baugh's face told Dudley DeGroot all he needed to know. In one quarter of play, Baugh had completed only one pass for six yards and he had looked impotent in failure.

"Filchock!!" boomed Dudley DeGroot, and Frankie Filchock rose out of the straw and went in to play.

The entrance of the healthy quarterback gave the Redskins impetus and in five minutes they had the lead. A simple flare pattern resulted in the touchdown, Filchock passing 38 yards to Steve Bagarus.

Nate Wallack moved in and out of the press box, ministering to aches and pains and needs. He was watching the crowd, too, and what he saw did not please him. "If there was any way to measure it," he said to one writer, "then I think this crowd will break the record for most liquor consumed per person."

What frightened Nate Wallack was that he knew the effect that liquor has on a human being in extreme cold weather. There is little reaction for a long time, regardless of the volume of consumption. But there is a point of no return and it can be a dangerous one.

On this afternoon, when the temperature was 26 degrees below the point when water will freeze, the attendance was 32,178.

Trailing 7-2, Bob Waterfield began from his own 30. He needed just six plays, three of them pass completions. The last was a 37-yard touchdown pass to Jim Benton.

It was 8-7, Cleveland, and Waterfield stayed in the game to try the extra point. In 1945, Bob Waterfield did all there was to do for the Cleveland Rams.

There was excitement in Harry Wismer's voice. "There's the snap," he said. "The ball is up, and it's..." For an instant Harry Wismer could not believe what he was seeing. For a literal instant, the ball teetered on the top of the goal post bar before falling backward and into the end zone for the point.

"It's good!" shouted Harry Wismer. "And let me tell you what happened!"

George Preston Marshall had insisted that his Redskin Marching Band be the featured halftime attraction. "They're the best," Marshall told Dan Reeves but the persuasion was unnecessary. Reeves knew the Redskin Marching Band was the best in pro football and one of the best anywhere. There was no question about who would be featured at halftime.

Bill John heard the sounds coming from under the stands, the agonizing toots and snorts of a band exercising. Leaning on a box railing, he said to Emil Bossard, "This should be something!"

And it was. The band came out of the tunnel behind the south goal posts and lined up in the end zone. The drum major came shooting out of the middle and the crowd howled. And there was no other sound except for the beat of the drums. The reeds and horns had frozen solid.

Halftime ceremonies had ended. It was two degrees above zero and dropping.

Franklin Lewis, the sports editor of the *Cleveland Press,* scraped a hole in the condensation on the press box window. Then he wiped away the instant wetness. Then he wiped it again. "I give up," he said to Nate Wallack. "I'm going to go sit in the cold. At least I can see what's happening." Half of the press box followed Franklin Lewis outside, out to the benches that held frozen typewriters.

There was fire in the Rams' locker room at halftime. Adam Walsh said he was not pleased with what he had seen. "You guys haven't shown me a helluva lot," he said.

The prodding lifted Bob Waterfield one emotional notch higher. At the start of the third quarter, he directed the Rams on an 81-yard touchdown drive, getting the final 44 yards on a pass to Jim Gillette. This time there was no crossbar to gather in Waterfield's kick. It was to the right. With less than 20 minutes remaining, Cleveland had an eight-point lead.

The commotion came from the upper deck. "My God," said someone in the press box. "A water main's broken up there and it's gushing down an aisle." It did not gush long. Instead, the water turned into a sheet of unpassable ice. Aisle 14 in Cleveland's Municipal Stadium was off-limits until the spring thaw.

Frankie Filchock brought the Redskins back to life in the final minutes of the third quarter, getting a touchdown on a nine-yard pass to Bob Seymour on fourth down.

Clearly, fate was on the Rams' side in the fourth quarter. Normally the steadiest of kickers, the Redskins' Joe Aguirre missed field goal attempts from 31 and 41 yards. And Frankie Filchock's final pass of the day was intercepted by the Rams' Albie Reisz.

At the final gun, it was Cleveland 15, Washington 14.

George Preston Marshall was leaving the press box when a ring of reporters moved in on him. "What do you think?" one of them asked, and Marshall grinned grimly and said, "I think it's good for the league to have the Rams on top."

Marshall moved toward the door. "That's all I have to say," he said.

Adam Walsh raised his arms to silence the noise in the Rams' locker room. "You were great all the way," he said.

The Rams finished with advantages in yards rushing and passing, totaling 372 yards to Washington's 211.

"Bob Waterfield is the greatest T formation quarterback in the world," announced Walsh and the words were lost in a wave of roars.

Outside the locker room, Dan Reeves admitted that he did not believe it. "I've been used to losing for so long," he said, "that I wasn't counting on anything until it was all over."

The one announcement Dan Reeves did not make was that the game was the Rams' last in Cleveland. After suffering $50,000 in losses in a championship season, the Rams would move to Los Angeles early in the next year.

Nate Wallack could only offer his final apologies to the numb-fingered writers who shuffled back into the press box area. "There will be bus service going back to the hotel every five minutes," he said.

Bob Waterfield signed autographs for only a short time. "We're all going to freeze to death," he said.

Later, in a car, he said, "I didn't notice the cold weather as much as I thought I would. All I know is that this was my biggest day."

Twenty years after that, when Bob Waterfield entered the Hall of Fame, he admitted that the memory of that day remained the strongest.

Bill John stood by a register again, soaking in the heat that poured out. "I can't wait to see what they say about this one in the papers tomorrow," he said to his wife.

It was 11:30 p.m.

by Joe Marshall

At Home on the Bench

His life is difficult to put in perspective now. It belongs to another age, to a placid, happier time when a man was the sum of his parts and when accomplishment was glorified in rather than dissected. Let us approach him then at the summit of his life. That would be April 16, 1962, the day that 44-year-old Byron Raymond White of Wellington, Colorado, was sworn in as the ninety-third Justice in the history of the Supreme Court.

Monday, April 16, is a clear day in Washington, a day with just enough hint of warmth to excite all the bright promise of spring, perfect weather for an Administration full of "vigah" and hope. The gloom of Vietnam is nothing more now than a small cloud on the horizon. This very morning the *New York Times* reports that a Pentagon study group has arrived in Saigon to "try to determine whether the approximately 6,000 United States military personnel assigned to the South Vietnamese forces...really know why they are here and what they are doing." But for the time being, ignorance is bliss. Cherry blossoms ring the Tidal Basin in front of the Thomas Jefferson Memorial while up on Capitol Hill the sun is gleaming off the white marble Corinthian columns at the front of the Supreme Court in seeming tribute to the splendor of Byron R. White's achievement.

Inside, White is chatting with one of his new law clerks, killing time until 10 o'clock, when he will become Mr. Justice White. He arrived at the Court shortly after 8, having prepared for this most moment-

ous day with a momentous breakfast: a banana, uncooked cereal, scrambled eggs, bacon, coffee cake, and coffee. Now he is waiting patiently in the chambers he has inherited from retiring Justice Charles E. Whittaker while the courtroom down the corridor is filling up with friends and relatives, among them his brother.

Dr. Clayton White is Byron's older brother by four and one-half years and was known simply as Sam when they were growing up together in Wellington, a town in those days of only about 350 people. Their father, Alpha Albert White, was a branch manager for a lumber supply company that had a yard there. Wellington is sugar beet country and the success of each year's crop determined the prosperity of the inhabitants. "I suppose you could say that by the normal standards of today we were quite poor," Byron White has said, "although we didn't necessarily feel poor because everyone was more or less the same. Everybody worked for a living. Everybody. You started working early."

Even then Sam White was setting a tough example to follow. He used to contract with farmers to do the field work, then hire other kids to help. And he was intent on getting an education, even though neither of his parents had gone through high school. His desires naturally filtered down to his younger brother. "I can't remember when I first thought of going to college," says Byron White. "My brother Sam was always going to go to college, and as far as I can remember I was, too...The state university passed out some academic scholarships to the first man in the graduating class of every high school in the state, so you made a noticeable effort to be first. That's how I was able to get to college."

Shortly before 10 o'clock Byron White dons his new black silk robe and walks down the marble corridor to the Justices' private conference room. In the courtroom the church pew-like rows of seats upholstered in deep red are nearly full. At the front sits White's wife Marion and his 8-year-old son, Charles. Nancy, 4, is at home.

Although they weren't married until several years later, the Whites met at the University of Colorado, where Byron's academic achievements were spectacular. In his junior year he won a Phi Beta Kappa key and in his senior year he finished first in the class and was Valedictorian as well as president of the student body. Like his brother Sam before him, he was selected as a Rhodes scholar from the state of Colorado. Harry Carlson, former athletic director of Colorado, remembers this brief exchange between a naval recruiting officer and White:

Officer: Mr. White, what about your studies?

White: I made a couple of B's.

Officer: What were the other grades?

White: A's.

To this day it would seem that the most difficult thing for Byron R. White to do is talk about himself. One of his two B's came in public speaking.

In the private conference room White is greeted by three retired Justices —Stanley F. Reed, Harold H. Burton, and Whittaker—as well as all the active Justices with the exception of Felix Frankfurter, who is in the hospital. Chief Justice Warren administers the oath: "I, Byron R. White, do solemnly swear that I will support and defend the Constitution of the United States against all enemies, foreign and domestic, that I will bear true faith and allegiance to the same, that I take this obligation freely, without any mental reservation or purpose of evasion, and that I will well and faithfully discharge the duties of the office of which I am about to enter."

In the courtroom the Court crier, George E. Hutchinson, pounds his gavel on the desk, the audience rises, and President John F. Kennedy enters through a side door.

White met John Kennedy for the first time while in England on his Rhodes scholarship. Kennedy's father, then ambassador to that country, invited the Rhodes scholars to several parties at the Embassy. Later, in the summer of that same year, 1939, the two young men met while touring Germany and spent a few evenings together in Munich.

The Oxford experience was unfortunately cut short in October, 1939, by the threat of war. White returned to America and entered Yale Law School. In his first year there he won the Edgar M. Cullen prize for the highest scholastic grades. But the war interrupted that, too. After two years of studying law, he enlisted in naval intelligence after being rejected by the marines because of color blindness.

White and Kennedy met again in the Pacific. In fact it was White who wrote the official report on the sinking of Kennedy's boat PT-109, a chapter of the President's life that was later made into a movie. White once told Sports Illustrated that "as a result of these encounters with the President, I began to get a strong feeling about what kind of fellow he was."

White was honorably discharged as a lieutenant commander with two bronze stars in 1945 and returned to Yale, where he received an LL.B. degree magna cum laude in November of 1946. He clerked for a year for Fred Vinson, then Chief Justice of the Supreme Court, before joining a law firm in Denver. There he settled, engaging in local politics, raising a family and practicing law. The years drifted by. Then in 1959, while driving from Boulder, Colorado, back to Denver, his mind wandered to the upcoming campaign, and he decided to back John Kennedy.

At 10:05 George Hutchinson smacks the desk again with his gavel and seven Justices walk through the red velvet hangings to their seats on the bench. "God save the United States and this honorable court," intones the crier. Byron White walks to the far right of the bench to the desk of the court's clerk, John F. Davis. The august nature of the room says more than enough about the solemnity of the occasion. The 82' x 90' courtroom is walled in "Ivory Vein" marble from Spain while the 24 massive marble pillars were fashioned out of a stone called "Light Sienne Old Convent" from the Montarrenti Quarry in Italy. Against that the heavy red draperies and the dark luster of solid Honduras mahogany are so imposing that one Justice once said that he and his compatriots looked like "nine black beetles in the Temple of Karnak." Yet despite this awing grandeur there is a relaxed air to today's ceremony, an air directly traceable to the presence of John Kennedy and his brother, Robert, the attorney general.

In early 1960, Byron White organized a Colorado Committee for Kennedy. Colorado was considered a key to Kennedy's success in the West. When White delivered 13½ of the 21 delegate votes at the Democratic Convention, Robert Kennedy, who was heading up his brother's campaign, asked if he would run the National Citizens Committee for Kennedy-Johnson. Impressed by his persuasive and organizational abilities, Bobby kept White on the team after the election by asking his brother to appoint him deputy attorney general. White was surprised. "I didn't get into the campaign with the idea of getting a job," he said. Nevertheless, he came to Washington and was serving in that post when President Kennedy made him his first appointment to the Supreme Court. In announcing that appointment the President said, "I have known Mr. White for over twenty years. His character, experience, and intellectual force qualify him superbly for service on the nation's highest tribunal. He has excelled in everything he has attempted—in his academic life, in his military service, in his career before the bar, and in the Federal Government—and I know that he will excel on the highest court.

And so all is hushed as Davis prepares to administer a second oath that will make White the first former Supreme Court clerk to become a Justice of that tribunal. Who would dare argue that the moment is not the supreme one in White's life or that the honor is not richly deserved? And yet there is a man in this august chamber who has a quibble, not with what is taking place but with a small oversight in President Kennedy's endorsement. That man is seated next to Ethel Kennedy now, directly behind the President, so close that, as he says later, "If there had been a louse on the head of the President of the United States, I could have snapped it off." Still, he seems a distinguished sort, with a strong, athletic face and a head of steel gray hair although his visage is not a familiar one to the assembled Washingtonians. Here indeed is a little mystery. Who is this stranger? He looks as if he could be a poet or a scholar perhaps, and in fact if you ask him his occupation, he replies vaguely, "Reading, studying, writing, meditating. Once meditation was an honorable occupation. Today, it would appear on a police blotter as a form of vagrancy, I suppose." He gives his name as John Victor McNally, but the stranger has a more identifiable handle, Johnny Blood.

Perhaps you have heard of Johnny Blood. For 22 seasons he was a professional football player, one so good that his playing feats won him election as a charter member to the Professional Football Hall of Fame. Yet he may have won more fame for his exploits off the field. There is a story that when he signed with the Packers, he asked for $100 a game. Coach Curly Lambeau came back with an offer of $110 a game if he would agree not to drink after Tuesday of each week. Blood countered with an offer to take the $100 he had proposed and drink through Wednesday. What is he doing in this venerable audience? It seems that Johnny Blood knows Byron White, has known him since the late thirties, and by a more identifiable handle, Whizzer White.

Johnny Blood became aware of Whizzer White about the time the rest of the nation did. It was the fall of 1936 and White was making a reputation the only way a junior in college could do in those days. He was playing football. A bad knee had kept him out of all but two games his sophomore season but by his junior year he was attracting a lot of regional publicity as a triple-threat tailback. It was a local sports writer, Leonard Cahn, who applied the sobriquet Whizzer. The nickname helped arouse national attention, particularly from Grantland Rice.

During his senior year he was the leading ground-gainer and scorer in college, scoring 16 touchdowns, 23 conversions, and the only field goal he tried.

"Byron was just plain mean and ornery and tenacious," remembers one of Colorado's assistant coaches. "He was the orneriest son-of-a-gun in the huddle I ever saw."

He was named to the All-America team as Colorado went unbeaten and untied and got to the Cotton Bowl. With final exams coming up, White took the lead in influencing the squad to vote it down, but at the urging of the governor and some other civic leaders, everyone reconsidered.

The game itself was a mismatch. Rice had far superior manpower but that didn't stop White from putting a big scare into the Owls. In the first quarter he led the Buffaloes on a long march, climaxing it with a nine-yard scoring pass. Shortly after that he intercepted a pass and sped 47 yards for another touchdown. He also kicked the two extra points and Colorado grabbed a 14-0 lead. But the rest was all Rice. The Owls eventually ground out a 28-14 victory but White had proved he was worth all the attention. And 16 years later he was named to the National Football Hall of Fame.

When the pro draft arrived, White should have been the prime candidate, but the word was out that he intended to follow his brother to Oxford. The Pittsburgh Pi-

rates, as the Steelers were then known, had the third pick and wanted to draft Boyd Brumbaugh from nearby Duquesne University but he was selected just before their turn came. Art Rooney told his player-coach to draft White. The player-coach explained about the Rhodes scholarship. "Pick him anyway," said Rooney. "I'll offer him so much money he can't refuse. I'll offer him fifteen thousand dollars. Which was a sum the player-coach could appreciate since in his dual role he earned just $3,500. And that began one of the least likely friendships imaginable. The player-coach was Johnny Blood.

Blood went to see his draft pick. "I quickly realized I was talking to a man, not a boy," he remembers now. "He was very impressive, but he had a great sense of humor. Success had not spoiled Byron White and it never has. He turned down the offer, even though he was waiting on tables at a sorority. He was set on going to Oxford because his brother had and he always wanted to be better than his brother." Blood returned to Pittsburgh empty-handed.

It was August of that same year when Johnny Blood next heard from Whizzer White. Blood was in Atlantic City with Art Rooney vacationing with Bert Bell at the latter's summer home when White called him and asked if the offer was still open. Sam had done some research at Oxford and discovered that his younger brother could come to England as late as January. Years later White explained his change in thinking: "Johnny didn't actually talk me into signing. It's just that I got so interested in Blood himself that I couldn't wait to follow him and see what happened."

It was a madcap year in Pittsburgh. The Pirates were miserable, finishing 2-9. They were a bad team, a fact Blood readily admits. "I ought to know how bad that team was. I coached it." "Sometimes," White remembers, "although Blood was a player-coach, he might miss a practice and explain next day that he had been to the library." Nevertheless, White led the league in rushing with 567 yards and was named to the all-pro team, and this despite rumors that his team wouldn't block for him at first because of resentment over his salary. "There was no truth to those rumors," says Blood. "The players loved him and they still do. We had a lot rougher life in those days, but he fit right in. He was a man with a hoe, you know. He's no ivory tower person; he isn't in any dream world."

"Of all the athletes I have known in my lifetime," said Art Rooney, "I'd have to say Whizzer White came as close as anyone to

giving one-hundred percent of himself when he was in competition."

In measured phrases Byron White repeats the oath being administered by the Court clerk. Johnny Blood is not the lone representative of pro football who is smiling proudly. In another row sits Fred Mandel, Jr., former owner of the Lions.

Fred Mandel bought White's contract from Art Rooney for a mere $5,000 when it looked as if the academic life had claimed pro football's leading runner. But then came the war and the impending draft and White decided to take the 1940 semester off from Yale and earn some money to make law school more affordable. The Lions were little better than the Pirates, finishing 5-5-1, but White once again led the league in rushing and was named all-pro in the same year that he had won the highest academic award at Yale.

He played just one more year, during which he was edged out by George McAfee of the Bears for all-pro honors. Then came the war and so ended pro football for Whizzer White. He had used sport the way it was supposed to be used—as a means to an end rather than an end in itself. "While athletics are a manufactured environment, there comes that moment when you stand face to face with doing," he said. "You either do or you don't. This kind of experience is valuable in maturing one."

In recognition of his achievement the NFL Players Association named an award in his honor, "to acknowledge our debt of gratitude to one of our own. Byron Raymond (Whizzer) White — scholar, athlete, patriot, humanitarian, and public servant—is the personification of the ideal to which professional football players aspire."

As he finishes the oath Byron R. White becomes Mr. Justice White. The Marshall of the Court, T. Percy Lippitt, escorts him to the high-backed leather chair on the opposite end of the bench. Of the principals we have encountered in the courtroom, all of whom now meet White's gaze as he takes his seat, only Johnny Blood dares dream past this moment.

And so we come to 1974. Justice White now ranks fourth in seniority on the Court and has long since acclimated himself to what the New York Times calls "the pageantry and the drudgery" of his occupation. He is still trim and athletic looking. Not long after he took office, a law clerk working late heard a loud thumping in the hall and on inspection discovered Justice White dribbling a basketball there. He still plays regularly with the law clerks in the basketball court on the third floor of the Supreme Court building. And at 57 he seems to have settled permanently into the lonely isolation of a Justice's life. He has chosen a middle path, not as liberal as many expected, yet not wholly conservative either. He is a contented prisoner to books, heavy legal volumes with place-markers that litter his desk and the floor of his office. But Johnny Blood has greater aspirations for his one-time comrade of the gridiron. He sees Byron White as President.

In 1972 Johnny Blood campaigned for Byron White. There were actually six men pushing the candidacy but Blood got the public relations job. The campaign, which judicial protocol demanded White take absolutely no part in, offered a compromise candidate, a name to be stored in the back of the mind, ''in the event that none of the present candidates is able to prevail at the Convention.'' In the case of a deadlock why not draft Byron White? The nominating committee made a strong case: ''Champion athlete, decorated naval officer, scholar, successful lawyer, former deputy attorney general and now a Supreme Court Justice, a man of iron integrity and with an exemplary record of solid achievement. Byron White is superbly qualified for the Democratic Party's nomination and for the Presidency itself. He can come to both, not the advocate of a faction, much less the prisoner of any special interests.''

So Blood stumped the country, as always appearing out of nowhere and vanishing back into it, caught up in a whirl of slogans and Shakespeare quotations: ''The dark horse is White . . . What fates impose, that men must needs abide; it boots not to resist both wind and tide . . . White for the White House . . . And the elements were so mixed in him that all the world might stand up and say, this was a man. I think that last is from Hamlet. On the other hand it might be George Halas of the Bears summing up his life.'' Blood is characteristically laconic about the whole effort: ''There's still 1976, and I'll only be seventy-two then.'' But these are dreams and it is not the age for dreaming.

Mr. Justice White has taken his place now. The ceremony has ended. President Kennedy stands and extends his hand up to the bench. Robert Kennedy gives the Justice a thumbs up sign, the court fills with smiles. Let us end with that moment. It seems the best perspective from which to view the man.

Dick Oden

There is more to the game than 60 minutes on Sunday, more than 22 men on the field and 60,000 people in the stands. The game is the strategy underlining the reckless abandon of the special teams. It is looking at the game through the eyes of an official. It is studying the mayhem from inside the pit, where the contest is won and the price is paid in the pain of twentieth century Goliaths. It is, simply, The Insights.

The Insights

by David Boss

Like a Living Thing

I was 10 years old when I saw my first real football game. On a warm September night in the Texas Panhandle my dad took me to a game between Amarillo and Denton high schools. The stadium was on the northeast side of Amarillo, out by the rendering plant, the grain mills, and the railroad tracks.

The stadium was a rickety, gray clapboard structure named Butler Field. Under the pale, yellow glare of lights that seemed to attract every moth and mosquito in the area, it took on the dimensions and complexity of a gigantic architectural wonder.

In truth, it was a small, prosaic arena, seating approximately 8,000 people. But it was like a living thing on Friday nights and Saturday afternoons when the Amarillo Golden Sandstorm—more affectionately known as the "Sandies"—met teams from Lubbock, Pampa, Borger, Childress, Plainview, and from as far away as Yseleta and Fort Worth. During those hours, it was not a skeletal wooden structure, ugly and uncomfortable, but an organism made up of a body of galvanized people who came to cheer their sons, brothers, and neighbors and—in a phrase foreign to 1942—let it all hang out.

I remember the spring of 1949, when Butler Field was razed after a championship season that had seen the Sandies go all the way to the state class 4A finals only to lose. The old structure came down and a few miles away, on the county fairgrounds, a new concrete bowl, one that would seat 12,000 people, was being finished for the 1949 season.

With progress, something kindred was stifled and subdued. With progress, an innocence—perhaps on a community's youth—was shrugged aside. In its place stood the future. And I have to admit it looked pretty glorious. There really isn't much sentimentality when it comes to creature comforts.

Three years later, I sat in the end zone of Cleveland's Municipal Stadium. It was an August night, warm and humid with a small, barely satisfying breeze ruffling pennants that hung from the roof.

Down below on the field were two teams, microscopic in my vision. I was watching the Browns and the Bears in a preseason game and it was my second pro football game. I was new to Cleveland, a big, sprawling city light years removed from my home in Texas.

The teams and players were equally removed from my understanding.

But that night I watched something that I still can see on memory's instant replay. I saw a game unlike any I had ever seen at Butler Field. It was played by people who still create conversation among pro football fans. I saw Otto Graham and George Blanda (yes, in 1952 George Blanda was quarterback of the Bears) lead their teams into the most amazing series of athletic wonder I had ever witnessed. And I realized, as I sat there fascinated, that I was not the only one screaming for more, that there were 78,000 other people who were there with me. The absurd truth struck my 20-year-old brain. The entire population of Amarillo was only 75,000. There were

Pittsburgh's Three Rivers Stadium

more people grouped into this one immense stadium than there were living in my hometown. And they were making a racket that was unbelievable.

In 1957, I climbed a stairway of the Los Angeles Memorial Coliseum with my brother. It was 11:30 A.M. on a Sunday in November, but the stadium was already crowded. I will never forget the sensation of first entering the Coliseum. It was one of this country's first monumental stadiums, and it still provides a special thrill to walk through its concrete tunnels. History is there, and it seems to permeate the place.

On this day, the Rams were meeting their arch-rivals from San Francisco and 102,368 people were there to watch a duel between Norm Van Brocklin and Y. A. Tittle. We sat in row 79, the last row at the top of the stadium, far above the playing field. Squashed together into a mass of wall-to-wall people, we screamed ourselves hoarse as we watched an apocalyptical game. We were sharing something special, my brother and I, and like everyone else in the Coliseum that day we knew it. We were a part of the largest crowd in the history of pro football.

Stadiums are the house of sport and each city boasts its own variety. As sport has progressed and matured, new stadiums have been built to celebrate a community's teams. Some are uncommonly lovely, like St. Louis's beautiful edifice designed by architect Edward Durrel Stone. Some are unbelievable, like Houston's Astrodome. Others are less imposing, like New England's Schaefer Stadium, built in less than a year in 1971. And others, like Pittsburgh's Three Rivers Stadium, Philadelphia's Veterans Stadium, and Cincinnati's Riverfront are so much alike in appearance that it literally is hard to tell one from another inside.

Still, it is better to be inside. There is nothing more depressing than to be outside a jammed stadium when the roar of the crowd is filling the air around you.

The fact is, the truth is, games are a way of life, not only for the player but for the spectator. In America we are not only gifted with this world's most unique team sport—football—but we are fortunate to be able to view it from the vantage points of some of the world's most luxurious sports stadiums. There are times when we take the comfort for granted.

Despite its commonplace availability, to witness a sports event is a rare and lovely opportunity. And for those of us who are never satiated, each occasion offers new opportunities to not only celebrate our city, our stadium, and our team, but ourselves.

In sport, one never grows old watching. We are forever young.

Washington D.C.'s Robert F. Kennedy Stadium

St. Louis's Civic Center Busch Memorial Stadium

Texas Stadium

Oakland-Alameda County Coliseum

San Diego Stadium

by Joe Marshall

What's in a Nickname?

Herewith a story of pro football nicknames—how and why they exist—a story, if you will, full of sound and fury (Lions, Eagles, Broncos, Raiders) signifying nothing. It is not a tale to be told in Shakespearian rhetoric or with Bronte-esque dark passion. It belongs more to the slapstick, pool hall, gashouse language of the twenties and to the modern day non-language of cereal box tops and newspaper contests.

For the older teams there is perhaps romance by association if one finds the days when ethnic neighborhoods grew by choice, and poverty was a force for unity romantic. They say the trolley car drivers in Brooklyn used to make strolling along the avenues a hazardous experience. Brooklynites became known as trolley dodgers and the baseball club acquired the nickname Dodgers.

But what of all this? Was poverty ever really romantic? Was dodging a runaway trolley car ever the stuff of merriment? Retrospect can be a powerful romanticizing force. Even the army seems fun in retrospect.

Where then do we begin in this matter of nicknames? Perhaps some ground rules are in order. With the exception of Thursday night bowlers who often mock their own incompetence with droll appellations, pro football nicknames generally honor power and speed (Jets, Lions, Rams), predators (Falcons, Eagles, Bears), good old aggression (Raiders, Vikings, Giants), or the particular city where the teams play (49ers, Oilers, Patriots). The point is to offer identification, to imply majesty, and to give that

poet-laureate of the newspaper, the sportswriter, a little kick in the vocabulary.

The only detectable trend in the acquiring of nicknames is a move toward majesty at the expense of identification. What, after all, does a Bengal have to do with a river port in Ohio? Buffalo Bill with a snowdrift in upstate New York? Falcons with Atlanta? The answer to the last is the logic of a Griffin, Georgia, schoolteacher named Julia Elliott: "The Falcon is proud and dignified, with great courage and fight. It never drops its prey, and has a great sporting tradition." Using equally impressive logic, Mrs. Robert Swanson gave Miami its nickname: "The Dolphin is intelligent and indigenous to the Miami area," reasoned this wife of a scientist. Now others suggested Dolphins—in fact hundreds did—but as a tie-breaker, contestants had to guess the outcome of that year's Notre Dame-University of Miami game. Resorting to methods less than scientific (she used her child's eight-ball toy), she announced that the game would be a tie. Neither team scored.

Contests produced the names of many National Football League teams, particularly the newer ones such as the Kansas City Chiefs, the New England Patriots, the Minnesota Vikings, and the Oakland Raiders. Occasionally contest winners backed their whims with reason. New Orleans takes its nickname from one of part-owner Al Hirt's favorite numbers, "When the Saints Go Marching In." Sentimentality ruled in Buffalo and Cincinnati, where the names of defunct teams were resurrected. In Buffalo in the late forties there were three professional teams with the name of Bison. When the confusion became too great, the pro football team, a member of the old All-America Football Conference, switched to, naturally enough, the Bills. Shortly after that the franchise folded, a fact which locals could never accept. When the new American Football League team arrived in 1960, people just thought of it as their old Bills come back to life. A new name was unthinkable. Denver, on the other hand, had never had a pro football franchise and wanted to signal its arrival with a nickname that wasn't familiar. Broncos was a natural. In Houston the answer was simpler: Owner Bud Adams was in the oil business.

The idea of town identification does still exist—hence 49ers and Patriots—but not in the homey sense that once prevailed. Curly Lambeau was a great quarterback at Notre Dame but he left school to take a job in Green Bay with the Indian Packing Company. The lure of the game eventually caused Curly to organize a team which the packing company backed with $500. The team had a fair to middling year, running up 565 points to the opposition's 6 (they lost the game in which they gave up the 6 to a team known as, believe it or not, the Fairies). Eventually the Acme Packing Company bought out Indian and advanced Lambeau $50 for a franchise in the NFL. They have been the Green Bay Packers ever since.

Then we have the St. Louis (nee Chicago) Cardinals, named not for the bird but for the color of some old faded jerseys belonging to the University of Chicago Maroons that former owner Chris O'Brien cut expenses with. At least they weren't ocher. Up until then they had been known, dashingly enough, as the Chicago Normals because they played in Normal Field. Their crosstown rival, the Bears, started life as the Decatur Staleys because they were backed by the Staley Starch Works. When Staley decided to concentrate on starch, George Halas picked up and moved to Chicago, where he named his team the Bears in remembrance of his favorite baseball club, the Cubs.

Some claim the San Diego Chargers were named by their original owner, Barron Hilton, when that hotel mogul was contemplating entering the charge card business, but in reality the name derived from the University of Southern California battle cry *CHARGE!*, which is popular in the Los Angeles Coliseum, the Chargers' first home.

In New York, the Jets presumably relate to nearby Kennedy and LaGuardia airports, although one suspects the mind of a poet lurks in the story. The Mets were already in Shea Stadium and now the American Basketball Association Nets have arrived. New York may play this game forever.

The reasoning behind some names is not always as simple as you might think. When Bert Bell moved the Frankford Yellow Jackets to Philadelphia, the eagle was more than a symbol of strength and speed. Those were the days when the country was trying to dig out of a depression and the National Recovery Act (NRA) eagle was the symbol of Franklin D. Roosevelt's New Deal. Bell saw a connection between that, his own new deal in bringing a franchise to the city, and the patriotic history of the city he had come to, so he called his team the Philadelphia Eagles. The Cleveland Browns, on the other hand, simply adopted the name of their first coach and architect, Paul Brown. The Cleveland Rams took their name from their first general manager's favorite college team, the Fordham Rams. The name stayed when they moved to Los Angeles.

In many cities the football team has taken a name from an older baseball franchise. New York's first football team shared a stadium with the baseball Giants and became the football Giants. For that matter there have also been New York area football teams called the Yankees and the Brooklyn Dodgers. In Pittsburgh, however, the team, which was originally the Pirates, found that system too confusing and derived a new identity from the city's steel works. For a brief period during World War II when they merged with the Eagles, they were known as the Steagles. In Detroit, the Heralds, Wolverines, and Panthers all failed before the Portsmouth Spartans arrived in town and, noting the presence of the Tigers, became the Lions: "The Lion is the proud monarch of the jungle, and our team will be the monarch of the league," it was reasoned. Alas, in 1942 they finished 0-11.

And finally the Bears, who may have settled for the most common team nickname, a plight which once caused an alumnus of similarly named Baylor to moan: "There are bears everywhere. There is Smokey the Bear and Barney Bear. There are teddy bears and bears at the zoo and bears on cereal boxes. There are an awful lot of bear rugs. There is a bear on firecracker packages and a bear on a tire billboard. There is Bear Bryant. I can't seem to get away from them. I dream a lot about bears and sometimes it seems I remember that there is a Yankee catcher named Yogi Bear."

The Redskins also copied a baseball team, the Boston Braves. George Preston Marshall started with his team in Boston on Braves Field. When he switched playing sites, he wanted to change names but keep the Indian motif. Since he was now sharing a park with the Red Sox and at the same time liked Harvard's crimson jerseys, Redskins seemed appropriate. Redskins they have remained, a proud tradition. Until a few years ago, that is.

It started when Russell Means, director of the Cleveland American Indian Center, went on the warpath against the Cleveland Indians' mascot, Chief Wahoo, which Means described as "a grinning clown." He attacked with lawsuits and subpoenas, and before he was through the Atlanta Braves' Chief Noc-A-Homa, who does a war dance after each home team home run, the Kansas City Chiefs, and the Redskins felt the slings and arrows of his outrage.

Means's reasoning pointed up the plight of the Indian's role in history. Would we think it funny, his arguments suggested, if after every Detroit touchdown a lion walked out and ate a defenseless Christian? Would we be kindly disposed toward that lion? Russell Means wouldn't think it was funny if after a Dallas touchdown a cowboy walked out and shot an Indian. Yet one suspects that there is some confusion here between result and intent. One doesn't adopt names for reasons of self-ridicule. Just ask Arnold Cream, Leonard Slye, and Archibald Leach. Or perhaps you know them better as Jersey Joe Walcott, Roy Rogers, and Cary Grant.

Yet for all this Means may have his day. The University of Nebraska at Omaha's Indians are now the Mavericks after a four-game stretch in 1972 during which they had no name at all. The changeover in uniforms and equipment cost an estimated $500,000. Stanford has dropped its Indian symbol. And now the battlefield is broadening. In early November, 1971 the University of Texas Senate passed a resolution to change the school mascot from the famous longhorn to the armadillo. The armadillo, it was reasoned, is a "peaceful and ecologically-minded animal." How long will it be before some old ladies' historical society in California protests the fact that youngsters think of 49ers only in terms of 270-pound behemoths who inhabit Candlestick Park? Must we learn to cheer for the pandas, titmice, and hamsters?

There is a precedent for all this. The Cincinnati Reds became the Redlegs during the Joe McCarthy era, but citizens have long since learned to take that baseball team's threat to democracy with a grain of salt. On the other hand, in England many of the football teams have no nicknames at all. But lest we go that far, remember the poor sportswriter. After all, his is a tale told by an idiom.

To the players, it's a hat. To the rest of us, it's a helmet. Whatever it's called, it's as much a part of football as…well, the football itself. Like the game whose rigors it protects against, the helmet has undergone quite a few changes through the years. The face at the right should be familiar. If Joe Namath had played in 1916, this is how he would have looked—before a game. It's safe to say that Joe's profile, had he played then, would not be the same Namath profile everyone knows today. What started only as a simple piece of leather today is a combination of plastic and padding that weighs as much as five pounds. Of all the equipment a player wears, he's most particular about his helmet. It has to fit right and look right—in short, be perfect in all respects before he will wear it. That's not to say it will necessarily be comfortable. "In the NFL, a helmet can save your life," says the Washington Redskins' equipment manager, Tommy McVean. "It's got to be tight at first. If it feels good, it's too big."

By today's standards, none of the early football helmets offered much protection. This model, popular in 1909, was very similar to the paratrooper helmet that became popular during World War I. It was made of leather, had holes for ventilation, and was secured with a strap that fit under the chin.

This is a cutaway view of the 1911 helmet. It had no internal protection of any kind. In fact, it was not until the early 1930s that helmets afforded the wearers any serious head protection. In the early days, blows to the head were absorbed only by the leather with which the helmet was made.

The helmet shown on Joe Namath (above) is one type worn in 1916. This is another, air-conditioned, style of the day. The forehead and ears received better covering than ever before. The top of the head, however, was not as well protected, due to a preference for increased ventilation.

The Evolution of the Helmet

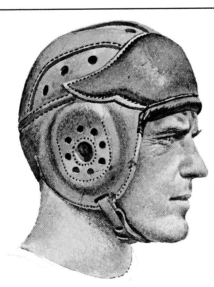

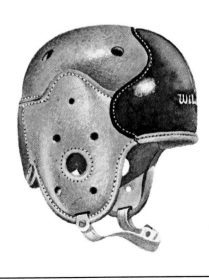

By the late 1920s and the early '30s, the players were bigger, the game was played harder—and better equipment became a necessity. This helmet, reinforced by leather bands across the top, became the forerunner of today's model. For the first time, the head was completely covered on all sides. The retail price was $7.50.

Dutch Clark, player-coach of the Detroit Lions during the 1930s, wore this helmet. It was a more streamlined version of the 1920s model, fit more snugly on the head, and was fitted with a better chinstrap. It was made of leather. Plastic helmets would make their introduction toward the end of the decade.

This leather model was used as early as 1934 by the New York Giants. It had a felt inner covering and offered more protection than any of its predecessors. It was very tight-fitting, however, and players of this era removed their helmet at every opportunity to allow their heads to cool off.

The NFL Official Rules Book stipulates only that helmets must be worn by all players on both teams (a 1943 addition), that helmets must be constructed only of plastic, and that all players on the same team wear the same color helmet. One exception to this latter rule is permitted: eligible pass receivers may wear a different colored helmet from their teammates, but if one pass receiver wears a different helmet, then all receivers must wear the same color. If, in the opinion of the officials, a helmet is similar enough in color to the football so as to give its wearer an unfair advantage, the solid color must be broken by at least two cross stripes of a markedly contrasting color at least one inch in width. In all cases, the officials are the sole judges as to the suitability of helmets or other equipment worn by players.

Since all available plastic products were used during World War II, plastic helmets, first introduced in 1939, didn't begin to appear until 1945-47. During and after the war, a variety of leather helmets were used, including this streamlined Wilson model used by various Chicago Bears into the 1950s.

While a member of the 1947 Chicago Rockets, Elroy Hirsch wore this early style plastic shell—until he sustained a serious head injury that nearly ended his career. In 1949, with the Rams, Hirsch returned to his old leather helmet for one game, but then adopted a safer plastic model for the remainder of his playing days.

This is the original Los Angeles Rams helmet, the first headgear to bear an insignia. Fred Gehrke, a Rams' running back from 1946-49, first designed and hand-painted the insignia on each of the team's helmets in 1948. Today, 25 of the 26 NFL teams have their own insignia. Cleveland is the exception.

The Inside of a Helmet

This is what the interiors of two modern helmets look like. The 16-web suspension model on the left is still the most popular with NFL players, as it has been for over 20 years. It features a series of elongated hexagons; the outer hexagon is riveted to the shell, while the inner hexagon is sewn to the outer one. On the right is the newer air suspension model, introduced in 1969. After a player is fitted, the helmet's component parts are blown up according to his size, assuring a perfect fit. The air cushion absorbs low to medium blows to the head. Medium to heavy blows are absorbed by a series of plastic sacs throughout the helmet containing a liquid known as ethyl glycol. Additional sacs containing sponge act as fail-safe protection for extremely heavy blows. Riddell, Inc. is the main manufacturer of helmets for NFL teams. Many veteran players still prefer the web suspension helmet because they are used to it. However, more and more younger players, who wore the air cushion model in college, are continuing to use it in professional football. Modern technology cannot always keep up with the rigors of the sport, however. Marv Hubbard, the Oakland Raiders' running back, says he broke six of the water-filled helmets in a single season. "I asked Dick Romanski (Raiders equipment manager) about it, and he told me the helmet I was using had been tested in college ball, and out of three thousand used, only three were broken. The only conclusion I can draw is that just because something is tested in college doesn't mean the same will hold true in the pros." Hubbard adds he didn't even know that he'd broken the helmet "until I went back to the huddle and the water was streaming down my face." Still, he will continue using the water sac model. "It's a lot more comfortable for me," he says, "and I don't feel the hits as much as with the suspension helmet."

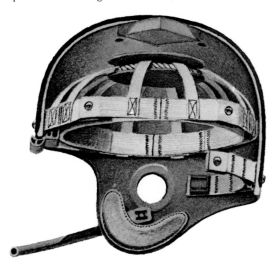

Otto Graham as he appeared in 1949 with the Cleveland Browns. Many players still wore the leather helmet and were reluctant to give it up, even when it reached the weatherbeaten condition Graham's did. Otto converted to the plastic model during the early 1950s, however.

Several college players in the late 1950s, notably those at Ohio State and Duke, preferred this helmet. It is like other plastic shells but it features a vulcanized protective strip which runs over the middle of the helmet. The Lions' John Gordy (above) used it, as does Kansas City's Willie Lanier today.

The pro football helmet, circa 1974. It is the product of over 30 years of technology and refinement. No helmet has ever protected its wearer as well as the modern one. Nonetheless, newly designed models are currently being tested by several NFL teams for possible use in future seasons.

The Evolution of the Facemask

Paul Brown is credited with being the first pro coach to insist that his players use some kind of facemask. On these two pages is the development of the mask.

Dr. M. T. Marietta designed this full-face lucite mask in 1948. When Joe Perry broke his jaw in the 1954 preseason, Joe used this mask until the fracture healed, then switched back to his regular mask, at the time a clear lucite strip.

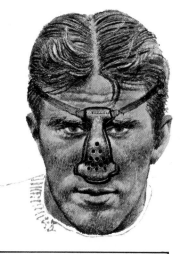

The earliest known facemask was this simple noseguard, used during the early 1900s.

During the 1940s and 1950s, linemen often handcrafted their own masks.

When Y. A. Tittle fractured his cheekbone, a strip of rectangular metal was added to his helmet for protection. Many players used the lucite facemask during the 1950s, but these were outlawed during the decade because lucite often shattered upon impact, gashing tacklers and ball carriers alike.

With the ban on lucite masks, most players switched to the single bar mask, the most common mask of the 1950s and early 1960s. Birdcages began making their appearance on linemen in this period, but single bar was most popular.

One of the last fulltime players to eschew the mask was quarterback Bobby Layne, who played primarily with Detroit and Pittsburgh. Layne finished his 15-season NFL career with the Steelers in 1962.

There is perhaps no greater distinguishing characteristic among players than the various facemasks they wear. It used to be that the position a man played dictated the type of mask he would use: birdcages for linemen, single- or double-bar for receivers, ball carriers or quarterbacks. No longer. The birdcage, or variations of it, is fast becoming a favorite of players at all positions. Joe Namath wears a birdcage that juts well below his chin, a testimony to his confrontation with Oakland's Ben Davidson a few years ago. Still, a few traditionalists abound. Washington's Bill Kilmer is one of only a few to use the single bar.

Wearing of facemasks is strictly a player's own choice. No rule exists that a player must wear a mask; however, the clubs themselves usually require all players to use one. The only stipulation is that the mask be no more than five-eighths of an inch in diameter and that it cannot be made of lucite or similar material.

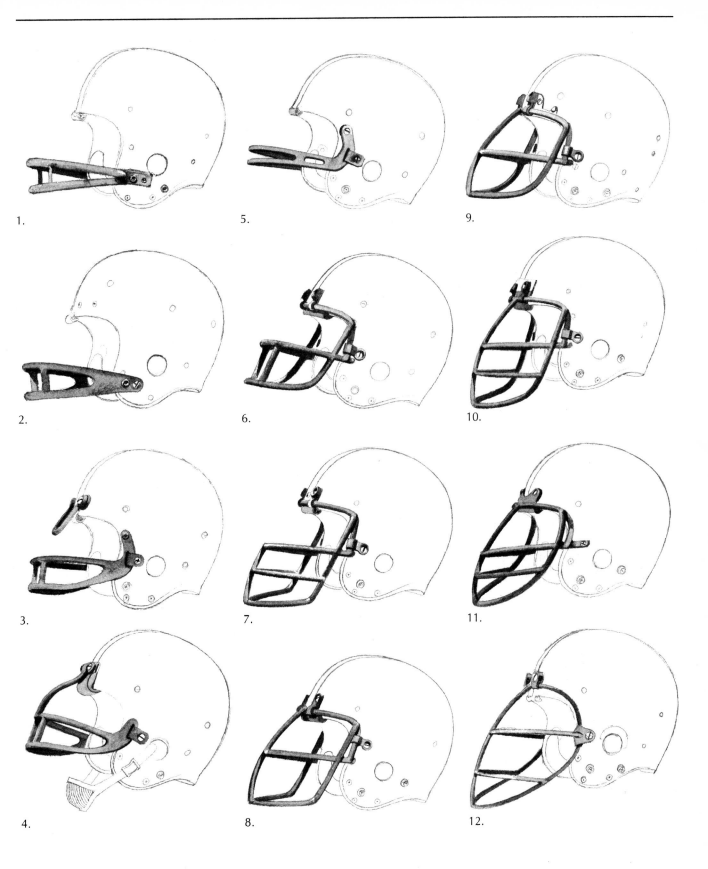

1.   5.   9.

2.   6.   10.

3.   7.   11.

4.   8.   12.

1.   Double bar — still the most popular facemask style among nonlinemen.
2.   A variation of the double bar. Used primarily by running backs.
3.   The horseshoe — protects the nose. Larry Csonka used this model.
4.   Double bar with face attachment. Ed Podolak prefers this mask.

5.   This double bar gives quarterbacks like Bob Griese optimum downfield vision.
6.   This elongated double bar has become popular with defensive backs.
7.   The half-cage. Used by some quarter-backs, running backs, and linebackers.
8.   Optimum vision cage. Many receivers use this, which still allows full vision.

9.   Rounded version of No. 8. Popular with linebackers.
10.   The cage. Used by all linemen and various defenders.
11.   Face bars are closer together on this model than on No. 10.
12.   The newest cage. Face bars are farther away from face.

by Jerry Magee

A Place in the Desert

An uninvited free agent showed up on the first day of practice that year, his patterns precise, graceful, ominous.

"Probably waiting for the first man to drop," said one veteran.

The buzzard continued its deadly circles over the rocks and sand of a spread in the San Diego County high country known as Rough Acres Ranch.

It was there where Sid Gillman took the San Diego Chargers in 1963 for what became the most unique exercise in preseason training ever conducted by a professional football team. Compared to Rough Acres, such places as Kerrville, Texas, Hattiesburg, Mississippi, Rensselaer, Indiana, and Thousand Oaks, California, outposts where National Football League clubs presently condition themselves, are pleasant meccas. Rough Acres—well, it was a reminder of another time when the niceties of living had not been developed. There were no television sets at Rough Acres Ranch. There wasn't much of anything at Rough Acres Ranch.

"Bob Burdick [then the Chargers' publicist] has a radio which brings in news from the outside world," noted one player.

The Chargers' journey east on Highway 80 to this implausible retreat began in 1962, when the team struggled through a most unrewarding season. The Chargers were 4-10 in a year in which 11 athletes were lost for all or part of the season with injuries and 12 others missed at least two games. The disappointment was compounded by the records of the years before. In the American Football League's first sea-

son, 1960, the Chargers were 10-4. The following year they were 12-2.

As the disaster of 1962 concluded, Gillman analyzed what had happened. In preparing for the season, his team had exercised and been quartered at the University of California at San Diego, which sits on a breezy mesa from which a splendid view of the city can be obtained. It also occupies a location within easy access of all of San Diego's civilized delights. Gillman decided the reason the Chargers had been riddled by injuries was that they had been lax in July and August. He was determined it wouldn't happen again.

San Diego is the most benign of cities. The Pacific Ocean fans it pleasantly in the summer. Winters are moderate. Smog is a condition known only in another area to the north. Go from San Diego to the east, however, and it becomes apparent San Diego lies on the edge of a desert. To the east the trees and greenery of the city are quickly replaced by boulders, scrub, and sand. Gillman looked in that direction for a training site.

Near Boulevard, he found it. Boulevard! There wasn't even a paved street in the place unless you counted the highway. What there were in that summer of 1963 were a post office, bar, a couple of truck stops, an antique shop, and, just outside town, McLain Road. And on McLain Road was Rough Acres Ranch.

Here, 60 miles from San Diego, 50 miles from El Centro and far from any worldly distractions, Gillman decided the Chargers should do penance for their 4-10 season of the year before. The coach talked grandly.

Glen Iwasaki

147

There would be a main lodge at which the players would be fed and in it there would be meeting rooms, quarters for the coaches, and a large recreational room for the players. Outside, there would be a golf driving range. In time, there would be a swimming pool.

Below the lodge would be the accommodations for the players: cabins, each sheltering four athletes. The cabins would be built across a mall, facing each other, and at the other end would be a locker room and training facilities.

"It's a perfect training site," Gillman argued to those who would question why a football team would train in the desert in the summer. "This isn't the desert floor; it's a three-thousand-foot elevation. The weather should be ideal. It won't be necessary for us to drill any harder or less hard than we always have."

The peak temperature the previous summer, he said, had been a tepid 91.

Up Highway 80, then, the Chargers traveled. This was an adventure in itself. The same route is now known as Highway 8 and it has been improved until there is only one stretch through which there are not four lanes. But in 1963, it was a narrow, high, winding road.

Through Descanso and Pine Valley, finally to Boulevard. And then the professionals found themselves at the gate of Rough Acres Ranch—a couple of pieces of lumber, tacked together.

Clearly, this place wasn't named what it was in order to lure tenderfoots to a layout for dudes. Neither was it anything like a Camp Runnymuck for children. It was, indeed, a rough land, dry because it rarely rains here in the summer, and yellow to match the color of the sand and the rocks.

Had a Chargers candidate stopped at the gate that first hot morning in July and looked to the south, he would have seen the hills of Baja, California. Where he was, was in a desert, albeit a high desert. For a person with a respiratory disease, it was an excellent place; for a football player, the atmosphere was, well, curious.

"Where is the employment office?" questioned Dick Harris, a pass defender, after viewing the field.

Green is the color usually associated with football. There was none of it here. On what was generously described as the field, there was no grass. Seed had been distributed but the sprinklers wouldn't sprinkle because there was little or no water pressure. Sand, rocks, and pine shavings, which had been spread to serve as a mulch, formed the playing surface. Though the rocks were combed away, the surface never did get better.

Accommodations for the players were luxurious, if you don't mind unfinished furniture with a quarter-inch of sand for a doily. Abe Lincoln must have learned to read in rooms like those.

The shower room for the players had no roof but it didn't need one because it never rained. And of course the chef prepared exquisite meals—when there was a chef.

"The most exciting moment of the day is when the chef plugs in the toaster," wrote Jack Murphy, sports editor of the *San Diego Union*. "Every time the toaster is connected it blows a fuse, and so does the chef."

Gillman is something of a gourmet and he had brought in a chef he expected to delight even his tastes. The poor guy couldn't stand the pressure, and Sid made his first cut in the kitchen.

Not that meals weren't an event. "I can hardly wait for the meals in the lodge," said one player after staring for weeks at the environment. "It's so nice to see all those people."

What animal life there was around the place was desultory. There were some horses and some cows but the heat and the thin air seemed to cause them to go through life in slow motion. "I noticed a good omen," someone said. "The cows are showing a little more life today."

Once a bell rang in the lodge while the players were disturbing the sand on the field a couple of hundred yards away. "Hey," screamed Paul Maguire, a linebacker, "the stage is in!"

There also was the time when a net was arranged on one of the goal posts so footballs would not skitter off into the wastes. This was important to the ball boys; there were snakes out there. A rookie pass defender, Dick Westmoreland, inquired about the net.

"It's to keep mosquitoes from coming on the field," said Maguire.

Among the Chargers that summer was their new quarterback, Tobin Rote, then 35. "Charlie Conerly played until he was forty-two but I don't think I'll try it," said Rote after arriving in the desert. "I just hope I live until September first."

Football players can live in conditions that would not be recommended by *Good Housekeeping*. In the preseason, their main preoccupation when they are not on the field or in the classroom is to restore their bodies with sleep. Even if the bed is made of unpainted wooden slats, they fall on it. Even if the preparation of food is unartistic, they eat it.

The thing that made life at Rough Acres an ordeal was the very air the players breathed. Since the ranch was at such an altitude, the place was as dry as a buzzard's throat. And it was hot.

Gillman usually went about announcing the temperature as 83 or something equally preposterous. Sid did so good-naturedly. From the start, he seemed to realize the training site he had selected was not exactly ideal—although he never publicly admitted it.

Because of the dryness, everyone complained constantly of being dehydrated. A soft-drink representative had supplied a dispenser in the main lodge. It was under constant siege. Ice was the most valued of commodities. Anything cold to drink was a prize.

Curfew was at 10:30 P.M. At about 9:30 P.M., the evening meetings would adjourn and the players would pile into automobiles and careen over the dirt roads two miles to Boulevard, to a place called the White Spot, where there was one shuffleboard game, one pool table, one juke box, and, blessedly, beer.

For company at the White Spot the players had a couple of sportswriters who had arrived there first, and construction workers who were building a stretch of highway around Boulevard and to the east, in the direction of the Imperial Valley. The athletes and the highwaymen got along well enough; the road workers didn't want to be where they were, either.

After a bit of this, life began to lose its disciplines for the Chargers. Some would stroll about the ranch totally naked. It was cooler that way and, besides, there wasn't a woman within miles.

Oh, there were diversions. It was noted in the San Diego press that a really deserving athlete could listen to Gillman's stereo set. The set was in his office, which was the only air-conditioned room on the ranch. Sid slept there. And there were two sagging pool tables in the lodge and a table tennis table on the porch.

Sam DeLuca was playing Ping-Pong one night. Now, Sam was from Queens, New York, and animal and serpent life, especially serpent life, was strange and frightening to him. On this night the table tennis ball rolled into a hole underneath the lodge. Sam reached for it—and found himself staring at the head of a snake.

Not long after that, Sam retired.

The summer's main diversion was when Gillman ordered a couple of buses and took his squad to a saloon in El Centro, where one of the Patterson-Liston fights could be seen on television. The fight ended in one round.

Later, the coach took his athletes to a country club. By this time, people were acting strangely. The highlight of the evening was when Ron Mix, usually the most gentlemanly of men, dumped a newspaperman into a swimming pool.

What the athletes could not have known up there in the country was that the Chargers were developing into possibly the finest team the AFL would see.

They came down from the mountains eventually and that was the year they won their only league championship. In the title game, Rote, Paul Lowe, Keith Lincoln, Lance Alworth, Don Norton, Ernie Ladd, Earl Faison, Chuck Allen, Ernie Wright, and Mix combined to defeat Boston 51-10.

But the Chargers did not return to Rough Acres Ranch. After their summer there, there was a lawsuit. The owner of the spread charged his property had been extensively damaged. The team reportedly settled out of court. The next summer it trained in Escondido, California, a beach city north of San Diego.

Recently, a man who was there at Rough Acres in 1963 was driving west to east from San Diego. He decided to pass through Boulevard. The White Spot wasn't there anymore, and the antique store was gone, too. The highway workers had done their job. They had taken away everything except the memories.

by Tom Bennett

The Invisible Men in the Striped Shirts

Not long ago an eager young man came to see Ben Dreith at Abraham Lincoln High School in Denver, Colorado, where Dreith is chairman of the department of physical education.

"Please tell me how I can become a referee in the National Football League," the young man said.

"Son," Dreith asked, "How old are you?"

"I'm twenty-one."

"Are you working as a football official anywhere now?"

"No."

"Go out and get yourself a job in a high school league. If you do a good job, you'll get moved up to a college league. Work there for a while. Then come back to see me in fifteen years."

Ben Dreith holds one of the coveted positions at the top of his profession; he is one of the 84 game officials of the National Football League. In January, 1974, he was the referee of Super Bowl VIII in Houston.

Television announcers are always forgetting the names of referees like Ben Dreith. Among the 14 men employed by the NFL as referees, only Tommy Bell and Norm Schacter have escaped the anonymity that covers the rest.

Dreith, 46, is one of five original American Football League officials still in professional football in 1974, 15 years after the formation of the AFL. Things are a lot easier now. For one thing, there's more money. In the early years of the AFL, officials signed a contract for $2,000 for the entire season; now Dreith is paid $500 for every regular-season and $300 for each preseason game.

Dreith officiates college basketball games in the Big Eight Conference during the off-season. He and Pat Haggerty, another NFL referee, teach physical education at the same high school in Denver.

On the opening weekend of the 1973 season, I joined Dreith and five other officials in Chicago to study their preparations for a game between the Bears and the Cowboys at Soldier Field.

The lobby of the Sheraton-Chicago Hotel bulged with travelers, stewardesses, pilots, basketball players trying out for the Harlem Globetrotters, members of the Chicago Philatelic Society, the Urban Research Corporation, the B'nai B'rith Women's Council, and the Chicago Playing Card Collectors. The Dreith crew gathered quietly in the middle of it all.

Umpire Art Demmas, 39, flew in from Nashville, where he is an insurance salesman. He was co-captain of the football team at Vanderbilt University a few years ago and ended his playing career in the 1955 North-South Game on a South team quarterbacked by Sonny Jurgensen. In his sixth year as an official, he has the most dangerous job on the crew. He works in the middle, in the vicinity of the middle linebacker.

"My first year," he says, "I read what I thought was a pass, and I stepped up in there. But then I saw it wasn't a pass play, it was a draw! I got wiped out.

"A couple of years ago, Ken Willard, Mike Lucci, Wayne Walker, and I all came together at the same time on the five (yard line) and ended up on the one."

Head linesman Frank Glover, 42, was a high school coach for 15 years; he now is a personnel specialist for the Atlanta public school system. He holds a Master's Degree in education from New York University. He is friendly and good-natured, and encourages jokes about the fact that he is the only black man on the crew of six.

"Look at the money I save," he says. "I don't have to buy stockings; I just put tape around my calves."

Line judge Mason (Red) Cashion, 42, is an insurance salesman in Bryan, Texas. He flies out of Houston each weekend to keep his officiating assignments.

Cashion is the new man on the Dreith crew. He is in his twenty-second year as a football official, but this is only his second year in professional football.

Glover and Cashion—head linesman and line judge—work on opposite sides of the scrimmage. They are arbiters of forward progress.

"It's the best example I know of selling," Cashion says. "You've got to *sell* those big monsters. They're so big and they're so *smart*. You put the ball down hard and you say it [forward progress] was *right there*."

Dr. Bill O'Brien, the field judge, is chairman of the department of recreation and outdoor education at Southern Illinois University in Carbondale, Illinois. He is 50. His Ph.D. is from Indiana University. He is a seven-year man, secretary-treasurer of the NFL officials association, and author of its code of ethics.

O'Brien is the alter ego of his partner, back judge Stan Javie. They officiate in the deep secondary, O'Brien 25 yards down in midfield, Javie 17 yards down. Away from the game, O'Brien is the target for an unending onslaught of jibes and good-natured kidding from Javie.

Javie, 54, is the senior game official in the National Football League with 23 years of service. He is a garrulous man, and his accent is pure Philadelphia; he is vice-president of a paint store there.

And he has forgotten more football than most people will ever know.

Javie smokes 28-cent Bering Plaza cigars. He buys them 10 boxes at a time. Because of the cigars, the five other members insist that the Saturday night meeting be held in Stan's room.

There was still some light outside when Bill O'Brien started threading the film. He pulled down the shades.

"The people in the apartment across the way must be wondering what's going on," he said. "Saturday night in a hotel room, six guys come in, set up a projector, and the shades go down."

Dreith had shed his tie, but he still wore the knit shirt in which he had arrived that afternoon. He turned through the heavily annotated pages of his rule book and the files he carried in his valise. The other members of the crew opened their own rule books, each one underlined, tabbed, and worn.

"Okay," said Dreith, "let's go over the things I got from Art when I called him today." "Art" is Art McNally, NFL supervisor of officials.

"One, double-check your cards. Some officials have been writing down their penalties for the wrong team.

"Two, one of us has to return the film Monday by fourth-class mail and insure it for $100.

"Three, this year we have to notify the coach on major penalties.

"Four, I have to call Stu Kirkpatrick Sunday night with activations." Kirkpatrick works in the NFL statistics department on Sunday nights.

"Okay," said Dreith, "let's look at that film now."

The projector was an old one and it gave O'Brien trouble.

"Somebody help that rookie with the projector," Javie said.

"As far as you're concerned," O'Brien countered, "if you haven't been in the League ninety years, you're a rookie."

"Do you remember that Bears-Eagles game?" Javie asked. "You were knocked cold. There was a fumble, and you were the only official who knew whose ball it was.

"I run over to you and I say, 'Bill? Stan. What was it?' I lift you up off the ground

and you say, 'White ball.' I say, 'Okay, you can go back to sleep now.' "

Demmas joined in. "Nobody could believe how sweet Stan was talking," he said.

"Yeah," O'Brien said, "When I woke up, I thought I was in heaven."

The movie was San Francisco versus Los Angeles, the final preseason game for both teams, and the first game the Dreith crew worked together in 1973.

The kicking reel showed that a special teams player for the 49ers was pulling the head of the Rams' center down as soon as the center snapped the ball for a punt.

"I told him to cut that crap out," Demmas said.

"But nobody shot the gap [taking advantage of the head-pulling action]," Javie said.

"That doesn't matter," Dreith broke in. "What happens if that center comes up slugging? That's why we've got to stop it."

In the 49ers' offense reel, a Rams' cornerback threw an elbow at a receiver.

"He said he didn't hit him," Javie said. "I said, 'I don't care. The next time you do it you're getting fifteen.' "

The Rams' offense was more interesting than the 49ers', since Los Angeles won the game 38-10. In the second quarter, Lawrence McCutcheon of the Rams sneaked two yards for a touchdown. On the film, Cashion rushed in to where McCutcheon had been stopped on the goal line. He hesitated, then threw up his hands, signaling touchdown.

"What could I do?" Cashion asked, as the film was stopped.

"You did right," Dreith said. "You waited until you could see the football, then you signaled. If the ball is over the goal line, it's a touchdown."

The film continued. In the second quarter, Dreith penalized San Francisco 15 yards when defensive end Cedrick Hardman roughed the Los Angeles passer, then 15 more when Hardman slammed his helmet to the ground in protest.

Dreith stopped the film again.

"My daughter [Laura Jean, a 22-year-old student at the University of California and the oldest of Dreith's four daughters] sent me this clipping from a San Francisco paper. It says, 'L.A. made the big plays and also got more than a modicum of help from head ref Ben Dreith.' Then it mentions the two fifteen-yard penalties. Does anybody know what 'modicum' means?"

The talk turned to the Hardman play again and I said Dreith must miss a lot of the action watching the quarterback, that being the referee's job all the way to the whistle and beyond.

"Yes," he said. "For example, we

worked that game last year when Joe Namath threw six touchdown passes and John Unitas two. There were several of those touchdowns I didn't see at all.

"That game Art mentioned earlier, the one at Detroit…After a pass play, I called for the ball. 'Right here, it's fourth down,' I said. Lucci says, 'Ben, they completed that pass.' I didn't know it. My responsibility is that quarterback, to see that he doesn't get a late hit."

On Sunday morning, Glover, Javie, and O'Brien went to early Mass. At eight o'clock, the crew sat down to breakfast in the hotel coffee shop.

"Four of us," Art Demmas was saying, "Ben, Bill, Stan, and myself, have been together for four years now, and we still review things over and over again."

"You can go for years without having a certain play occur in a game," said Dreith. "Then it will happen. You'd better be ready for it."

In the pregame meeting later in Dreith's room, the six officials correctly anticipated several out-of-the-ordinary decisions they would make later in the game. Some of the predictions were the result of careful planning. One came in an intelligence report from an official who wasn't even a member of the crew. And two of the predictions bordered on crystal-ball reading.

Dreith began by saying that he would be standing on the left side behind the offense when Bobby Douglass of Chicago, who is left-handed, was quarterbacking, and on the right side when Roger Staubach of Dallas was quarterbacking.

The new man, Cashion, brought up the play when the quarterback is hit as he passes, and the ball pops loose.

"If the arm is coming forward, it is a forward pass," Dreith said.

Javie broke in. "Don't worry," he said to Cashion. "This guy [Dreith] is the best in the business. You'll know."

Dreith said, "If it's an incomplete pass, I'll call it off right away. If it's a fumble, I won't make a signal [the ball is live]."

O'Brien said both quarterbacks were scramblers, so there would be more pushing and shoving by receivers and defensive backs. Receivers would be fighting to get open while quarterbacks were running around behind the line of scrimmage.

"And when one of those quarterbacks keeps," said Javie, "who's going to take all that wash behind them, all that contact?"

"I've got it," Dreith said. "It's mine."

Dreith went around the room, giving each man a chance to talk about his area of responsibility. Then he turned to Cal LePore, an NFL head linesman (he was line judge of Super Bowl II) enjoying his one

Sunday off during the 1973 season—by joining the Dreith crew as chauffeur. Now he was asked what he knew about the Bears and Cowboys. Among other things, LePore said the Bears occasionally ran from punt formation.

The conversation moved to the ball-slapping incident of Super Bowl VII; a Washington player had flailed at the football as soon as Miami snapper Howard Kindig raised it to center it to punter Larry Seiple.

"You cannot slap the ball or bat it, at any time," Dreith said, "You can reach in and take it away, provided the man is on his feet. But you can't bat it."

The pregame meeting was over. The Dreith crew was ready.

Stan Javie turned his white official's pants inside out, taped the bottoms around his calves, and sat on a bench in front of his locker, elbows on knees, staring straight ahead, without pulling his pants up. He has been in this league since 1951, worked hundreds of games, thrown down thousands of flags, and worn out a dozen whistles. Yet now he was as silent as if he were about to call his first game.

So was Bill O'Brien. The two of them sat without saying a word, brooding, staring, thinking.

Suddenly, Javie erupted. "Smiley," he said to O'Brien, "they wouldn't make any money selling comedy pictures to you."

"Stan," O'Brien said. "If you opened your shirt, your heart would fall out."

The officials' dressing room at Soldier Field is a narrow room under the West stands. There are lockers, a bench, a table, a coffee machine, a hot water heater, and, at the far end, two showers, and a toilet.

Dreith's crew arrived before 11:30 for a one o'clock game. The six men found lockers and began opening their small suitcases, taking out their uniforms and their working paraphernalia: whistles, wrist stopwatches, flags, beanbags, clocks, and elastic straps to go around fingers and keep track of downs.

At 11:40, Dreith and Demmas, still in street clothes, left to check the field. They looked for uneven seams in the artificial surface, insufficiently padded goal posts, and missing end line and goal line flags. They favor artificial surfaces. With it, there are fewer measurements for first downs; yard lines aren't washed away.

They are glad to be starting the regular season; they have worked preseason games when groundskeepers balked—but later relented—at putting down the required six-foot border around the field because it would still be on the grass during the next night's baseball game. Dreith and Demmas recalled a game at Municipal Stadium in Kansas City when a pitcher's mound was still in place and had to be removed. At another city, they were astonished to see a groundskeeper busily taking up end-line flags during the fourth quarter; he explained to them that he had lost his flags to thieves during earlier games. The officials told him to put the flags back.

At 11:45, Dreith and Demmas returned to the dressing room. Dreith told Cashion that the Bears had activated defensive tackle Dave Hale and deactivated running back Roger Lawson. Cashion left to tell the Cowboys.

George Rennix of Northbrook, Illinois, the NFL observer who would make a report to the league on the crew, entered. He had been a referee for 15 years and worked the 1965 title game (Cleveland at Green Bay) with Stan Javie. He was greeted warmly. There was kidding and small talk.

At 11:50, Cashion left for the CBS television truck beneath the stadium, to learn the official time of day, and then report it to each locker room. A Bears' ball boy brought 12 footballs in a large canvas bag to Dreith. The referee punctured each with a gauge to insure that each was properly inflated: 12½ to 13½ pounds.

At noon, Dreith began to dress in his official's uniform. He pulled on two pairs of white sox, then black stockings, and taped them over his calves.

Dan Desmond, public relations director of the Bears, came in to arrange a code. Only Desmond would be allowed to telephone the referee in his dressing room during halftime or after the game for a rules interpretation. To ensure that no imposter attempted to contact Dreith, a code was necessary. Dreith agreed to speak on the phone only when he heard Desmond say "Colorado twelve." That was chosen as the code because Dreith is from Colorado and wears number twelve on the back of his striped shirt.

Cashion returned. He said he had reported the Hale-for-Lawson activation to Cowboys coach Tom Landry. He said Landry made no activations, and that information had been reported to Bears coach Abe Gibron.

At 12:05, Bob Stenner, director of the telecast of the game for CBS, entered. He introduced the network's sideline representative, Paul Arndt, a stage manager at station WBBM-TV in Chicago. They discussed television time outs. Arndt said he would be stationed on "the Bears' north forty-five [yard line]" and would be wearing white gloves to make it possible for Dreith to spot him quickly.

They went over the signals for commer-cials. Arndt said both arms crossed against his chest would mean, "I need a commercial;" one arm dropped to his side and the other remaining against his chest, "the commercial is in progress;" and, the second arm dropped to his side, "the commercial is over."

Stenner said the number of commercials would be the same as in past CBS telecasts: "three-four, three-four," meaning, three commercials in the first quarter, four in the second, or if four in the first, then three in the second, and so on.

At 12:10, Jack Pittges, the Soldier Field timer, entered with a .22 caliber pistol and blank cartridges for Cashion. The pistol would be fired to end each quarter and the game. Line judges used to carry them on airplanes, but that ended with hijackings and the new, strict security measures.

At 12:25, the door opened again. "Red Cashion!" a voice said. "I oughta say 'Mason Cashion' instead."

It was John Mulhearn, the stadium announcer.

Mulhearn's comment about whether to introduce Cashion as "Red" or "Mason" had relieved the doubts anyone in the room might have had about his official status. But then he asked for "Mr. *Dreeth,*" mispronouncing the name of the leader of the crew.

Dreith identified himself. They discussed penalty signals. Mulhearn said he would announce from the east side of the field, at ground level. Dreith said he always gave signals to the main pressbox atop the stadium, on the west side. The announcer said there would be no problem, he would be able to get the signals anyway.

At 12:27, the crew emerged from the dressing room. Soldier Field was alive with noisy activity. CBS announcer Pete Retzlaff greeted the crew. They chatted for a moment. Demmas left to check equipment, one of his first duties as umpire.

Dreith assembled the captains—Glen Holloway, Carl Garrett, Dick Butkus, and Doug Buffone of Chicago, and Staubach, Rayfield Wright, Lee Roy Jordan, and Cornell Green of Dallas. They stood together at midfield. Ben introduced his crew, then tossed the coin. Chicago won the flip and elected to receive.

At 12:40, Glover gave instructions to the chain crew and ball boys. Dreith chatted with the head coaches. He spotted Rudy Custer, the Bears' business manager, on the sideline and told him benches too near one of the end zones had to be moved. Custer said he would get it done right away.

At 12:50, the crew returned to the dressing room. Dreith went over last minute details.

"Gibron complained about Dallas cracking back," he told them. "He said his players are going to turn away from the block [to draw a clipping call]. I told Landry, and he said, 'Fine. If they turn, we won't even block them.'"

Dreith began a pep talk. "Be aware of what is going on out there today. We are going to work every game like it's the Super Bowl. I want you to hustle all the time. And don't say anything; don't talk back to anyone. If someone hollers, let him."

The sideline press box representatives, Art Robbins and Jim Custer, arrived. They wore bright vests so they could be seen in the crowd. Dreith assured them that he would report all numbers of players committing major penalties to them, so the information could be telephoned to the press box. The officials returned to the field.

At 1:05, the coin toss was reenacted for television. The starting teams were introduced. The National Anthem was played. The officials' names were announced. Mulhearn pronounced "Dry-th" correctly. It was game time.

Two elements of the crew's preparation paid off before two minutes had been played. On fourth down, the Bears ran from punt formation, as Cal LePore had said they would, and succeeded with the maneuver, making a first down. Running back Carl Garrett fumbled on the next play, however, giving the ball to Dallas. Staubach brought his arm forward on his first pass of the game, only to have it blocked, the ball falling to the ground. Dreith immediately called it an incomplete pass. It was the play that had concerned Cashion.

Dallas couldn't move and punted. Chicago's punt returner was downed and the ball was whistled dead. Dreith looked across the field to Arndt and, seeing the technician's arms crossed against his chest, signaled an official's time out—arms straight out to the sides, hands in fists. For 60 seconds, Dreith stood transfixed, staring at Arndt. When the second white-gloved hand of the technician finally dropped, Dreith looked away, put the football down, blew his whistle and said, "Okay, men, let's go."

This crew was methodical. Umpire Demmas unfolded the pileups, peeling away bodies to get to the football, while Dreith ran to the spot or to the hashmark and Glover and Cashion spotted the ball. A dry football came in from the sideline and Glover or Cashion relayed it to Dreith. He put it in place, bellowed out "second down," reached up in the air as if he were grabbing for a light switch, and pulled. Glover and Cashion mirrored Dreith's light-switch pull and Glover repeated his call of "second down" and Glover waved

the boxman of the chain crew to his new station—the forward point of the football.

Far downfield, field judge O'Brien watched Dreith reaching for the light switch. When Ben's arm fell, O'Brien started the stopwatch on his wrist. The offense now had 30 seconds to call its play and snap the football; if they exceeded it, O'Brien would call delay of the game.

The earlier banter between O'Brien and Javie was forgotten. Now, they were all business. Javie, for example, could put himself in position for any play, pass or run, by movement of 10 or 15 yards up and down the sideline. His long years of experience were evident; in the language of officials, he has great "mechanics."

Two green beanbags hung from O'Brien's belt, one more than the other officials carry because he is more likely to have two possession changes to mark; a punt might be fielded at one point, then fumbled at another.

He has lost beanbags on NFL fields, so he wraps a thin strip of white tape around them. Once, the bags were all white, but they confused fans, who saw them flying and thought they were penalty flags. So the league changed to green beanbags.

O'Brien's equipment differs from that of the other officials in another way. He is one of the few who wears his whistle on a metal clasp around his fingers. "I have to bring it up to my mouth to blow it," he explained. "That way I know I won't have an early whistle."

It is a luxury that referee Dreith cannot afford. He carries his whistle in his mouth; any motion bringing his arm up to his lips might be misinterpreted in the pressbox as a signal. Every move an NFL official makes during a game is scrutinized by someone.

The Bears and Cowboys swapped field goals before two Staubach touchdown passes to Otto Stowe and Bob Hayes made it 17-3 Dallas at halftime.

In the dressing room, Dreith spoke to his crew. "We've talked about a lot of things," he said, "but now we're down to the nitty-gritty. That's all I've got to say. Let's just get a little more sharp."

They sat quietly, sipping coffee and munching hot dogs and fried chicken brought by the guard-attendant.

When it was time to return to the field, Dreith finished his coffee and pulled on his white cap. "Okay, men," he said, "this is going to be tougher."

On Dallas's first possession of the second half, left tackle Ralph Neely forgot the snap count, came up from his stance, and set up in pass protection. The rest of the Cowboys' line was still in three-point stances. Demmas threw a flag as soon as it happened. Illegal motion at snap, five

yards. Neely retreated to the huddle talking to himself.

In his place just behind the defensive line, Demmas looked like a beagle, hunched-over and intent. On pass plays, he executed a whirling motion, watching the scrimmage action until the ball flew overhead, then turning on his heels to hone in on the receiver.

"On a low pass," he told me later, "a receiver might hook in front of Stan or Bill and they couldn't see the catch. I can."

Eight plays into the second half, Dreith made the call of the game. Dallas's Jethro Pugh, rushing Douglass, slapped the football out of the quarterback's hands. Dreith was standing no more than two yards away. He threw a flag. Fifteen yards for "unsportsmanlike conduct."

"Ben, what about it?" receiver Bob Hayes asked when Dallas's offense returned to the field a few moments later.

"Bob, you can't bat the ball, at any time," Ben said patiently, and that was the end of the discussion.

The pregame meeting had paid off again.

Chicago tied the score 17-17 on a 15-yard run by Garrett and a 59-yard punt return by Ike Hill. With four minutes left in the game, the Bears again ran from punt formation on fourth down. This time, however, they came up short by two yards. Dallas took over and Toni Fritsch kicked a 10-yard field goal to win the game 20-17.

"A helluva call on that slap, Ben," observer George Rennix said as he entered the officials' room after the game.

"Yes, a very good call," Javie agreed.

"What airport are we flying into next week, National or Dulles?" someone else said. (The crew's assignment for the next week was the New York Jets at Baltimore.)

"Dulles," someone answered.

Each man's penalty cards were handed in to Dreith. He would transfer them to the game report and mail it to McNally. A CBS official came in to say goodbye. Everybody left $2 apiece for the attendant. Pittges, the timer, walked in to reclaim the pistol from Cashion. "You guys really worked a nice game," he said. "Real fine."

Heavy traffic engulfed O'Hare International Airport as Cal LePore's 1967 Cadillac approached, bearing members of the Dreith crew to their airplanes. They neared the "Arriving Flights" and "Departing Flights" juncture.

"Cal, take the left," someone said. "It's quicker."

"No," Dreith said. "Go right."

They argued for a moment. Then LePore said, "Ben made the call." He turned the car to the right.

The Defensive Tackles

by Ray Didinger

There was a time—once upon a leather helmet—when no one noticed the defensive tackles in professional football. No one, that is, except the offensive guards who had to notice them as a matter of self-preservation.

The defensive tackles were obscure masses, buried deep in the push-and-shove, gouge-and-claw mayhem of The Pit. The fans cheered the quarterbacks and the runners and the graceful receivers who made the spectacular plays anyone could appreciate. The bloody struggle for supremacy at the line of scrimmage went largely unnoticed. Only the players and coaches recognized the enormous contribution of the defensive tackles.

However, the twentieth century finally has caught up with the big men of pro football. The increased interest in the game and the superior technology of televised football has shifted a long-deserved spotlight on athletes like Joe Greene, Manny Fernandez, and Mike Reid.

These three represent a new generation of defensive tackles. They are at last sharing in the public acclaim once reserved for the Jim Browns, Joe Namaths, and Raymond Berrys. When Joe Greene tramples his way through a double-team block and wraps his massive hands around the windpipe of a $250,000 quarterback, the fans at home are now shown the process step-by-step. A color commentator points out things like the quickness of Greene's feet, the fast, sure use of his hands, and the technique of leaning in one direction and veering the other to shed his blocker.

"We're not doing anything tackles twenty years ago didn't do," said Reid, the brilliant 26-year-old Cincinnati Bengal, "people just notice us more now, that's all."

Reid, Miami's Super Bowl hero Manny Fernandez, and Pittsburgh's Joe Greene discussed today's pro game and their role in it.

First of all, would you each discuss the qualifications—mental and physical—required to be a defensive tackle in the NFL today?

Greene: "I'd say size is number one. I suppose someone two-thirty-five or two-forty could play the position but they would have to be exceptionally quick or make up for their lack of bulk in another way.

"You might be hurting yourself when you get as big as I am [6-4, 275 pounds], too. I say that but I don't do anything about it [losing weight]. I've tried to get lighter but I feel like I'm hurting myself."

Reid: "It's easy for you to say size, Joe, because you don't have that problem. Manny and I, though, are right at the borderline [Reid is 6-3, 250; Fernandez 6-2, 240]. I'd say the most important thing to me is quickness off the ball. The ability to get the first step across the line and be the one initiating the contact is very valuable. More valuable, I'd say, than sheer bulk."

Fernandez: "I hate to put one thing ahead of another. I'd say there are four qualities a defensive tackle needs. One would be strength, another would be quickness, a third is determination, and fourth is size. I'm not necessarily listing

Mike Reid
Joe Greene
Manny Fernandez

them in any order. I would minimize the size since that's the one area where I'm most lacking.''

If you had to put more emphasis on one over another, what would it be?

Fernandez: "Size is necessary—I agree with Joe, nobody under two-forty could stand up under the pounding week after week. But I'd make strength and quickness my top two. I'd say those are my two best areas and I've been able to get by pretty well.''

Greene: "I agree with you guys about quickness. I think it's essential for a defensive tackle to be quick. Quicker than the guard blocking him, that's for sure. If he gets the jump on you, you'll have a heckuva time getting past him, especially on the pass rush. But I think you have to make a distinction between quickness and speed.''

Reid: ''Right.''

Greene: ''These guys know what I mean. Lateral pursuit—in other words speed from sideline to sideline—is important and all the great tackles have it, but the distance a tackle has to be concerned with is those ten yards from the line of scrimmage to the pocket where the quarterback is setting up. Now, moving those ten yards is a matter of quickness, not speed. And quickness is determined in the first two steps a man takes. That's where you say a dude is quick or he isn't quick. Those first two steps make the difference between great tackles and so-so tackles. The first step is the one where you get off the ball like a coiled-up cat—and the second step is your counter-move. If the guard is hitting you, which he will be ninety percent of the time, that second step is a counter-move. In other words, it's your reaction. You have to know where to go with that second step to get rid of the blocker and make your play.''

Reid: ''The whole thing boils down to a matter of physics. You can figure it out by the equation, force equals mass times acceleration. Therefore, the force with which I rush is that much greater the faster I can get my two-hundred-fifty pound mass into motion. I have to put my maximum force against my man and stymie his charge. I have to take for granted one thing—let's say there is an eighteen-inch space between the offensive guard and the defensive tackle when they line up over the ball. If I can assume I'll travel twelve inches to his six inches once the ball is snapped, my force will be greater than his and I should control him rather than vice-versa. It's a basic law of physics but it's a brutal truth on the football field. If a man has nothing but pure bulk, he will be beaten constantly by smaller, faster blockers.''

Fernandez: "You need a certain amount of bulk, though. Your quickness can get you there first but if you don't have the leg drive to sustain it, you wind up going backwards.''

You're talking about being purely outmuscled. Has it ever happened to you?

Fernandez: ''You bet it has. The third preseason game of my rookie year, I was playing defensive end against the Philadelphia Eagles. That put me smack across the line from Bob Brown. That was like climbing the side of a battleship.''

Is there anyway to offset his strength?

Fernandez: ''If there is, I didn't find it. He just came off the ball and buried me. I tried everything I knew but nothing worked. When he comes at you, he blocks out the whole horizon. And, remember, I was only a rookie, too. One thing saved me. It was a preseason game at the Orange Bowl and I was in better shape than Bob was at the time. The heat got to him and he only played little over a half. But, by the time he left the game, I was so beat up I wasn't worth a damn either.''

Do you think the men who played defensive tackle twenty years ago could have handled today's faster, more wide-open game?

Greene: ''I like to think the really good ones could. Looking at it the other way, I like to think I could have played their game, too. I wouldn't like to play the three-yards-and-a-cloud-of-dust game as a regular diet, but once in a while—like in a goal line stand—I kind of enjoy it. It's really a man-to-man, hand-to-hand battle. None of that fooling around with traps and draws. Just me and the guy across from me, trying to blow each other out of there.''

Reid: ''The answer, of course, is pure conjecture. The obvious tendency is to say the men who played tackle twenty years ago were a bunch of behemoths with little or no mobility. But I'm reluctant to say that. A statement like that tends to negate a man's competitive spirit and that's a very powerful factor. If a man was truly a great player twenty years ago, I believe he could be a great player today. I'd hate to think the game has changed that much. If it has, perhaps the game is wrong.''

You mean if a great defensive tackle of the 1940s needed today's speed, he would find some way to develop it?

Reid: ''Exactly. Either that or he would find another way of contributing to a team utilizing the skills he does possess. Nobody is ever going to convince me, for example, that Big Daddy Lipscomb or Ernie Stautner couldn't play today. That's nonsense. I'll grant you that today's game is faster—the backs are faster, and, by necessity, the defensive linemen must be faster, too. But the skills that made one era of players great are still enough to make the same player great today.''

Fernandez: ''Mike's right. The basic skills haven't changed that much. The lineman today has to be quicker than ever, mostly for the pass rush. The emphasis on the passing game now requires that a defensive tackle be able to catch a scrambling quarterback like Fran Tarkenton or Greg Landry or Roger Staubach. You can look pretty foolish plodding along after those quick, nifty guys.

''I'd like to add something to what Joe said, too. The goal line stands today aren't even what they used to be. At least, in Miami they're not. Now we (the Dolphins' defensive linemen) are taught to bury ourselves, just go as far under the offensive line as we can on a goal line series. We try to stack up the blockers and let our linebackers and safeties come over the top and push the runner back.''

How's it working out? Do you have any problems?

Fernandez: ''Heck, no. I'm so short it's easy for me to slide under people. It's like they thought this up just for me.''

Greene: ''It's pretty hard to argue with the record, right?''

Reid: ''Yeah, who can top seventeen-and-oh and two Super Bowl victories?''

Greene: ''You know, Manny brought out a good point about size. I think it's possible for a guy to be too tall to play inside [defensive tackle]. A tall guy is conscious of keeping blockers away from his knees. You know that your legs are a bigger and more inviting target when you're six-five or six-six than when you're six-one or six-two. And if you spend your time bent over swatting the guys away from your legs, it's like playing on crutches 'cause you're always hunched over.''

Fernandez: ''Joe, you're tall enough that you can draw those conclusions. I don't know. I can see what you're saying but I think it all depends on the individual. If a guy is gonna be 'knee-conscious,' that's one thing. But look at guys like Buck Buchanan [6-7 Kansas City tackle] and Bob Lilly [6-5 Dallas tackle]. They are two of the greatest, right? They don't have much trouble. I guess it's an individual thing. If you're gonna be gun-shy you'll be gun-shy no matter how big you are.''

This talk about being knee-conscious leads to another point. Is there much ''dirty play'' in the NFL? In the middle of the line, it would be an easy thing to hide.

Greene: "Yeah, except somebody would remind you fast."

Reid: "That's right. I think we all know that if we pull something dirty, it's so easy for the other team to retaliate. Brutally, if they want to. If somebody intends to retaliate at you, the thing that makes it so lethal is you don't know when it's coming."

Fernandez: "I've found very little dirty play in pro ball. I've found a lot of vicious play and hard-hitting but, hell, that's the nature of the game. If a guy doesn't like that, he'd better get out. Much of what might appear to be dirty play from the stands is actually unavoidable. It's a contact sport and maybe I'll hit some guy when he's off-balance or halfway down. To some fans, that looks vicious but I'm just doing my job. I understand that and if you could ask the guy I'm hitting, he'd back me up. You know, I've never been charged with hitting a quarterback late. Never. I'm kinda proud of that but there are some guys who might think it's a strike against me."

How so?

Fernandez: "There are some guys around the league who think that it's good to rough a quarterback up occasionally just to keep him honest. I don't buy that. I've averted I don't know how many late shots on the passer by veering off or diving into the ground instead of hitting the guy when I see he has already thrown the ball. To me, it's smart football anytime you can avoid a fifteen-yard penalty. Hell, how do I know what's happening downfield? My late shot at the quarterback might nullify an interception. I'd really look like a jerk then. Besides, I think most of these quarterbacks are immune to the late shots. Namath gets hit late as much, if not more, than anybody but they'll step off the fifteen yards and Joe'll throw a touchdown pass on the next play just to stick it to you."

Reid: "It's a matter of conscience to me. The rusher has all the advantage. He's coming full-speed drawing a bead on the quarterback. The quarterback is just sitting there, off-balance after throwing the ball. It's not an equal situation. It would be too easy to hurt a man that way. Besides, like Manny said, any quarterback who has any guts will just get madder after a late shot and he'll become more determined to beat you. Any quarterback who's made it this far isn't going to be intimidated."

Greene: "There's a lot being said out on the field during a game. One player often winds up calling another player 'cheap shot' from time to time. Larry Brown [the Redskins' running back] talks about taking cheap shots but what he means to say is 'illegal shots.' In my mind, there's no such thing as a 'cheap' shot. What Larry is talk-

ing about are late hits [after the whistle] and hits that he takes out of bounds. Now those, I'll admit, are illegal and if a ref sees one, he should throw the flag. But if a guy can put a hurt on a back like Larry Brown, it's anything but a 'cheap' shot. That kind of shot can turn a whole ball game around."

Fernandez: "Frequently, in the turmoil of a game, a guy can get all keyed up and take shots like that. He might not mean it but this is a contact sport and sometimes the difference between right and wrong becomes a little distorted. I think the one thing that keeps us all under control is the knowledge that the guy I am playing against is simply earning a living on the field the same as I am. There is an unspoken mutual respect that exists. It's like, 'I don't want you chopping at my knees so I won't go chopping at yours.'"

We've thrown some pretty heavy vocabulary around here and it's got me thinking. Do you guys feel the public has stopped viewing football players–and defensive linemen in particular–as a pack of big, dumb lugs?

Greene: "I hope so because I'm getting pretty paranoid about it. I'm always having people look at my size and say, 'Hey, you must play football.' It bugs me. I'll say, 'Why do I have to play football? Can't I be a doctor or a lawyer or a writer? Just because I'm big, why do I have to be a football player? Sometimes when I'm in a bad mood, I'll catch people looking at me and I'll feel like saying, 'What are you staring at? This isn't some freak show.' I don't think a dumb man can survive in pro football today, the game is too complex, there is too much to learn. After a game, I'm physically beat but the worst drain I feel is from the mental pressure. That big, dumb football player bit might have been true a long time ago but it doesn't apply now. In fact, I'd like to see the people who think we're so dumb try to learn what we have to learn."

Reid: "We have to live with this giant credibility gap. Within that gap there is this belief that we all fell out of trees and at some point in our lives someone put shoulder pads on us and led us to a football field. There, for the first time, we began to contribute to society in a constructive way. Very seldom am I recognized as homo sapiens. Almost everyone relates to me as a football player—some big, hulking mass in pads."

Are people legitimately surprised when you play the piano?

Reid: "Yes, quite surprised. And they tend to be condescending. If I do a recital that is not up to what I consider my usual standards, they'll still give me this tre-

mendous hand which, to me, says, 'How nice that a football player can play the piano.' I don't go for that. I want to be received critically on the basis of my performance, just like any other concert performer. Size has nothing to do with a man's emotional content. The biggest of men have fallen to their knees and wept. You know what I enjoyed most about my first Pro Bowl game? It was meeting Joe Greene. Until then, he was just the eternal enemy but once I got to know him, I found out what a deep, sensitive, kind person he is. But how does the American public at-large know him? Mean Joe Greene, right? *Mean Joe Greene*—it sounds like some kind of movie monster. This guy is anything but mean but he's stuck with the name anyhow. It's unfair."

Are you bothered by people who stare at you because of your size?

Reid: "It depends on my mood. I'll generally be most evasive on a plane flight. People will say to me, 'Are you a football player?' If I want a peaceful flight where I can relax, I'll tell them 'No.' I've assumed roles plenty of times. I've been everything from a plumber to a man who operates a lumber yard just to discourage conversation. Not that I'm a hostile person, understand, but there are times when I just can't stand hearing the same old questions."

Like what?

Reid: "Well, the favorite one is, 'How are the Bengals going to do this year?' A guy asked me that on the street once and I said, 'I'm glad you asked me that question. I have just finished making a complete study of the situation, taking into consideration our won-lost record of the past three years, the won-lost records of our opponents, the number of artificial as opposed to grass surfaces on which we will play, the combined won-lost records of the various head coaches we will be facing and the projected weather forecast for each of the weekends on which we have games and I have come to one inescapable conclusion—we will not win a single game.' The guy was so stunned, he couldn't think of another word. He walked away and I guess he must be thinking now, 'What a fool that guy Reid is,' but it was one put-on that I just couldn't resist. I always wanted to do it but I never got around to it until then. I don't know but I might have cost the Bengals a season ticket holder."

by Floyd Little, with Dick Connor

A Day in the Life of Floyd Little

In 1966, when I was playing at Syracuse and they came out with those annual evaluations of runners for the pros, they said I could never make it. It was in *Sports Illustrated* and all the magazines and there was a writeup in the Buffalo newspaper. I was up there for the Hickok dinner in Rochester and Frank Robinson got the award that year. I can remember it verbatim. Some newspaper people interviewed me and one guy was really something. I almost decked him.

"You're just a little guy, aren't you?" he said.

I told him, "Well, my heart is the same size as a guy three-hundred pounds. That's all that counts."

But he wouldn't quit. "You can't play pro ball," he said. I told him that remained to be seen. When his story came out, it was to the effect I was too small, I couldn't make it in pro ball, I wasn't big enough, I didn't look as though I was strong enough, that kind of thing.

That's why every time I put on a uniform, I try to show that guy. And everybody else that didn't think I could make it. I'm only five-ten and about one-ninety-five—I think I'd be six-two if my legs were straighter —but what that guy said in the paper that time is one of the reasons I'm intense about everything I do.

I even dream about it. I don't sleep too well before a game. I'll watch television until midnight or so when I'll finally doze off. I'll dream. In the early years, when I was on punt and kickoff return teams, I always dreamed of taking it back all the way. That's inevitable for any returner if he has his mind on the game. But in 1971 I wasn't on those teams. So now I dream of getting the ball on the twenty after they've kicked it into the end zone. And now I dream of going eighty yards on the first play.

And the next morning, well...that's where it's all at for me.

The Locker Room

It's very, very quiet in the locker room before a game. You can hear that tape being ripped off by the trainer and a few low voices. It's not like during the week before practice with people talking and joking.

I had a slight shoulder separation in 1971 and we had to tape on a protective shell to help reduce blows on it. For the most part, after we get taped and suited up, we just sit in our stalls and look at the floor and try to concentrate on what we're going to have to do.

After that, like the other guys, I try to think about what I am going to do. I'm a running back, so I think in terms of running plays. For instance I feel I have to run a play three or more times before I can make it work right. The first two times I might get creamed. But I'm learning each time how they are defensing it. The fourth time I run, I'm going to make some yards.

So you think of these things. Then, after we've had a little prayer, there's usually still some time, and I'll go around and wish my teammates luck and relax those guys who need it. Sometimes it's my teammates who relax me. Like Roger Shoals, a special friend. Roger retired after the 1972 season. He was a real pro for nine seasons.

Fred Kaplan

Just before we go out, I say a little prayer to myself that nobody on either team is seriously hurt during the game. I've missed parts of three seasons due to injuries and the thought that this could be your last game is always there.

I guess I don't have the problems some other players do. In fact, mine is just the opposite—for the most part, people don't recognize me. Even a lot of people from Denver. It's because of my size.

They're looking for a guy six-two, two-hundred-fifteen pounds, something like that. That's the size a pro running back is supposed to be. That's what they think Floyd Little is. I've walked right by a lot of people who were waiting for me. But they looked past me—that was just another little guy who went by them. It was the same in college at Syracuse. There would be people waiting and I'd walk right past them and they wouldn't know.

I don't mind the attention from fans when it comes. I think it is an honor to have somebody ask for your signature. That's true in any business, and especially this one we're in. It's part of your duty…and you should enjoy it. You should be willing to give your signature. It doesn't last too long.

The Pregame

The coin flip is kind of a special time because it gives you a chance to say hello to old friends. We were playing the Oakland Raiders this day and I guess I don't have to tell you about Jim Otto, the Raiders' center. I'm glad he's on offense. He's tough.

This was the final game of the season for both of us and it's hard to describe the feelings that were there. Neither one of us was going to be in the playoffs and we both wanted to win…but that feeling you have in a championship game wasn't there.

The Game

I played this game pretty much the way I play all games—instinctively. It's like in golf, when you're playing you really can't be thinking of every step, every physical action, or you'll blow the shot. It's the same in football. What you do in a game has to come from all the times you've worked, practiced, and drilled.

Oakland likes to play an uneven defense against us, shut off any action to our right, cut it off, and turn it up inside where their safety makes the tackle. But we feel there isn't anybody we can't run on.

We have run on everybody. They expect it and play a thirteen-man line but we go after them anyhow and we did against Oakland. They won twenty-one to thirteen,

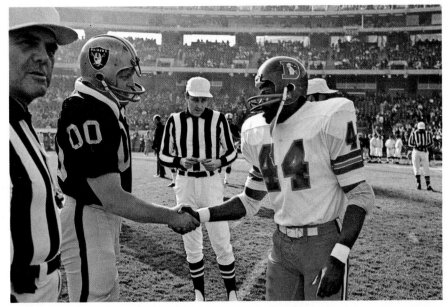

even though we had thirty-three more plays than they did. It was that kind of game. We obviously had our chances.

Afterwards

When you have a good day in a winning cause, it's ecstasy. A good day in a losing cause is all washed out, and leaves you feeling that way, too. We lost at Oakland and that was really all I was concerned about. I could have had twelve touchdowns and all kinds of records. But we 'lost.

You walk off after a game like that, and you spend a few minutes maybe talking quietly to guys you've played against so hard for three hours—like Clarence Davis—and you feel good about that.

And it's always nice to get a kind word from the fans.

I found out right after that that I had gotten seventy-nine yards in the game, which was enough to give me one-thousand one-hundred thirty-three for the year and the NFL rushing title. I didn't know I had won the title until a television man told me afterward in an interview.

But you're so tired, and go in and get in that hot shower and suddenly, hey, what's this? The water stings and you feel a hip and find out you've had a whole big piece of skin stripped away and didn't even know it. You might feel a bump at the time, but you're so intense during the game you don't realize it unless it's a major injury.

We normally don't keep our door closed too long after the end of a game, and then the press comes in for interviews while we dress. It's hard sometimes, especially when you've lost, to go over it again in answering questions.

I thought 1972 was my best as a pro. I played with a bad shoulder and led the league in rushing yards for the second straight year. But at the same time, with all those good things that happened to me, I wished that the team could somehow have shared them with me. They were responsible. I left that final afternoon wishing we could have had a better year. This individual thing is great, but I want so badly to be on a winning team—to play on one. And they do, too.

I'll tell you, this game doesn't owe me anything. This game has been tremendous to me. I've got a lot of respect for it. I love the game and enjoy everything associated with football. And when it's over, when I don't feel I'm contributing anymore, it's not going to be with a feeling of relief that I'll leave it.

I'm just happy to have been part of it for all this time.

by Bob Oates, Sr.

What's So Special About Special Teams?

A Yale football coach of several years ago, the late Herman Hickman, is reputed to have been the inventor of the contrivance known in the National Football League as "special teams."

During his biggest season at Yale, Hickman was asked one day to explain his success.

"In modern football," he said, "you can't win with iron men any more. I have three special teams—one for offense, one for defense, and one to hit the books."

In its NFL manifestation, the spirit is the same but the interpretation is different. There are now nine distinctive, uncommon, specific, and unique special teams on a pro football club. They punt and return punts, kick off and return kickoffs, attempt placekicks, and attempt to block placekicks.

Thirty or more of the 40 athletes on an NFL squad are involved these days in the tug o' war of the kicking game, which in the opinion of the coaches who emphasize it the most—such people as George Allen, Don Shula, Hank Stram, and others—is one-third of football. The amount of time devoted to preparation reflects this.

They all agree with Hickman that offense and defense are the other two-thirds.

Some special team performers achieve great fame. The Oakland and Miami kickers, George Blanda and Garo Yepremian, will never be forgotten, no doubt, although a partial explanation for their prominence is that both have also been known to throw the ball.

Those who kick it and return it are, nonetheless, the only special team members whose names and faces are generally recognized in the sports community. Offensively you can get famous running, catching, or throwing footballs; and on every NFL defensive platoon household names rush the passer and play linebacker or cornerback. The uniqueness of an assignment to the special teams is that it is a ticket to obscurity.

Those who do most of the work in the department considered one-third of the game are perhaps the most anonymous athletes in sports today. Does anybody in the audience know Rich Saul? Mickey Zofko? Charlie Crist? Ray Hester?

Consider what Hester did in 1972. He was in on one-half of all the tackles made by New Orleans's kicking teams—despite the fact there were always 10 other tacklers going down the field with him.

Saul's contribution in Los Angeles, Zofko's in Detroit, and Crist's for the Giants have been similar.

Their importance—and also their obscurity—are an accepted fact of life on the special teams of pro football. It has always been so, ever since the NFL began stressing the kicking game.

That wasn't long ago. Shula, coach of the Miami Dolphins, was among the first to take an interest in the third platoon as something more than an aspect of the game that had to be put up with—and Shula has only been coaching little more than a decade.

When he was in Baltimore, Shula appointed the NFL's first special team captain, Alex Hawkins. The importance and obscurity of his status are summed up in the

nickname given Hawkins: "Captain Who?."

Paul Brown, of course, had preceded Shula in scientifically organizing special teams. Brown, then in Cleveland, now in Cincinnati, has been the inventor of much that is scientific in football.

Although Clark Shaughnessy is responsible for most of the philosophy and also the style of both offense and defense as now played, Brown is the coach who organized and systematized Shaughnessy's theories—much as Einstein's formulae were systematized in laboratories under the University of Chicago's football stadium in the 1940s.

Brown, strangely, has not always been widely known for his interest in the sensibilities of his players. This is Shula's long suit. It is not an accident that Shula had the first special team captain. He is a coach who thinks largely in terms of morale and motivation.

In those years Baltimore's kicking units won more than one important game.

Washington's Allen, another big winner during the past few seasons, carried Shula's thought one step further. Allen was the first coach to hire an assistant to coach the special teams exclusively, with no other assignments.

This was Dick Vermeil, who left Allen in 1970 but returned to the special teams in 1973 under Chuck Knox in Los Angeles before taking the head job at UCLA. Knox's dispositions differ from Allen's in that Vermeil had two assignments, kicking and the offensive backfield.

Some coaches (including Shula and

164

Brown) still divide up the special teams among their assistants. It is done many ways in the NFL.

Vermeil's way (as originally outlined by Allen) remains the model on which the kicking game is now structured in pro football. Nobody else does it exactly his way, but because he was the first, his is the standard, the starting point.

In Vermeil's system in Los Angeles, special team players were graded in four areas (assignment, technique, effort, and block or tackle).

On the kickoff-return team, for example, the blocker assigned to L1 receives one point if he gets him and no assignment points if he blocks L2. But if he knocks L2 down, he can still get one point for effort and one to three points for a good block. For special team performance above and beyond the call of duty, Vermeil has an RBI category worth five points.

The maximum is 11 points (one each for assignment, technique, and effort, three for making the block or tackle, and five for an

skilled, aggressive, and reliable tacklers.

The ideal athlete for a punt-and-cover position is a linebacker. Linebackers are the surest tacklers on most teams. Speed is also a linebacking requirement. Most NFL punting teams include as many linebackers (including regulars) as the coach in charge can persuade the head coach to give him. Defensive backs who like to tackle also find themselves on punt-and-cover teams as a rule.

The only backfield blocker on a punting team, known as the fullback, is a "safetyman," who is supposed to pick up any opponent who breaks through the line. Occasionally two or more break through. Thus the fullback's most critical job is to block the right man—the player most likely to get in the way of the punt.

For this reason, NFL teams don't deploy their meanest or most aggressive people at fullback on the punting team. They put their most reliable big man there, one who won't panic against a determined rushman and one who will instinctively hit the right

can try to block the punt, or it can try to give it a long ride back.

There usually isn't much difference in the personnel between punt-return and punt-blocking teams. With a drastic change in personnel, the receiving team would be tipping its intentions. But if possible, special team coaches insert a specialist or two if they hope to block the punt. If they intend to run it back, they may add a specialist or two of another kind (those with an aptitude for open-field blocking).

Specialists who return punts are also chosen for their open-field or broken-field prowess. Punt running is something like running sweeps from scrimmage, and so punt runners are usually the best running backs on the squad—provided they have the hands to catch a ball falling from a height.

3. Blocking a punt

The deployment of the players differs slightly if the objective is to block the kick. The most common technique is the

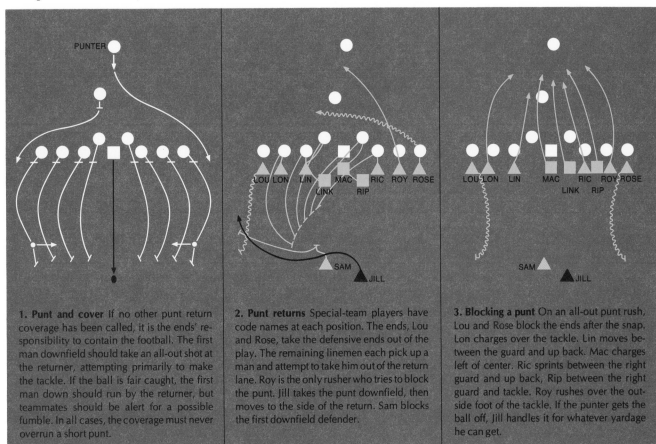

1. Punt and cover If no other punt return coverage has been called, it is the ends' responsibility to contain the football. The first man downfield should take an all-out shot at the returner, attempting primarily to make the tackle. If the ball is fair caught, the first man down should run by the returner, but teammates should be alert for a possible fumble. In all cases, the coverage must never overrun a short punt.

2. Punt returns Special-team players have code names at each position. The ends, Lou and Rose, take the defensive ends out of the play. The remaining linemen each pick up a man and attempt to take him out of the return lane. Roy is the only rusher who tries to block the punt. Jill takes the punt downfield, then moves to the side of the return. Sam blocks the first downfield defender.

3. Blocking a punt On an all-out punt rush, Lou and Rose block the ends after the snap. Lon charges over the tackle. Lin moves between the guard and up back. Mac charges left of center. Ric sprints between the right guard and up back; Rip between the right guard and tackle. Roy rushes over the outside foot of the tackle. If the punter gets the ball off, Jill handles it for whatever yardage he can get.

RBI performance). A player with a sprinkling of 11s on his report card is apt to wake up with a raise next year.

1. Punt and cover

Except for the punter and the fullback, these are principally defensive players. The chief function of a punting team is to tackle the safetyman who catches the ball; hence the object is to load the coverage lineup with

enemy if two or more opponents are drawing a bead on the punter.

The man who kicks the ball is chosen first for his ability to get it high, second for his ability to hit it far, third for his ability to kick it fast.

2. Punt returns

When the other team is in punt formation, the receiving team has two choices. It

"overload"—massing more players than expected against one part of the line. In an effort to get the punter, all 10 available members of the team (all except the safetyman) are sometimes assigned to the rush.

Punting teams correctly guessing a rush sometimes counteract with surprise plays: passes or runs.

Punt blocking is a science requiring split-second timing. If a personnel change is advisable, the most common substitution is in the middle. The club's toughest man may be sent in to terrorize the center—who can't be bothered by anybody he sees regularly but may panic temporarily if he suddenly sees Deacon Jones on his nose.

During his Rams career Jones was frequently used in situations when Allen felt a greater compulsion than usual to block a punt.

4. Kickoffs and coverage

The most aggressive players are lined up on this team. It is the most spectacular of the kicking teams, attracting athletes with the spirit to race downfield and attack recklessly. The other requirements—mobility and speed—rank far behind natural aggressiveness.

Members of the kickoff team are assigned special positions to the left or right of the kicker (L1, 2, 3, 4, 5 and R1, 2, 3, 4, 5) based on two criteria. Those with the most aggressiveness line up closest to the ball shading out to those with most speed.

Aggressiveness is needed in the middle to pound the wedge; outside speed is needed to run around it.

Some teams occasionally "offset" or position the kicker near the sideline—perhaps one-third or one-fourth of the way in instead of one-half. The purpose here is to restrict the options of the receiving team to go both left and right as well as down the middle.

5. Onside kickoffs

The objective is to recover the ball instead of kick it away. Thus the demand is for the quickest athletes on the squad as well as those with the best hands.

These changes are often made in the L4 or L5 positions (or R4 or R5), depending on which way the ball is to be kicked. Sometimes, however, they are not made; to avoid tipping the other team, the coach may decide to retain most of his regular kickoff personnel.

Such decisions are not arrived at easily. The players with the best hands are obviously the starting receivers—who are not typically assigned to the kickoff team. The question is whether to give yourself the best chance to recover the ball or whether to make a mystery of your intentions to kick it away or onside left or onside right.

6. Recovering onside kickoffs

The same doubts are felt here in onside kickoff situations. But the shrewdest coaches tend to play it safe. They assume an onside kick is coming; therefore, they deploy their best hands (receivers and defensive backs) up near the ball.

If the other side kicks away, they breathe a sigh of relief and accept the ball anywhere they can get it, reasoning that possession is nine-tenths of football.

7. Kickoff returns

In kickoff returning there are three components on an NFL field—two runners in the area of the goal post, preceded by a four-man wedge (in the neighborhood of the 20-yard line) preceded by five other blockers (widely spaced out in the area between the wedge and midfield). Most personnel is from the offensive platoon, skilled in blocking.

The "wedge" normally includes a fullback (to catch short punts) and the three biggest men on the squad, who have a knack for open-field blocking. It isn't easy. Charlie Cowan, an offensive tackle for the Rams who has run with the kickoff wedge for years, is 6-4 and 265 with the durability implied in those dimensions, plus an agility that has foiled scores if not hundreds of would-be wedge-breakers.

The contest on a kickoff, the main event, is between the wedge and those who would break it. A kickoff runner who slips unscathed through a hole in the wedge is hard to bring down short of midfield.

Kickoff runners have a different job (and hence different qualifications) from punt runners. The latter tend to be offensive backs, usually halfbacks. Kickoff returners are drawn from the ranks of various positions (offensive backfield, wide receivers, defensive backfield, etc.) because there are two requirements: speed and courage.

It is so desirable to bring the ball out to the 30- or 35-yard lines on kickoffs that those who can do it occasionally are carried as specialists along with kickers on some teams.

But the straightaway speed required eliminates most candidates, and virtually all the others are eliminated by the courage requirement. Nothing in football takes as much courage as running full speed into a tackler (or into a running back) in the open field.

8. Field goals and conversions

Most members of this team are offensive linemen who are used to holding off a rush. Offensive guards, who on many teams are smaller than other linemen, are occasionally replaced by defensive linemen—who are not only larger but taller. For many years, Merlin Olsen, the all-pro defensive tackle, has played guard on the Rams' placekicking team.

Placekickers come in two models, American and soccer style. Most NFL critics believe the day of the American field goal kicker is on the downgrade. Soccer stylists, as a group, tend to be more reliable.

Says Harland Svare, former coach of the San Diego Chargers: "There's less room for error in soccer-style kicking. An American hits the ball with his toe, a European with his instep. Placekicking the American way is like a punch shot in golf. A soccer kicker gets his foot on a larger surface of the ball. The soccer action is also more natural—like a golf swing—and easier on the leg."

The transition from American to European has taken longer than some football men expected because most of the early imports, Garo Yepremian and the others, were not first-division (major league) soccer players in Europe. The newer ones, including Toni Fritsch of Dallas, are experienced veteran pros merely changing one continent for another. Yepremian, the man who attempted one of the few passes thrown by anybody in Super Bowl VII, played only amateur soccer in Cyprus.

American kickers still have many fans in the NFL. Some coaches believe soccer kickers need too much time and kick the ball on a trajectory that is too low.

"There's only one important question," says Vermeil. "Can the guy get it through the uprights?"

9. Blocking FGs and conversions

Most members of this team are defensive linemen used to rushing. In some franchises, special rushmen are inserted—usually reserve defensive backs and reserve receivers. They are typically placed on the ends of the line.

According to most coaches, a blocked field goal is always a mistake by the kicking team. The mathematics of the timing are such that with a good snap, hold, and kick, it is impossible for any defensive man to penetrate before the ball is in the air.

If the blocking is reasonably competent, the rushing team is just going through the motions. The longer the kick, or course, the greater the need for a determined rush. Most kickers take a second or two longer to hit the ball from the 45-yard line than the 15. And more kicks are blocked out around midfield (undoubtedly because of the extra time) than on the goal line.

The determining point on whether the rushing team is thinking of a runback is the 30-yard line. From the 30 out to midfield, the return is on. Inside the 30 it isn't.

On some teams the special teams member will make fat bonuses. The players (and coaches) often throw $1 or so in a hat before the game and award it to the guy who gets in the day's best hit.

The winner isn't always easy to determine. Those who play well on the special teams love the action. They're a special breed of athlete whose philosophy is summed up by Rich Saul:

"Football is hitting people and I like to hit people. When you hit a man, you can let it all go. Like any fan, I like to see the good backs run and the passers pass. But running and passing and catching aren't football. Hitting is what the game is all about.''

Considering the number of plays in a football game and the number of blocked kicks, it doesn't seem worth the time of most coaches to practice the latter at great length.

In an average NFL season, the special teams are on the field for about 5,000 plays—but it's a rare year when 20 punts are blocked. Field goals are deflected more often, but always fewer than 50 times a year.

The figures for 1971: 4,995 plays, 62 blocked kicks (15 punts, 47 field goals).

For 1972: 4,982 special team plays, 59 blocked kicks (18 punts, 41 field goals).

There are valid reasons, however, to practice the other aspects of special team play. Mathematically, the kicking game is one-fifth of all the plays in pro football.

The 1971 figures: 26,951 total plays, of which 4,995 involved the special teams—or 18.5 percent.

In 1972: 27,010 total plays, with 4,982 involving special teams—or 18.4 percent.

Accordingly, the kicking game is accorded status as a third platoon on most pro clubs, and the players are taught and graded in a fashion identical with those on the offensive and defensive platoons.

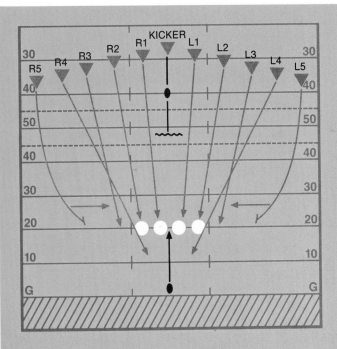

4. Kickoffs and coverage The kickoff team contains five two-man L&R units and the kicker. L&R 1 takes on the middle of the return wedge, L&R 2 the tackles in the wedge. L&R 3 slide inside, maintaining leverage on both sides of the field. L&R 4 are free to go around the wedge, but fold back inside if the wedge breaks inside. L&R 5 have the prime containment responsibility. It is their play if the kick returner goes outside. The kicker fills in the running lane.

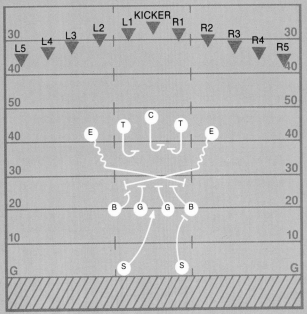

7. Kickoff returns The center and tackles drop back, keying on coverers L1, kicker, and R1. The ends cross block on L2 and R2. The back on the side of the safety handling the ball becomes outside man on the wedge. The other back becomes part of the wedge blocking straight ahead. Both backs should be ready to field the short kick to their side. The guards set the wedge. One safety handles the ball. The other forms as outside man on the wedge.

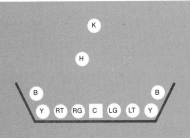

8. Field goals and conversions The holder lines up seven yards behind the line of scrimmage. On the snap, the tight ends (Y), tackles, guards and center charge at the rush line. Their objective is to deliver a sound hit, keeping the defense off balance and away from the flight of the ball. It is important to keep the initial momentum so the defense can't get its hands up. The up backs handle any outside rush.

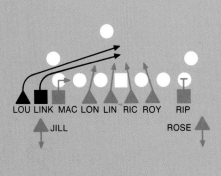

9. Blocking field goals and conversions Mac and Rip pull the ends inside, opening the way for Lou and Link to block the kick. Lou sprints to outside shoulder of covering halfback. If HB blocks down on Lou, Lou pulls, making room for Link. Link lines up on outside shoulder of the end. If HB blocks down on Link, he pulls to make room for Lou. Whoever has a shot at the ball should keep coming, aiming for a spot in front of the placement.

by Bob Oates, Jr.

The Zone Defense

There is something monstrous loose in NFL-land, a stifling, shape-shifting point-eater that is choking off touchdowns in major cities coast to coast.

This horror show vision is seen by many people, especially offensive people, when they think about that rapidly spreading threat to big yardage totals and quick scores: the zone pass defense.

Listen to Paul Warfield the all-pro wide receiver for the Miami Dolphins: "They're going to have to do something about the zone. If teams get good at it, the passing game may become extinct."

Warfield feels that many people don't realize the threat that zones pose for civilized offense because they don't fully understand the nature of the beast. "You hear all the time that the zone stops the long pass," he says, "and that's true. Those guys hang back in the deep zones and you just can't get past them. But what most people don't realize is that the zone shuts down the ten-to twenty-yard pass, too. All the linebackers get back in that area with the cornerbacks, and a passer has to have an arm like a sniper to get the ball through the mass of arms."

Listen to Bud Grant, coach of the Minnesota Vikings: "It's not only the passing game. Think how much better the zone is against draws and screens. None of our linebackers or deep backs ever has his back turned to the play chasing a receiver man-to-man. They are all in their zones facing the ball. They see a delayed play the instant it starts. The pursuit is tremendous."

In the view of many qualified observers, the mid-1970s will be crucial years in the evolution of football strategy. Paul Warfield's quarterback, Bob Griese, feels that the offense will catch up to the zone. "These things run in cycles." Griese says. "A few years ago the offense was way ahead of the defense. Right now the zones are causing us some trouble, but we'll solve them pretty soon."

To accomplish this comeback, offensive thinkers will need to effectively answer three questions: (1) What is a zone defense? (2) How do you "read" the zone?—that is, how do you tell just what variation of zone is being used on each play? (3) How do you beat the zone?

What is a zone defense?

The basic idea of a zone is deceptively simple. Seven defensive players—the three linebackers and four deep backs—each run to a prearranged area of the field, a zone. They stay in the effective center of their zones, more or less regardless of where the receivers go, until the ball is thrown. But once the ball is in the air, they converge on the receiver.

"A zone can be pretty scary," says Randy Vataha, the watch-fob wide receiver for New England. "You never know where you are going to get hit from. With the other kind of defense, man-to-man, that's not a problem. Take Oakland for instance. When we played the Raiders in 1971, I knew one man would cover me everywhere I went. Their cornerman, Willie Brown, will follow you over and sit down on the bench with you. I always

know where he is and where he'll hit me from. But in a zone, that's not true. They just sit out there and wait and when you get the ball, they come at you from all directions. You can get your head torn off."

For the defensive back, playing a zone is a completely different experience from playing a man-to-man. According to Grant, the two defenses almost require different personality types.

"A successful man-to-man defender must be a great athlete," says the Vikings' coach. "He needs great reflexes and great speed. You usually find that these people are very self-confident, even cocky. They're not afraid to go out and challenge anybody.

"But in a zone defense," Grant continues, "a back has to subdue those aggressive tendencies. He has to lay back, watch the play, and have the discipline to stay in his zone even if receivers cross right in front of him. Discipline is the word I always come back to. The zone is not an easy thing to learn."

It is the lack of head-to-head competition that upsets receivers such as Warfield. "There's no place for a zone in professional sports," he says. "It doesn't take much ability to just stand and wait for something to happen. These are the big leagues. If the defensive backs are supposed to be the best possible players, then they should be expected to go out and use their abilities man-to-man."

Grant smiles at that. "I can understand Warfield's complaint," he says. "He may be the best receiver there is. I don't know anybody who can handle him one-on-one.

But I can't agree with him about the athletic ability needed in the zone. I know that on our team the defensive backs are probably the best athletes we have, as a group."

Until recently, there were only two teams playing much zone defense. Grant's team, Minnesota, was one, and Baltimore was the other. The Colts have been using it the longest, since the middle of the 1950s, and the Colts have pioneered most of the basic ideas of the zone.

In any zone defense, there are two basic types of zones covered—short zones and deep zones. A defensive player assigned to a short zone is responsible for an area roughly 10 to 20 yards down field. A man assigned to a deep zone has a much larger responsibility. He must cover all the way back to his own goal line, if need be, and he must never allow a receiver to get behind him.

When the Colts first started playing zone defense, they used an alignment with four short zones spread across the field and three deep ones behind them. This is called a "rotating zone" for a reason that is obvious when you look at the diagram on page 171. The defensive players rotate in a circle as they run to their assigned zones.

Don Shula is now head coach of the Miami Dolphins, but he started as a player and then became head coach of the Colts. He learned to play the rotating zone as a defensive back, and then he coached it for a number of years. In 1968, however, while he was still in Baltimore, he began to play with another type of zone which he has used increasingly.

"We call it the double zone," Shula says (see page 171). "Basically, there are two deep zones and five short ones. The three linebackers take short zones inside and the two cornermen come up to cover the short outside. The safeties split and take the deep outside zones."

The double zone is extremely difficult to throw against in the middle ranges, as Warfield pointed out. There are five defensive people spread out about 15 yards downfield with only about eight yards between them. Throwing the ball between them is like trying to throw through a picket fence.

"Still, I was afraid to use it at first," Shula says. "There is a big hole deep in the middle and I thought we'd get burned a lot. But as I've used it more, I've gotten confidence in it and we run it often now with the Dolphins. Recently we've come up with another variation, too, where the five short people all cover one receiver man-to-man, while the safeties still take the two deep zones. That makes it harder for the offense to throw short to the backs because we have somebody specific waiting for them."

The zones, with all their many variations, are making it difficult for the offense in general. The question now is what can the offense do about it?

Reading the Zone

Before a quarterback can attack a zone, he has to know what zone he is facing. Often the defense changes from play to play, going from rotating zones, right and left, to the double zone, with many minor variations on each.

To figure out what he is facing, the quarterback has to "read" the zone as the play starts by watching the moves that the defensive people make.

Baltimore quarterback John Unitas has been reading zones every practice day of his pro career. His own Colts defense has been playing zone since John came up in 1956.

"The first guys you read," says John, "are the safeties. If they're going to cover deep zones, they have to go right away. You should see the basic coverage as you step away from the center."

If the two safeties go to the right, it will be a rotating zone to the right. If they move left, it's a rotating zone to the left. If the safeties split, it's a double zone.

"After you check the safeties," Unitas continues, "you watch the linebackers. If the deep backs are rotating to the right, the linebackers in the middle and on the left will have a long ways to run to cover back on the left side. You can pick that up right away, too. Usually, by the time you throw the pass, you've checked all seven guys back there."

The quarterback accomplishes all this in about three seconds.

Sometimes it is possible to read the defense even before the play begins. Virgil Carter, who completed 62 percent of his passes for the Cincinnati Bengals in 1971, thinks that's the way to do it all the time. "The defense has to commit itself by the way it lines up," he says. "If the safety is going to have to run all the way to the deep outside zone, he'll show it by lining up closer to that direction than he would normally. He only has to cheat a foot or two for you to pick it up after watching him over and over on film."

Of course, diagnosing the defense is only part of the problem. As Unitas says, "After you read what they're doing, you just hope you have something on that you can use." If the quarterback doesn't have the right play called for the defense he sees, it's no more help to read the safeties than it would be to read Sanskrit.

Beating the Zone

Which brings us to the question of how to beat the zone. Or maybe first, *can* you

beat the zone? Many wide receivers, such as Warfield and Gene Washington of the San Francisco 49ers, say no. They think it should be outlawed. But then, the zone is definitely hardest on wide receivers.

When the question is put to quarterbacks, a different feeling emerges. Unitas gives a fatalistic answer typical of his career-long attitude. "Changing rules is not my department," he says. "My department is beating what I see. You just do the best you can."

Other passers seem to enjoy the thought of attacking a zone and Jim Plunkett, New England's sensational rookie of 1971, flatly states, "If I have the time to throw, I think I have more success against a zone than I do against man-for-man."

Getting time to throw isn't easy these days, of course, not with the huge pass rushers who seem to materialize in greater numbers each season. As former Cleveland quarterback Bill Nelsen says, "Don't bother making the zone illegal. We can do things with it. What I want is a rule against those big guys coming in at me."

But assuming the time to throw, what can the offense do? There seem to be many different answers. During his two beautifully crafted drives in the second game against Miami in 1971, Unitas gave a textbook example of one method. He used up 17 minutes on those two drives, each of them longer than 80 yards, and his main weapon was short dump passes to his running backs (see page 171). "Their backers dropped off so deep into their zones," Unitas says, "that we just threw in front of them. A zone team sits back and waits for the offense to make mistakes, but in this case we threw short, easy passes and let them make the mistakes trying to tackle our runners."

Plunkett, in two 1971 season-end victories against Baltimore and Miami, went another route. "We took out our tight end and put in a third fast wide receiver, Hubie Bryant. With Bryant sprinting down the center of the field, we forced their deep backs to drop so deep that big holes opened up between the short zones and the deep ones. Bryant and our wide receivers hooked into these big spaces and my line gave me time to throw the ball. In fact, the first seven plays against Miami were all hook passes and all complete."

Virgil Carter points out two other elements which he feels are important. "The first one might surprise you," he says. "It's scrambling. Most people think that when the quarterback takes off to run, it's just haphazard. But there are some high-faluting theories of scrambling. I like to scramble against a zone. The linebackers don't know whether to come up and get me or stay back and play their zones. They get caught flat-footed while our receivers get a lot of time to run deep and stretch the zones out of shape.

"The second point is that you have to make sure your team keeps patient. You can't go out and score quick on 'strikers'—long passes. This is something the quarterback has to handle personally. He has to stay calm and keep his team calm and patient. Most games where the teams use a lot of zone will be low-scoring and fairly even to the end. You just have to be ready for this."

Throwing to the backs, using speed at tight end to stretch the zones, adjusting patterns, scrambling—these are a few of the passing theories available to beat the zone. But it isn't all a passing problem, as Bud Grant points out.

"It used to be that some teams could make a living by passing," he says. "But against a zone team, that's not true. You can't hit long touchdown passes against the zone. And you can't count on marching up and down the field on ten-yard passes. You may hit three or four in a row. It happens all the time. But eventually something happens. The rush gets you or a linebacker shows up in the wrong place. You can't do it on passing alone. To beat a zone, you have to run."

Statistics bear out Grant's point. In 1971, with more teams using the zone than ever before, NFL offenses ran 56 percent of the time and passed 44 percent, a marked turnaround from previous seasons.

And running the ball is not simply a surrender to the zone. It is also a useful way to attack it. As Carter says, "If you have a credible running threat, you hurt a zone."

The zone is here to stay. Not all of the teams will use it all the time, but most will use it some of the time, and the character of the game will change as a result. There will be fewer "cheap" touchdowns—long passes that depend only on the brilliance of one or two offensive players or the mistake of a single defender. Instead, there will be more emphasis by the offense on full-team coordination, efficiency, subtlety, and patience.

Teams will have to work harder to score points, but under that pressure they will have to refine their skills and broaden their approach. The result should be a more balanced and integrated offense.

The zone is a hard teacher for the offense. It may seem like a monster for a while. But when the offenses have learned the necessary lessons, football will have moved another step on its evolutionary path as the most highly refined and coordinated of all team sports.

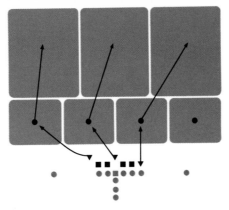

Rotating Zone The defense divides the passing area into four short zones and three deep ones. The three linebackers and one of the backs (usually a cornerman) take the short zones. The other three backs—two safeties and a cornerman—retreat into the deep zones. Since the linebackers retreat in one direction and the safeties move in the opposite direction, the effect is one of "rotation." In this case, the defense is rotating in a clockwise direction. Each man has an exact spot that he is to move to. In the past, several teams have used the hashmarks and numbers painted on the field as reference points. But that will have to be revised this season because the field markings have changed and the hashmarks have been brought closer together.

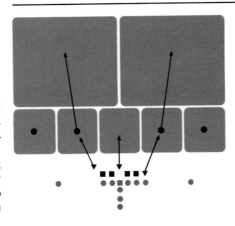

Double Zone In this alignment, the defense divides the field up into five short zones and only two deep ones. Both cornerbacks and all three linebackers play the five short zones, putting up a thick picket line about 15 yards down field. The two safeties divide and cover deep zones, paying particular attention to the wide receivers, since the double zone is primarily aimed at checking off wide receivers both short and deep. Both the left side linebacker and the middle linebacker keep track of the tight end.

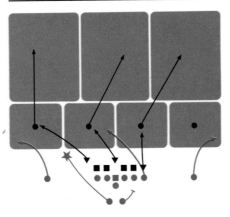

Throwing Underneath The easiest way to attack the zone is with short passes to the backs. Often the patterns are run after a slight delay. Since the linebackers in any kind of zone must turn and hurry 15 yards downfield, it is easy for the backs to slip out and catch a pass about five yards down, "underneath" the linebackers. If the runner then dodges one tackler, he can get as big a gain as if a wide receiver caught a pass further down field. That is why running backs catch so many passes against a zone.

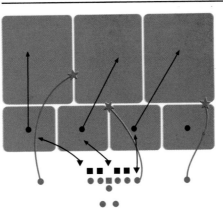

Hitting the Seams A zone defense, especially the rotating zone, has space or "seams" in between the four short zones, and also between the short zones and the deep ones. The receivers can run downfield 15 to 20 yards and hook into these dead places in the zone, if the quarterback can get enough time to throw the ball. If a zone defense does not get a pass rush and make the quarterback throw badly, then it will get torn apart at the seams.

Football needn't always be viewed from a 50-yard line seat, binoculars in hand, program rolled and tucked under one arm. It isn't meant to be analyzed as science, scrutinized under a microscope. It is a game. An expression of joy, an outburst of emotion. It is a game for us all to interpret for ourselves. For sophisticated artists, for children who scrawl pictures, for photographers who interpret in different ways. From them, comes The Unexpected View.

The Unexpected View

by James Dickey

In the Pocket

```
                    Going backward
                   All of me and some
        Of my friends are forming a shell      my arm is looking
                  Everywhere and some are breaking
                        In      breaking down
                      And out      breaking
              Across, and one is going deep      deeper
         Than my arm.      Where is Number One hooking
                   Into the violent green alive
      With linebackers?      I cannot find him he cannot beat
                  His man      I fall back more
                Into the pocket      it is raging and breaking
              Number Two has disappeared into the chalk
         Of the sideline      Number Three is cutting with half
            A step of grace      my friends are crumbling
                   Around me the wrong color
                  Is looming      hands are coming
                     Up and over between
      My arm and Number Three:      throw it hit him in the middle
            Of his enemies      hit move scramble
                 Before death and the ground
            Come up      LEAP STAND KILL DIE STRIKE
                          Now.
```

by Dr. A. Craig Fisher

Sport and Masculine Identification

It was said of the Old West that in it men were men and women were women. You know how it went. The men were the ones who rode on the range and sat in the saloons. The women were the ones who baked the bread and took care of the young'uns.

The masculine and feminine roles seemed easily defined. But then maybe that's only because Dr. David Reuben and Germaine Greer weren't around to question them.

The Old West is, perhaps sadly, a memory. It left along with wide-open spaces and stagecoaches and log cabins. They call the Santa Fe Trail "Route 66" now and it is only one long day's journey from Albuquerque to Los Angeles.

These days, the standards for judging men as men and women as women are different ones, although it is no less important for a man to be masculine and woman to be feminine in order for each person to be authentic. If one is to get along with other people, it is necessary to portray the appropriate role. There is, however, a greater range of accepted behavior for each sex.

Sports participation and appreciation is a measuring stick of our time, particularly in a sport that is conceived as being masculine. Football would seem to be the epitome of that kind of sport.

Football provides a clearcut definition of appropriate male behavior. Whether the accent is on the toughness of the sport or the identification and interaction with male images is immaterial. The results are the important thing. And in a study of game preferences of children in the past 60 years,

football was found to be a sport that still clearly differentiates the sexes.

Origins of masculinity are significant and multidimensional. They come from an integration of biological, sociological, and psychological variables.

And it is not an all-or-none concept. One's behavior, emotions, interest, and preferences all can vary in their degree of masculinity. Masculine orientation really is the degree to which an individual adopts and exhibits characteristics associated with the majority of the male population. The characteristics often are related to a particular culture.

Daniel Brown, a psychologist who has focused much of this research in the area of sex role development, stated that the nature of one's sex role development in childhood appears to bear a direct relationship to the individual's eventual sexual orientation and adjustment in adolescence and adulthood. Brown claimed unequivocally that one of the most important conditions is for the individual to feel safe, secure, and satisfied in his emerging sexual identity. Whether these feelings can be promoted depends upon a great many variables—the cultural, psychological, and even the biological appropriateness of his behavior.

At a time in our society when much attention is being given to women's liberation, one should also realize that at the same time the young American males are undergoing a degree of feminization. Patricia Sexton, in her book *The Feminized Male*, documented factors that impinge upon the masculine identity of males.

Ignacio Gomez

Very often institutions such as the home and the school stunt the young male's growth toward the masculine way of life because they are so matricentered. Females are nearly wholly responsible for rearing the children and female elementary school teachers do much of the early teaching.

In referring to various feminizing factors of masculine development, Dr. Karl Menninger, the renowned clinical psychiatrist, stated:

"That these devices actually do have the effect of crippling the masculinity of the boy, every psychiatrist knows from clinical experience. It is the sort of thing that has happened in childhood of men who consult us many years later because of impairments of masculinity which may show themselves in an unsatisfactory sexual life, such as alcoholism, hypochondriasis, neurotic illnesses, all kinds of marital conflict, and even actual psychoses. Call them the extreme cases if you like, but they are extremes that indicate what I believe to be an increasing trend of a most malignant sort.

"Biological sexual identity is predetermined at birth but sociological sexual identity is for the most part learned."

There are indications that one's sociological sexual orientation is formed as a result of modeling influences, i.e. parents, peers, heroes, and the like. Psychological sexual identity is derived mainly through interpersonal interaction, i.e. group situations. In the psychological literature one can find several proponents of the idea that appropriate sex role orientation is facilitated if male children adopt the games and master the skills associated with their sex.

Karl Bednarik, the Austrian scientist, stated that the field of sports offers the best opportunities for projecting the male image. This is especially important since the personal interaction and feedback realized from peers is instrumental in developing the male sex role orientation. Myron Brenton, in his book, *The American Male,* affirmed the previous comment but in much stronger sentiments. It is his impression from his in-depth survey that masculinity is really put on the line when one engages in sport. Dr. Arnold Beisser leaves no doubt about his feelings on the subject:

"In sports, male and female are placed in their historical biological roles. In sports, strength and speed do count, for they (often) determine the winner. As in pre-mechanized combat, women can never be more than second place in sports. They can cheer their men on, but a quick review of the record books comparing achievements in sports of men and women confirms the distinctness of the sexes here."

It is small wonder that the American male has a strong affinity for sports. He has learned that this is one area where there is no doubt about sexual differences and where his biology is not obsolete. Athletics help assure his difference from women in a world where his functions have come to resemble theirs.

In 1969 the National Football League published a widely acclaimed book entitled *The First 50 Years: The Story of the National Football League.* The book's description of the game of football bears repeating:

"It is a sport that demands unusual dedication. The many men who have tried it and failed have found unmistakably that it takes more than the promise of a pay check to encourage participation. The game challenges a man to discover the very source of his competitive spirit, forcing him through pain, adversity, and the despair of defeat. The very difficulty of the game is a call to excellence, an invitation for a man to express himself violently and powerfully while achieving the acclaim of victory."

The question now arises as to which human characteristics can be delineated as being more masculine and to what degree does football enhance these qualities. Dr. Lionel Tiger has expressed an intriguing belief. He asserted that male bonding is the central organizational feature of sport, especially those involving physical contact. This congregational behavior of males is another universal need, on the same plane as hunger and thirst. However, this need can only be satisfied by real social contact with other males.

Beisser expands on this concept and explains why a sport such as football contributes positively to masculine orientation:

"In a subtle way, these super-masculine 'frontier rites' allow for the expression of warmth and closeness among men which society compels them to disown. In sports…with full cultural approval and without detracting from the supermasculine atmosphere, men can satisfy either physically or vicariously their needs for close male companionship like that which they expressed in their childhood. In this context, physical contact, either aggressive or friendly, is applauded rather than condemned, and in the frenzy of American sports, males are purged of their femininity, and at the same time provided with an outlet for close male contact."

The male bond in sport is important both to players and spectators alike—both are active participants in football. To claim that football fans are passive would be far from the truth. Players satisfy their male bonding needs on the field by personal interaction with peers, whereas the spectators satisfy their needs vicariously through the modeling influence of the athletes. Males are more deeply involved in football than are females in that they internalize the game to a much greater degree. For the average female fan, the game only reaches a very superficial depth of appreciation and understanding. Male bonding in football undoubtedly enhances certain modes of masculine identification.

Vince Lombardi looked upon the game of football as a struggle emphasizing controlled violence and expressed the opinion that it was man's nature to be aggressive. Regardless whether you attribute the male's added aggressiveness to innate or environmental factors, the point remains the same—males, generally, are more aggressive and violent than females. Football demands both a toughness of mind and body, something that is not *culturally relevant* for American females.

Football is an aggressive way of life both for the players and the spectators. Larry Wilson, retired St. Louis Cardinals safety, was certainly cognizant of this when he stated: "This [football] is one way for people to release their aggressions. I see them coming out of the stands, they are wringing wet with sweat, they are mad, they have played a football game, and they look as beat up as the football players on the field."

Paul Brown reiterates a previous point made regarding female participation and attitude toward football: "I've known women who thought football was worthless and brutal. But they just don't understand the nature of the male."

The constant struggle of every football play is not very meaningful to the female; to the male it is a highly ritualized masculine endeavor.

Physical strength and athletic skills are highly prized by American males and are predisposing factors of masculine development. Strength and power are male qualities which are very much a part of football. Interviews with former and current professionals such as Mike Ditka, Forrest Gregg, Howard Mudd, and John Niland reveal that there is some enjoyment to be gained by physically defeating an opponent. Ditka asserted that you have to enjoy the contact and have confidence in your own body and abilities. All of this gives one a feeling of power. Gregg expressed similar emotions concerning the elation of overpowering an opponent. Mudd saw football as an agency which gives him the opportunity to display himself and be recognized for his qualities. Niland put it very succinctly by saying that it is simply a satisfaction to block a man to the ground and know that you are responsible for him being there.

Bravery is another male quality. This aspect of football is evident on every play. Picture the 190-pound halfback fighting off the block of the 250-pound guard; or the free safety one-on-one with one of the behemoth tight ends. The ensuing collison may well resound to the top rows of the stadium. There are few situations remaining in our society where daring and courage play a significant part. Sport, and especially football, is one area where such masculine qualities can be exhibited—indeed, must be exhibited to survive.

Mastery and self-proof are qualities that are attributed more to males than to females. In our culture, males are constantly being tested and are constantly testing ground for many male characteristics. In football, one finds out very quickly if he has credentials to master the game. He receives a supreme test every Sunday.

As so aptly stated in *The First 50 Years:*

"Their own self-image is continually tested: their pride, their courage, the meaning of their pain, the reality of their hostility, their need for group affection, the level of their ability, their worth to other people."

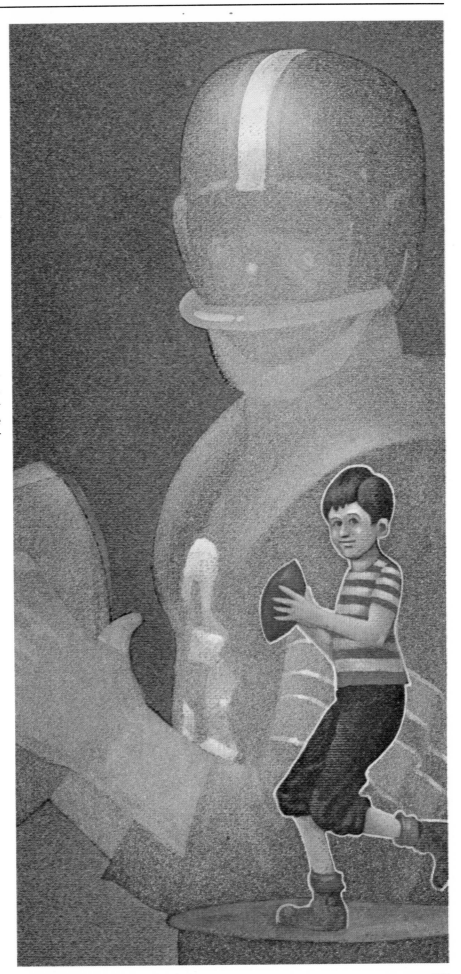

A Child's View of Football

Give a child a paint brush.

Pass around some water colors. Some pastels. Some felt-tipped pens. Some crayons. Some pencils.

Watch them work. The improvisation. The imagery. The freedom. The spontaneity.

A child cuts through the facade of things and gets to the heart of the artistic matter. Inevitably, the end result is something simple, something basic, something appropriate.

CRUNCH

Bill Sims
Age 9

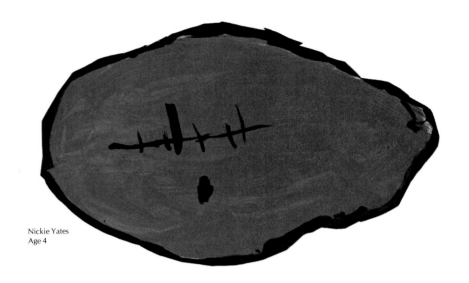

Nickie Yates
Age 4

A football lies in dirty mud
    and on the cold cold snow.
When the referee blows the whistle
    it is time for the ball to go.
At kickoff time it sits on the tee
    and waits to sail through the air.
The coach wants his team to win
    but does the football care?

—REED CHAFFEY, AGE 10

Kris Gaines
Age 6

Dong Sook Suk
Age 9

Keith Davis
Age 10

by
Keith Dav

Mike Prock
Age 8

by David Morcom

Symbiosis

We met, it seems, so long ago that autumn day
Ablaze with red and gold and yellow.
It was the first you'd met me, the game,
But, oh, how you played for such a little fellow.

And as you grew your dreams grew, too,
The roaring crowds were a part of you.
Then came that gleaming sunlit day when
    college halls and ivied walls were finally
    left behind.
By then we'd been friends for many years so
    you turned to me to find…
A way.
And there were things I demanded from you.

For in that summer sunfurnace you worked
    as you had never worked before.
The steel in you lifted, strained, and ran and
    melted and through it all you swore.
You fell to earth and rose again to battle
    emotionless machines.
You knew that this had played no part in
    those long-gone boyhood dreams.
Finally, there came that September day when
    you raced out to claim the glory you
    thought you'd earned
And how you railed at me when I said,
    "There's still a lot more to learn."

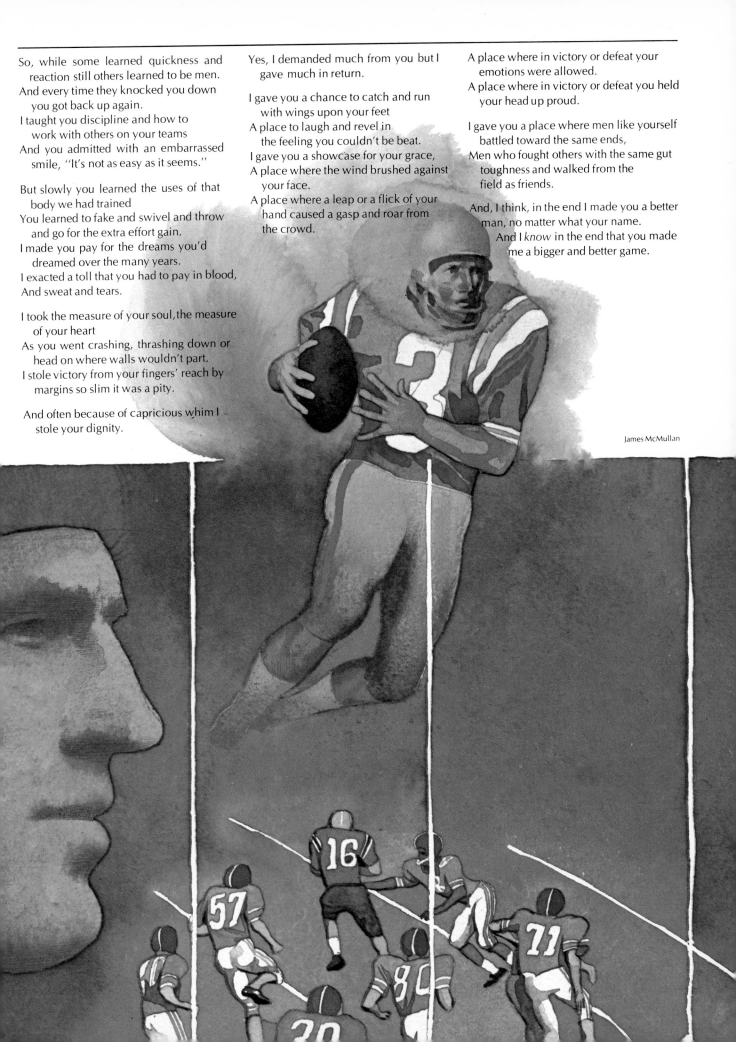

So, while some learned quickness and
  reaction still others learned to be men.
And every time they knocked you down
  you got back up again.
I taught you discipline and how to
  work with others on your teams
And you admitted with an embarrassed
  smile, "It's not as easy as it seems."

But slowly you learned the uses of that
  body we had trained
You learned to fake and swivel and throw
  and go for the extra effort gain.
I made you pay for the dreams you'd
  dreamed over the many years.
I exacted a toll that you had to pay in blood,
And sweat and tears.

I took the measure of your soul, the measure
  of your heart
As you went crashing, thrashing down or
  head on where walls wouldn't part.
I stole victory from your fingers' reach by
  margins so slim it was a pity.

And often because of capricious whim I
  stole your dignity.

Yes, I demanded much from you but I
  gave much in return.

I gave you a chance to catch and run
  with wings upon your feet
A place to laugh and revel in
  the feeling you couldn't be beat.
I gave you a showcase for your grace,
A place where the wind brushed against
  your face.
A place where a leap or a flick of your
  hand caused a gasp and roar from
  the crowd.

A place where in victory or defeat your
  emotions were allowed.
A place where in victory or defeat you held
  your head up proud.

I gave you a place where men like yourself
  battled toward the same ends,
Men who fought others with the same gut
  toughness and walked from the
  field as friends.

And, I think, in the end I made you a better
  man, no matter what your name.
  And I *know* in the end that you made
    me a bigger and better game.

James McMullan

Photographs by Malcolm Emmons
and Tony Tomsic

Snow

Down it comes, spilling over and white, weaving an animated veil that swirls and curls before the yellow-bright overhead lights.

The field becomes a broad chalk-on-pearl plain, flat, and horizontal, without dimension or boundary. Beckoning.

Little boy sounds of crunching snow, and flakes falling upon the nose and cheek, becoming a trickle and triggering fond remembrances of soggy wet wool mittens.

The little boys are grown and now assembled, forming their familiar dotted patterns, like black coal stones, as intimate as the eyes, nose, and mouth of snowman.

The contest unfolds as though on a different planet—Armstrong and Aldrin on the moon perhaps. A bizarre landscape upon which is acted an old yet strangely new pageant.

Big men loom even larger, dark-bright silhouettes against the unyielding white.

Now a loud close voice rasps, ''Ball!'', and the crisp blow of a sinewy forearm brings urgent awareness to resentful flesh.

There is a game here, make no mistake, but in a slow motion dimension where clocks turn slowly through a day dark as night.

by Ray Bradbury

All Flesh is One: What Matter Scores?

The thing is this:
We love to see them on the green and growing field;
There passions yield to weather and a special time;
There all suspends itself in air,
The missile on its way forever to a goal.
There boys somehow grown up to men are boys again;
We wrestle in their tumble and their ecstasy,
And there we dare to touch and somehow hold,
Congratulate, or say: Ah, well, next time. Get on!
Our voices lift; the birds all terrified
At sudden pulse of sound, this great and unseen fount,
Scare like tossed leaves, fly in strewn papers
Up the wind to flagpole tops:
We Celebrate Ourselves!
(Sorry, old Walt.)
We play at life, we dog the vital tracks
Of those who run before and we, all laughing, make the trek
Across the field, along the lines,
Falling to fuse, rising amused by now-fair, now-foul
Temper-tantrums, sprint-leaps, handsprings, recoils,
And brief respites when bodies pile ten high.

All flesh is one, what matter scores?
Or color of the suit
Or if the helmet glints with blue or gold?
All is one bold achievement,
All is fine spring-found-again-in-autumn day
When juices run in antelopes along our blood,
And green our flag, forever green,
Deep colored of the grass, this dye proclaims
Eternities of youngness to the skies
Whose tough winds play our hair and rearrange our stars
So mysteries abound where most we seek for answers.
We do confound ourselves.
All this being so, we do make up a Game
And pitch a ball and run to grapple with our Fates

On common cattle-fields, cow-pasturings,
Where goals are seen and destinies beheld,
And scores summed up so that we truly *know* a score!
All else is nil; the universal sums
Lie far beyond our reach,
In this mild romp we teach our lambs and colts
Ascensions, swift declines, revolts, wild victories,
Sad retreats, all compassed in the round
Of one autumnal October afternoon.
Then winds, incensed and sweet with dust of leaves
Which, mummified, attest the passing of the weather,
Hour, day, and Old Year's tide,
Are fastened, gripped and held all still
For just one moment with the caught ball in our hands.
We stand so, frozen on the sill of life
And, young or old, ignore the coming on of night.

All, all is flight!
All loss and ept recovery.
We search the flawless air
And make discovery of projectile tossed—
The center of our being.
This is the only way of seeing;
To run half blind, half in the sad, mad world,
Half out of mind—
The goal line beckons,
And with each yard we pass,
We reckon that we win, by God, we win!
Surely to run, to run and measure this,
This gain of tender grass
Is not a sin to be denied?
All life we've tried and often found contempt for us!
So on we hied to lesser gods
Who treat us less as clods and more like men
Who would be kings a little while.
Thus we made up this mile to run

Beneath a late-on-in-the-afternoon-time sun.
We chalked aside the world's derisions
With our gamebook's rulings and decisions.
So divisions of our own good manufacture
Staked the green a hundred yards, no more, no less.
The Universe said "No"?
We answered, running, "Yes!"

Yes to Ourselves!
Since naught did cipher us
With scoreboards empty,
Strewn with goose-egg zeros
Self-made heroes, then, we kicked that minus,
Wrote in plus!
The gods, magnanimous,
Allowed our score
And noted, passing,
What was less is now, incredibly, more!
Man, then, is the thing
That teaches zeros how to cling together and add up!
The cup stood empty?
Well, now, look!
A brimming cup.

No scores are known?
Then look downfield,
There in the twilight sky the numbers run and blink
And total up the years;
Our sons this day are grown.

What matter if the board is cleared an hour from now
And empty lies the stadium wherein died roars
Instead of men
And goalposts fell in lieu of battlements.
See where the battle turf is splayed
Where panicked herds of warrior sped by,

Half buffalo and half ballet.

Their hoofmarks fill with rain
As thunders close and shut the end of day.
The papers blow.
Old men, half-young again, across the pavements go
To cars that in imagination
Might this hour leave for Mars.
But, sons beside them silent, put in gear,
And drive off toward the close of one more year,
Both thinking this:
The game is done.
The game begins.
The game is lost.
But here come other wins.
The band tromps out to clear the field with brass,
The great heart of the drum systolic beats
In promise of yet greater feats and trumps;
Still promising, the band departs
To leave the final beating of this time
To older hearts who in the stands cold rinsed with Autumn day
Wish, want, desire for their sons
From here on down, eternal replay on replay.

This thought, them thinking it,
Man and boy, old Dad, raw Son
For one rare moment caused by cornering too fast,
Their shoulders lean and touch.
A red light stops them. Quiet and serene they sit.
But now the moment is past.
Gone is the day.
Amd so the old man says at last:
"The light is green, boy. Go. The light is green."
They ran together all the afternoon;
Now, very simply, they drive away.

Alan E. Cober

by John Wiebusch

A Captive Audience

It sits there on a finger that juts into San Francisco Bay, up from Sausalito and Tiburon, a monolith of mottled grays and whites. A fist on which the knuckles are the turrets and the turrets the reminders that you cannot always go where you want to go and do what you want to do.

Big Q.

They call it that inside, on the other side of the turrets, in the yard and up on the north wing and the south wing and in the place where Johnny Cash comes to sing.

San Quentin.

The ills of man are there. Greed. Lust. Hate. Where time waits for all men and all men wait for the time.

And the waiting is the worst part. It is hell for Robert Thornton, whose fate lies in appeals and supreme courts. Robert Thornton lives on Death Row. It is hell for John Severnson Watson, who laughs to keep from crying and cries to keep his sanity. John Severnson Watson may spend the rest of his days in Big Q.

An everyman of prisons. Attica, Leavenworth, Stillwater, Sing Sing, Joliet. Only the names have been changed to protect the guilty. Or the ones so judged.

And how it is, is lonely. The outside, only a visitor. A face on the other side of a window. A letter. A television program. Mostly a television program.

The remembrance of things past are there in "As the World Turns" and "Let's Make a Deal" and the six o'clock news. They are there in the basketball games of the winter and the baseball games of the summer and the football games of the fall. They are there, always a hand to hold. And

always there is someone reaching out.

Television is the mansitter of our time. In prison they watch it because they want to and because it is there. Perhaps they are not unlike the rest of us.

And in the prison watching there is a caste system. John Severnson Watson gets to watch color television. Robert Thronton has to watch black and white. It is a difference of life and death.

A paragraph from a letter from Robert Thornton:

"We have a control box in each cell to change television channels. As you can imagine, I have to view television through the bars. I have acclimated myself."

A paragraph from a letter from John Severnson Watson:

"They also serve who only sit and watch."

Watching. Watching anything. Waiting, though, for one thing: for pro football.

That's what John Severnson Watson and Robert Thornton both say.

Watson, former sports editor of the *San Quentin News,* was asked to explain the popularity of pro football in prison.

The question: "I'd like to get your feelings on why pro football is so popular with people on your side of the bars."

The reply: "Well, it's like this…the bartenders like it because it's good for business and the customers like it because …what? Oh, *those* kind of bars."

If you get the impression you are being conned, read on:

"I've asked many, many cons in the past twenty-four hours the question you asked me. Pro football has many meanings for the men in blue. It's a mental escape from the concrete and steel. They definitely like the body contact and the controlled violence. They like the game for the exciting action. Some feel it gives the pro football athlete a chance to pit his skills, physical and mental, against the best players in the world. Others expressed the sentiment that any team can win (or lose) on any given Sunday.

"Still others compared it to a chess game (the quarterback constantly probing for a weakness in the opponent's defense). But the controlled violence was the reason most often given for liking pro football. Maybe an amateur psychologist could make a lot out of that. But that's the way it is."

That's the way it is with John Severnson Watson. This is the way it is with Robert Thornton:

"Cons are more or less islands unto themselves. But with pro football, or sports in general, they are more apt to leave their islands and temporarily show their true emotional qualities. The con can relax from his diurnal guarding of emotional outlets in order to remain strong in the eyes of his peers.

"Prison tends to segregate men. To cause them to shrink from their fellows and into themselves. Football allows them to open up and share a common experience of a spectator's excitement for the two or three hours of a game.

"Football gives them a temporary outlet for emotions that are normally being repressed by the very existence of prison.

"Football watching is also one of the most effective means of escaping the prison setting temporarily because of the high degree of emotional involvement it engenders."

There are some things you should know about John Severnson Watson and Robert Thornton.

You should know, for example, that John Severnson Watson has killed three people. He tells it better:

"I was born at an early age in Pittsburgh. My parents were Canadian and the family returned to Ottawa shortly after I was born. Lived in Ottawa until I was eighteen, when I joined the U.S. Air Force.

"Got married to my high school steady and spent half of the next seven years on overseas assignments. Killed my wife in 1956 and came to prison.

"Discharged in 1966. Couldn't get a job and lived on Skid Row in San Francisco. Met and married a hooker. Told her what happened to my first wife and why—that she was sleeping in strange beds.

"About six months later, second wife started doing the same. I couldn't handle it,

so here I am again. [A companion of the second wife also was shot and killed.]

"Summary: Good middle-class family background [they talk about a traffic ticket at the supper table for two weeks], good service record, no juvenile trouble, two arrests in entire life—and a stupid, idiotic moron for committing virtually identical homicide a second time.

"Diagnosis: Subject will spend the rest of his life in prison—deservedly so—even though the judge gave sentence of 'Life with possibility of parole,' which means, technically, I'm eligible for parole again in six years. I've been here nearly four years this time."

That is the way it has been for John Severnson Watson. This is the way it has been for Robert Thornton. The *Los Angeles Times* of December 2, 1967, said:

"A young aircraft worker, whose case some day could result in a landmark Supreme Court decision outlawing capital punishment, was sentenced to die Friday for his 'bestial' sex attacks on three women.

"Robert Emmett Thornton, 24, of 9210 Compton Blvd., Bellflower, was condemned to death by Superior Judge Herbert V. Walker.

"A jury voted the death penalty last April 14 after convicting Thornton of kidnapping for the purpose of robbery with bodily harm and a series of other sex crimes, including forcible rape and sex perversion....

"The frail looking Thornton...maintained, as he did during the trial, that he is 'totally innocent' of the offenses of which he was convicted."

Although he no longer lives on Death Row, Thornton continues to maintain his innocence.

A lot of people had never heard of Robert Thornton until he wrote a poem on hearing of the death of Vince Lombardi:

Vince Lombardi was a man
Who climbed Mt. Everest,
As few men can.

Bard is a word in his name,
Vince was the poet of the game.

Reverence he commanded with great rife,
Cancer was the severance of his life.

Vince's life is not yet done,
For his acumen was left for everyone.
His life was a gift to me,
Because I savored his history.

Thornton showed the poem to a friend and the friend sent a copy to John Hall, sports columnist for the *Los Angeles Times*. A lot of people heard about Robert Thornton after that.

To read his letters and his poem is to be stirred by the seeming irony of the report of a probation officer nearly four years ago:

"[He is] beyond the scope of rehabilitation procedures. The defendant's savage antisocial behavior in this matter indicates that his character structure is totally devoid of human feelings and beyond restoration."

On June 3, 1971, Robert Thornton wrote:

"Emotionally speaking, I enjoy reading stories, articles, and books on various athletes. Such as the story of Gale Sayers and Brian Piccolo in a national magazine and their wonderful relationship, not as a black man and a white man—although at first it may have been just that—but as two individuals who felt what each had to offer the other. When Mr. Lombardi died, I felt very hollow inside; a feeling I have only felt once before. That time being when my brother died of polio twenty-odd years ago.

"I never played football in school as I was too small (about ninety-five pounds at eighteen years of age) and could not pass the mandatory physical because of my smallness. But I played tackle football on the dirt lots and paved streets of Butte, Montana, where I grew up.

"As I believe is the case with most young fellows, there was a vast amount of competitiveness among my friends, which I believe is another reason I love pro football. Pro football is highly competitive and very much parallel with man's incessant desire to move forward....

"I hope I have been as lucid as possible in expressing my thoughts to you. Quite simply, I enjoy pro football because I can identify with these people that I admire. I can temporarily escape from my quasi-hermitically sealed existence. And most of all I just love sports."

"I hope I have been helpful. I hope that your life is a peaceful and happy one."

And then there is John Severnson Watson, a man who has spent more than a third of his life behind bars. John Severnson Watson, who writes:

"Nowadays, colleges are emphasizing education. One university has become so strict that it won't allow a basketball player his letter until he can tell which one it is."

And: "If you're a sucker for punishment and want still some more material, drop me a line. Preferably about a hundred feet in length."

He is a man of wit and wisdom and a pro football seer of uncommon perception. Before the 1970 season began, he made his selections for the Super Bowl. People told him he was crazy. Dallas and Baltimore? Sure. Crazy like a fox.

So if we can have a little quiet in the audience, it gives me great pleasure to introduce, in his first national forum as a sportswriter (he said he wanted a big buildup)...JOHN...SEVERNSON...WATSON!!!

"During the autumn months there are more pools in San Quentin than in Beverly Hills. Big pools, little pools, medium sized pools. And tickets that have more combinations than a Bank of America safe. Caliente could learn something from *our* bookies about the number of ways to empty a patron's wallet.

"The cons follow baseball, basketball, hockey, golf, boxing, tennis, and bowling. But the most popular by far is college and pro football, with the pros the big favorite.

"There are a number of valid reasons why the cons get so involved in pro football. They know it's honest (which can't be said for boxing) and they're certain to see and hear exciting action. Most importantly, it's the only sport that excites them to the degree that even if they lose a couple of packs of cigarets (or more) it doesn't hurt quite as much as when they lose on other sports.

"The cons know if Roman Gabriel has a hangnail or if Donny Anderson has had a fight with one of his seventy-three girl friends. That information isn't in the papers or on radio or television, but the prison grapevine is more knowledgeable and accurate than CIA reports [which, come to think of it, really isn't saying much].

"The pro pigskin parade is taken so seriously here that a Raquel Welch movie comes out a poor second to Merlin Olsen, Deacon Jones, Cedrick Hardman, and Charlie Krueger on the television screen. And none of those four behemoths are noted sex symbols.

"Next to the Super Bowl and a heavyweight championship fight, the Rams-49ers wars create the most interest and excitement. Even the exhibition game between them—er...ah...pardon me, Pete Rozelle...preseason game—takes on the importance of World War III.

"The rivalry is intense during those 49ers-Rams games. It's the northern California cons against the southern California cons as each side cheers and jeers the jocks. Witty, sarcastic comments fly back and forth about the ancestry and playing habits of the hated rivals. The cons' favorite team has forty all-pros on the squad and the enemy force is filled with forty spastic athletes—if you can believe such unbiased opinions.

"Players who were signed as free agents from such renowned points as Gerkie's Corners U. and Platinum Tech become instant heroes if they perform well against 'those bums.' However, the same players might drop a key pass or fumble a handoff and become 'butterfingered dummies' in the next series of plays.

"The final gun sounds. Blueclads all over San Quentin deliver lost cigarets, drink countless cups of water, and perform hundreds upon hundreds of pushups as punishment for the blundering, lame, ineffective performances of their hometown heroes.

"But the smokes, the gallons of water, and the zillion pushups are the easy parts of the payment. The verbal slingers have to be tolerated around the clock until the 49ers and Rams meet again. And with the many sharp, caustic tongues in action about the ineptitude of the losing team, the next scheduled game between Los Angeles and San Francisco seems light years away."

John Severnson Watson closed his story about pro football with a note to the editor:

"Well that's it. Be honest now. Was it good, very good, exceptional, outstanding, or stupendous? Seriously [as if I wasn't]..."

And in a P.S.: "Don't take me too seriously. I'm really a wonderful, unique, talented, and modest guy."

A captive audience. A captive audience seeking mental escape in pro football. That is the way it is everywhere where men are surrounded by four walls and iron gates.

In Big Q. In the cloistered place where John Severnson Watson lives. In the claustrophobic place where Robert Emmett Thornton lives.

Two men (and men, incidentally, who have never met) caught up in a game. Two men who ask, really, for very little.

Oh, well, a few things maybe.

Like letters. (Watson's address: B-11037, Tamal, California 94964; Thornton's address: B-12151, Tamal, California 94964).

And the 49ers and, oh, say, 3½ points.

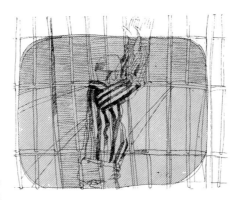

Photographs by Jack Zehrt

Football as Structure

Football, like most other phenomena, is what you think it is. To some it is war and violence, to some, chess and strategy, or color, or motion, or maybe just entertainment. We are even used to seeing football differently. The three dimensional immediacy of the game in the stadium differs from the flattened pointillistic image of television or the frozen moment offered by a photograph.

Photographer Jack Zehrt here sees football as structure. The photograph of the Cleveland Browns in huddle resembles nothing so much as the prehistoric monoliths of Stonehenge and the Cardinals' tackle of a Vikings' runner a teetering arrangement of children's blocks.

And the game seen as structure makes sense. For football, like structure, consists exactly as "interdependent parts in a definite pattern of organization."

The image then is the reality.

by Bob Oates, Jr.

The League Where I Can Play Quarterback

Bob Gomel

It was late in the fourth quarter of the championship game last December. The Rams were behind 14-13 and there was just enough time for one more drive—one calm unhurried drive to a title.

On the first play the quarterback faked a handoff and faded back. Under a rush, he threw out to his left. It was a weak pass. A linebacker intercepted. The return carried to the Rams' 12-yard line and in three plays the game was out of reach, 21-13.

The team that lost that day was the New York Rams, the champions of the Gotham Division of the New York Semi-Professional Football League.

The quarterback who threw that interception was me.

Even if I were a master of time and space,

with galaxies streaming from my fingertips and all creation's happenings subject to my will, I would never wish away the experience of that moment.

"I keep asking myself when I've got pulled muscles and battered ribs, why am I doing this? But it gets ahold of you. Football is the last really physical thing in this civilized society. When I take that ball, I run right at people. I'm trying to do something they can't stop. They know it's coming but they can't stop it."

—HOMER WRIGHT, ART DIRECTOR AND FULLBACK.

I have found the league where I can play quarterback.

You wouldn't think it is a very impressive league, probably. Our fields sometimes have no stands, and where there are stands, there usually aren't any people. The socks on our uniforms don't always match and an ungodly number of snaps fly crazily over punters' heads.

But we have our pride. The New York Rams run every formation you are likely to see on a Sunday in front of your television and we operate some pass patterns the pros haven't yet heard of. We wreck some plays. We get some weird bounces. But we run off some classy stuff, too, plays you'd like to see.

It took me 26 years to find my league and 28 to get good enough to blow a championship, but it was worth the work and the wait. Like millions of Americans, I spend my Sunday afternoons trying to figure out what my favorite team ought to do next.

And when I call a 32 Inside Trap, that's what we run.

I dump my uniform out on the cement in front of the lockers and it scatters out in motley disorder. Thigh pads don't match, shoulder pads are taped together across the back. I've forgotten the wrist bands again.

I sit down on the bench and begin my transformation by taping my own ankles. It's a sloppy job, but I've never had a sprain. I pull on the long green stockings, stretch them tight and clip them around my calves, high up, with more tape. Pads are shoved into pants, strapped around hips and ribs, buckled onto shoulders.

I wear everything that seems feasible on my puny body. In addition to the normal equipment, I wear elbow pads, rib pads, and the bulky three-bar face mask of a linebacker. I saw Joe Namath wear the rib pads and the three-bar cage. That's where I got the idea to wear them, and also the courage. In one of my other incarnations, as a sportswriter, I once asked Namath about the extra protection. "Why not?" he said.

Adjusting all the gear takes some time, and while it happens the cramped space around me is filled with excited people getting themselves ready. Preston Smith is sounding off about what he's going to do to the Bears' star flanker. Nick Lerakis calls out, "This is the *Rams'* day, baby." Gordon Heaton tapes up his knee slowly and precisely and worries with me about how I want to handle the trap block against stacked linebackers. Willie Paige is hurting again, even dressing with a slightly pained expression, but that's good. Willie plays better hurt.

It's an amazing time, a magic time, as 40 diverse people unify themselves in green and white.

I'm always one of the first players dressed. I have to go out and get my arm loose and usually Nick and I are alone on the field for a few minutes. Nick's hero is Raymond Berry. "Do you know that Berry had eighty-eight different patterns?" he says. He has mastered most of them. In practice he catches every ball with stylish concentration and he does it the same way in a game, in a crowd. It's like throwing to a vacuum cleaner. Nick and I have been working together for three years now. I don't see him much off the field but we have one of the better relationships I know about.

We start by throwing back and forth. Then he runs easy slant-ins. After five or six he runs his first turn-in, a 12-yard pattern, and I start pulling my head into the fine points of steps and timing. I can feel it building inside me.

It's Sunday again. I get to play a football game.

Most people who play semipro football have no thought of turning professional some day. The idea that every sandlot quarterback is dreaming of the big time is partly a conceit of the professionals and partly a basic misconception of what it is to engage in sports. It is not necessary to be *the* best in order to feel *your* best.

Most people who play semiprofessional football do it for another reason altogether. They do it because they're a little crazy.

The New York Rams are the greatest football team in America. We practice in Central Park and in the summer the kites fall on us, the frisbees slice over us, the dogs cut up in the huddle, and little kids stop more sweeps than linebackers do.

People from all over Manhattan come to Central Park on summer Sundays, and that's how we recruit our team. We see guys with excessive elbows in the touch games, or guys see us chasing ourselves around trying to miss the dog leavings.

The team was founded several years ago by Robert Engle, cover editor of *Newsweek,* but by now it virtually operates on spontaneous combustion—a true New York team, continuously reforming on the green fields of the island's geographic center, and comprising every type of male the city provides. We've got Poles, Greeks, Blacks, Italians, Germans, Puerto Ricans, Jews, and WASPs. We've got doctors and butchers and ad men and students and taxi drivers and cops and narcotic agents and long-hairs—although there's only a couple of us in that last category.

The amazing thing, the beautiful thing, is that this weird bunch of people generate so much togetherness. We only see each other two or three times a week, playing football and hanging out afterward at Hanratty's. But we love each other. We do. I'd like to find a more sophisticated way to express it, but nothing else really seems to fit.

Longer than anything else that happened last season, I'll remember the moment when our defensive team came off the field after I'd set up the losing touchdown in the championship game. One of our defensive tackles is the federal narcotics officer I mentioned. Since my personal style is cliche hippie, you wouldn't expect Carlo and me to be very close, but he's one of my favorite people on the squad.

As he came off the field with the rest of the defensive team in that gray, cold moment that crystalized our loss, he hollered out to a silent bench, "It's our fault. They scored that touchdown on the defense. We've got no one to blame but ourselves." I looked up as he went past me. He's a teammate of mine.

Most of us on the team are what our friends might call marginal athletes, but we have some good ball players, some hitters, and some dancers. The man who sets apart, however, the man who makes us an exciting team, is the physical genius who plays left halfback.

Bill Bryant runs a football like nobody you ever saw. The truly great runners never look the same. Bill Bryant swoops and slashes and makes blind cuts into suddenly open spaces and I stand behind the line screaming, "Do it, Will," as if I were sitting in the stands.

And Bill Bryant has *style.* I once threw him a deep swing pass. He had called the play and sure enough he was striding free down the left sideline, high-stepping after the catch with the joy of living shining off him. The safetyman was angling over hard but it was clear he would arrive a yard too late. As Bryant sped into the end zone he crooked his right arm out toward the safety, palm up. What could the guy do? He whacked Bryant's hand a soul slap as the two flashed past each other. A spectator on the sidelines slumped to his knees, stunned at the audacious perfection.

I'd pay to watch Bryant play football.

A football field is a hostile environment for a skinny quarterback. The ball slaps back into my hands and I become an instant focus for the physical aggressions of

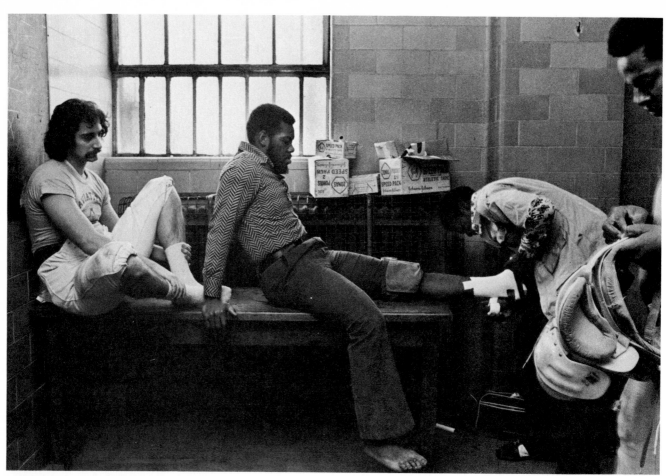

11 psyched-up opponents. Every step I take I'm followed by a swarming, grunting mass that spews forth powerful people aimed at my head and gut.

It's intense. Every reflex is hair-trigger, every nerve is fine tuned. You don't last if you can't operate at maximum efficiency using the hormones provided by the fear overload—transmuting lead into gold.

In that zapping energy field, with possible pain and injury hurtling in every direction, my friends and I have performed many beautiful acts together. The high we get is indescribable.

"When I'm running that ball, that's the greatest feeling in the world. I'll be out there laughing out loud. I just put a beautiful move on somebody, and I know it was beautiful, and I can't be mad at a time like that. It feels so good. I'll be laughing and getting ready to do it to the next guy."

—BILL BRYANT, PHOTOGRAPHER AND HALFBACK.

Once last season, in the fourth quarter of a close game, we came up to third and nine. I knew just the play I wanted. I had seen a weakness earlier and filed it away for this exact situation. Their left safety sucked up fast on a pitchout.

I took the snap and wheeled around clockwise, faking a pitchout left. The safety went to my halfback like iron filings to a magnet, and my left end crossed into the open area the safety had abandoned. My left end is the best friend I have on the team, a man who can smile and make you remember why it's fine to be human. Jody loves football so much he has made himself into a receiver with the sole attribute of an indomitable will.

He slanted in and I finished my wheeling fake pitchout and tipped my cleats into the ground just so, reversing my momentum perfectly. As the crashing linemen closed in I gunned out a pass, flat and knife hard, a pass to build a life around, and Jody was sprinting for it and then he was diving out as flat as the path of the ball and he had it on his fingers and slammed into the other safety.

The catch was beautiful; the collision ugly. We had the ball on the 1-yard line and in two plays Homer Wright leaped completely over a tackler and scored.

After holding for the extra point, I came off the field and started for the water. Jody and I saw each other. You could have walked on the light between our eyes. We grabbed each other and our pads clattered together.

I don't know what to tell you.

There is one glorious blessing to semi-pro football that is not true at any other organized level, even high school or kiddie football. In semipro, there's not much pressure to win.

"There are so many restrictions on you in this society. People are always telling you, 'You can't do that. You can't be like that.' But on a football field you are free. When I go up to catch a pass—I am. I'm there totally. No hangups. No distortions. It's all coming out at once."

—JODY FRIEND, TAXI DRIVER AND WIDE RECEIVER.

That's not to say that we don't die to win. The great effort for victory is what the game is all about. I would feel cheated if the people on defense all fell down and let me walk to the end zone.

But if we don't win in our league, there is no major catastrophe. In the first place, it has nothing to do with money. "Semipro" means, in our case, that if there were ever any profit we would split it—and profits appear in our league about as often as 220-pound, 9.1 halfbacks.

In the second place, people who play at our level are people who just like to play—even after they have given up on impressing women or making the Pro Bowl. I don't play football in order to be a "winner." What I am after in football is my experience with my teammates and the emotional rush that happens out on the field. It's an exciting way to be alive.

The biggest plus for winning that I can see is that you get to party afterwards. I love to party, but I usually don't need that much excuse to get into it. And Sunday isn't the best night anyway.

"My wife told me last year that if I didn't stop wasting my time on this stupid football team, she was going to leave me. I told her to be sure and write me her address."

—LOU LAVENDER, MAINTENANCE SUPERVISOR AND LINEBACKER.

I've been there in the clutch with the clock winding down and the defense clawing at me. I've thrown some good passes in that pressure. I've helped us pull out some last-minute wins. I've also blooped out a miserable, sick-looking ball that flopped into a linebacker's stomach and beat us out of a championship.

But I don't mind. It all comes with the package. And I like the guys on the Brooklyn Mariners anyway.

The thing is, I was there when it happened. It wasn't something I saw and nobody had to tell me about it. I could feel it in my mind and body as that pass slipped away.

I was there.

It's a place I love to be.

by Stan Lee and John Buscema

Beware the Linebacker!

Fasten your safety belt, frantic one, 'cause here they come! They're the superheroes' superheroes—strong, smart, savage, and swift.

You know their names. Nobis, Butkus, Lanier, and Wilcox. Curtis, Robertson, Jordan, Villapiano, and Siemon. Call 'em the linebackers…pro football's dazzling defenders, magnificent marauders who battle against incredible odds every game of the season.

Now know them as we know them through the world of fantasy. Let's watch these real life superstars with their superhero counterparts from the pandemonious, power-packed pages of marvelous Marvel Comics.

Lee Roy Jordan / Captain America
Jordan and Cap are proof positive that man improves with age. They're the marvels of the 1970s, both living it up after more than a decade of cataclysmic combat. The ol' shield-slinger, resurrected from comics' Golden Age of the 1930s and 1940s, came back in the 1960s, bigger and bolder than ever. At the same time, Jordan began to cop red, white, and blue honors as a leader of the Cowboys' famed Doomsday Defense.

Dave Wilcox / Dr. Doom

Every once in a while someone makes the scene who's so totally powerful he can do almost anything. Dr. Doom is that kind of someone, and he's dead-set on conquering the world. However, the 49ers' Dave Wilcox isn't quite as ambitious. He just wants to conquer the football world. Which shouldn't be all that hard for a powerhouse like him. But don't tell 'im we said so. We've enough to do now, protecting the world from Doom!

Phil Villapiano / The Silver Surfer

The silver-skinned Surfer is a space-born adventurer, exiled on earth where he spends his time trying to make sense out of the woebegone, whacky, and warlike nature of our primitive civilization. In the process, he manages to tear things up pretty good. That ol' marauder from Oakland, Villapiano, does pretty well in that department himself. And he doesn't need super powers to convince the opposition that roughing it with Phillip is an invitation to instant annihilation!

Tommy Nobis / The Thing
A guy with a grinnin' good nature can still come out swinging like a pounding piledriver. At least that's the rollickin' rule of the Falcons' red-haired Nobis and the orange-skinned Thing. Blue-eyed banter and cherubic chuckles go out the window when the famous battle cry "It's clobberin' time!" fills the air. That's when lesser men take to the hills as their agonized adversaries bite the dust — and even the stadiums tremble!

Isiah Robertson / Black Panther
Super Speed, pulsating power, awesome agility, and dauntless dedication are characteristics of both the linebacker and the superhero. The Rams' Robertson and his avenging alter-ego, T'Challa, have it all...plus the natural nobility of men who tower above their contemporaries. "Butch" and the Panther — electrifying examples that not *all* men are created equal!

Jeff Siemon / Thor

Don't let his soft yellow curls throw you. The Viking God of Thunder, with hammer in hand, is no one to mess around with. Jeff Siemon is the Vikings' God of Thunder, too...and his foes swear they were hammer-struck. His favorite hues are black and blue, and ball carriers throughout the NFL can show you examples of this valorous Viking's thunderous attack!

Willie Lanier / Iron Man

Poor Tony Stark. Because of his ailing heart, this swingin' millionaire industrialist had to design himself some iron threads to offset the frailties of mortal man. The Chiefs' Willie Lanier aches a lot too — just ask him. But, when he pulls on his helmet and pads, look out! He doesn't need Stark's electronic gizmos to clobber the foe. His bare hands do all right.

Dick Butkus / The Hulk
When you're the strongest rampager on earth, you've got something going for you. When you're also the angriest, let mankind beware! Meet the Bears' Dick Butkus and the Hulk. These two titans have a lot in common — they think everybody's always picking on them. And what they do in the name of self-defense would make an H-bomb yell "uncle!"

Mike Curtis / Spider-Man
Peter Parker's sensational spider powers are the result of an accident in an atomic lab. Where Baltimore's Mike Curtis got his is a mystery. Both are a couple of pussycats, trying to get along in an unsympathetic world where there are always some bad guys stompin' around, making life miserable. So, what else is there to do but whack 'em around a while, and then try to pick up the threads of a simple life that's always turning the corner to new adventure.

by Michael Katz

A Frenchman Looks at American Football

Pierre Doutreleau

In a motel room someplace in Oklahoma a Frenchman with nothing better to do turned on a color television set and has been turned on to football ever since. In 1971, he brought his vision of the game back to Paris. It was an enormous success.

Imagine Joe Namath posters plastered from the Champs-Elysées to the neighborhood cafés on the Left Bank. Joe Namath would not have recognized himself in the poster, as if that would have mattered to the poor people of Paris who are not hip to red dogs and white sneakers.

The posters were advertising an art exhibit by a French painter whose subject matter, of all things, was—still is—"football Américain."

Pierre Doutreleau's vision of football is colored by the fact that he is an artist. He cares not the least for pass rushes and flares; he does not know the rules. But with his artistic sensitivity, this young (33) native of Arles, in the rugby and bullfighting country of the south of France, managed to capture the excitement that fills stadiums all across the United States.

Freezing the action with his stop-action artist's eye. Doutreleau filled canvas after canvas with scenes of America's favorite sport. He may not know the rules, but in oil after oil he was able to catch the essence and the beauty of the game.

Linemen clash, bodies entangle, and Doutreleau sees a web of color. The offensive line moves with the ball and the quarterback half turns to make the handoff; Doutreleau sees harmony.

"It is magnificent," he exclaims. He speaks in gushes, and not as a sports fan—but as an artist. He loves football the way Degas loved ballet and Dufy horse racing.

Doutreleau's love affair started in U.S. motel rooms when his wife, a former Christian Dior model, was away. It was late 1968 and Doutreleau was accompanying his wife, then a designer for J. C. Penney, on an American tour. While his wife was out working, Doutreleau was alone with a television set.

He had always looked upon the television screen as a reproduction of what he calls a "two-dimensional, flat world." But earlier in 1968, the screen jumped alive with the student riots in Paris and the Olympic Games in Mexico. Until then a "classical" painter of still lifes and still-water seascapes, Doutreleau became interested in capturing—"speed."

"Some of the color television sets were not too well regulated," he recalls, "and I saw that with a little digeting with the dials, I could make the picture blurred, just like an abstract.

"It was marvelous. All those oranges and blues, it was already on canvas."

But what really "astonished" him was the beauty of football. "It just fills up the canvas," he says. "It's so much better than rugby, for example. Or baseball. In baseball, there's all that empty space —ugly. And in rugby you only have heads and hair; in football, you have *helmets*. And those shoulder pads! There's a rhythm to those curves. The colors are fabulous and the movement is in all directions. And with such violence, *mélange,* brutality —it's all very pictorial."

Doutreleau was obviously hooked: "Wheels started to turn." He began snapping pictures of the television set and buying up copies of sports magazines so he could go back home and analyze his new-found "movement" in detail. The result was a major six-week show at the posh Galerie de Paris. Eighty oil paintings, and most were of football (his interest in "movement" was also expressed in paintings of rugby, auto racing and motocross).

The motif of the show, of course, was "movement" and "speed." He chose sports, and especially football, as the best means of expressing it. The handsome, mod-looking, shaggy-haired artist has virtually stopped his production of still lifes and has taken up easel and brush to joust with the problem of getting movement on canvas. His latest work (he is rather prolific, producing more than 150 canvases a year) has carried his early football paintings literally one step further. Whereas the early works gave only the hint of "movement"—basically, they were stop-action portraits—Doutreleau's latest oils "blur" the action. For example, by putting a player's left foot in two places at once—where the foot was and where it now is—he gives the blurred impression that the player's foot is "moving" on the canvas.

Doutreleau admits to a rather skimpy knowledge of the game. "I discovered football because I painted football," he says. "It was not my intention at first to show a sport. But now I want to be a *'pro de football'.*"

He claims to understand the basic *"tactiques"* of the game—"I don't know sport and I don't know American football, but it is easy to understand what it means when the quarterback goes back"—and says that "any country can understand the game, even if you do not know the rules."

But occasionally, an American spoilsport will point out 12 players on a team in a single painting. Doutreleau counters by saying that in one of his paintings of rugby ("which I used to play as a youngster") two members of the same team have different colored socks.

"Of course it's not accurate," he says, "but if I use blue socks here, like the other player has, it is not good art. I need red to balance the painting."

Looking around the dozens of canvases strewn about the attelier of his fashionable apartment a block away from the Champs-Elysées, he recently observed: "I certainly constructed a different game in my head. It's evident I don't know the rules."

Not that it matters to the French. Take for example, this conversation between two elderly women at the Galerie de Paris during Pierre's exhibit. Staring at a canvas where an unidentified Baltimore Colt is heading for a hole in the line after taking a handoff from a number nineteen (Johnny Unitas, whom Doutreleau does not identify, probably because he doesn't know who number nineteen is), one of the women knowingly turned to the other and explained:

"See, that's a picture of ice hockey."

The other woman, turning to a huge canvas of a Denver Broncos' scrimmage (the only "live" football that Doutreleau has seen has been a Broncos' practice), she nodded: "Oh yes, I see—that's the water."

Few of the visitors to the exhibit could be classified as sports experts. Doutreleau laughingly points out another reaction: "The idea of painting American football annoyed all the French rugby players." One gallery visitor literally turned his back on the football paintings and looked only at the rugby. He was Walter Spanghero, the Joe Namath of French rugby.

Then again, how could the French be expected to understand paintings entitled, "Deacon Jones," "New York Giants," "John Mackey," "21-Yard-Line," or "Dallas Cow Boys" (sic). Obviously, Doutreleau isn't trying to make football a replacement for soccer or the Tour de France bicycle race. He is more than content with reactions like that of the chic girl who looked at another Broncos painting and didn't see a handoff, but "harmony, balance, and color."

What Doutreleau does not achieve, according to at least one critic (an English painter), is emotion. "I don't understand American football either," said the Englishman during a visit to Doutreleau's show. "But look at that painting. There are no faces, just gray. To me, it would be more interesting to visit the players in the dressing room and capture their emotions, not only their motion. Of course, this suits his style."

Doutreleau agrees. And disagrees. Take, for example, the painting of Joe Namath, which was sold during the show to a West German movie star, Helmut Berger (maybe in Germany, football is understood not only for art's sake). "Joe Namath" has a face mask, not a face. He has neither white sneakers nor a number twelve on his jersey (which is, incidentally, identifiable as that of the Jets). But what would shock Weeb Ewbank and all the Jets' fans is that this "Namath" is pictured *running* with the ball. It may be good art, but coach Ewbank for one might shudder at the very thought of his frail-kneed quarterback running into the waiting arms of a tackler whom Doutreleau has accurately portrayed as not intending Mr. Namath any good.

The artist apologizes for calling the picture "Joe Namath," which he said he did because somehow he knew Namath was a star. Not surprisingly, most purchasers of the poster at the Galerie de Paris never heard of Namath—said one: "I am buying a poster of Doutreleau; who this Joe Namath is doesn't interest me."

The artist shrugs off this type of criticism by saying, "I'll change the name . To me, it has no importance for the painting; of course, it's important for the truth if it really doesn't look like Joe Namath.

"But I'd rather someone look at it and like it or not just as a painting. If the Mona Lisa weren't called the Mona Lisa, would it be any less of a masterpiece?

"And besides, my painting was meant only as a general homage to a great player—any great player. I am a foreigner. I recognized, though, the qualities of the players. When you are interested in the *tactiques,* you look with a different eye."

Yet Doutreleau agrees with the English painter that "Joe Namath," or whoever he is, "does not express emotion, at least in the usual sense. But he sees emotion slightly differently.

"I am interested in light, land, man," he says. "Emotion, what is it? I see emotion in flowers. I can see in a flower all the drama and life of the world.

"When I paint a flower, I'm not painting a flower that's going to die tomorrow—I paint all flowers for all time. When I paint a great player, I do not paint a star that is going to fade tomorrow either. We know tomorrow there will be another star. Joe Namath will be gone and in his place maybe there will be..." he gropes for another name, "...maybe Deacon Jones. But the qualities of greatness remain forever."

Then he thinks some more and concludes: "I work more closely to the literal truth now. If I paint Joe Namath again, it will be him."

Illustrations by Bart Forbes

Only a State of Mind

What it is like, watching the clock and knowing that each second is one second less in which to do your job? To overpower your opponent. To succeed. To win.

That is what it is all about. All of the tension, all of the clenched fists, all of the looks of agony.

Pressure is a state of mind but it is more than that. It is the reality of the scoreboard, of teammates' faces, of threatening sounds coming down, loud, out of the stands.

First and ten, do it again...and again...and again. Driving, ignoring pain and adversity. Knowing that this time there must not be failure...

Eighty yards away. Three minutes left to play. Trailing by four points. Last chance. Trying to stay loose in a situation forced by tension.

Okay, here we go. First and ten...

Afterward

The game ends, not with
a whimper or a bang, but with a tissue streamer.
The people move to the exits and it is not long before there is a
sound vacuum where earlier there was a sound
stage. The afternoon is over and the stadium is quiet…
except for the sounds of the cleanup crew.
Without the people the stadium is a fossil, an empty cavern that
evokes melancholia as much as memories. The stadium
will come alive again with the next game.

Index of Authors, Illustrators, and Photographers